Classical Presences in Seventeenth-Century English Poetry

Classical Presences in Seventeenth-Century English Poetry

GEORGE DeFOREST LORD

Yale University Press
New Haven and London

Published with the assistance of the Frederick W. Hilles Publication Fund.

Permission to include material previously published by the author is gratefully acknowledged:

From chapters 1, 2, and 3 of *Homeric Renaissance: The* Odyssey *of George Chapman,* Yale University Press, 1956; "Milton's Dialogue with Omniscience in *Paradise Lost,*" *The Author in His Work: Essays on a Problem in Criticism,* ed. Louis L. Martz and Aubrey Williams, Yale University Press, 1978; "Folklore and Myth in *Paradise Regain'd,*" *Poetic Traditions of the English Renaissance,* ed. Maynard Mack and George deForest Lord, Yale University Press, 1982; "Homer, *Paradise Lost* and the Renaissance," *A Milton Encyclopedia,* 8 vols., Associated University Presses, 1978–80; "Pretexts and Subtexts in 'That Faire Field of *Enna,*'" *Milton Studies* 20 (1985), The Pittsburgh University Press; "From Contemplation to Action," *Philological Quarterly* 46 (1967). Copyright by The University of Iowa; Introduction to *Andrew Marvell, Complete Poetry,* Everyman's Library (1984), J. M. Dent & Sons Ltd; "Satire and Sedition: The Life and Work of John Ayloffe," *Huntington Library Quarterly,* 29 (1966); "Innocence and Experience in the Poetry of Andrew Marvell," *The British Library Journal* 5 (1979); introduction to *Poems on Affairs of State: Augustan Satirical Verse,* 1660–1714, vol. 1, Yale University Press, 1963; introduction to *Anthology of Poems on Affairs of State,* Yale University Press, 1975; pp. 59–77 and 110–21 from *Heroic Mockery: Variations on Epic Themes from Homer to Joyce,* Associated University Presses, 1977.

Set in Garamond No. 3 type by Huron Valley Graphics, Inc., Ann Arbor, MI.
Printed in the United States of America by Hamilton Printing Company, Rensselaer, NY

Library of Congress Cataloging-in-Publication Data

Lord, George de Forest, 1919–
   Classical presences in seventeenth-century English
poetry.

   Bibliography: p.
   Includes index.
   1. English poetry—Early modern, 1500–1700—History
and criticism.   2. English poetry—Classical influences.
3. Classicism.   4. Epic poetry—History and criticism.
5. Mock-heroic literature—History and criticism.
6. Classical poetry—History and criticism.   I. Title.
PR545.C67L67 1987   821'.4'09142   86–22438
ISBN 0–300–03815–1 (alk. paper)

The paper in this book meets the guidelines for permanence and durability of the Committee on Production Guidelines for Book Longevity of the Council on Library Resources.

10 9 8 7 6 5 4 3 2 1

Contents

Acknowledgments

This volume includes material from books and articles that I have published during the last thirty years, revised, cut, rethought, augmented, and often provided with new contexts. Nancy Wright, a scholar in Renaissance studies, proposed the idea that significant generic, thematic, and stylistic patterns, mainly derived from Greek and Latin models, could be traced among apparently heterogeneous studies. She is to be credited with organizing my work on Chapman's translation of the *Odyssey;* on Milton's two epics of paradise lost and regained; on Marvell's lyrics, his elusive and playful mockery of metaphysical extravagance in *Upon Appleton House,* his remarkable poems on Cromwell, and his mock-heroic Restoration poems; on Dryden's lifelong pursuit of the theme of restoration, most exquisitely expressed in *Absalom and Achitophel;* and on Homeric mock-heroics in Milton and Pope. She convinced me that out of these apparent disjecta membra might emerge a volume that was more than a selection of essays on seventeenth-century English poetry. She also suggested that the seemingly most recalcitrant material, *Poems on Affairs of State,* could contribute to an understanding of the triumph and the subversion of the heroic tradition in the turbulent years that extend from the 1650s to the death of Pope. Needless to say, she bears no responsibility for my deficiencies in developing her plan.

The literary and sociopolitical subculture of which John Ayloffe is a striking example reflected a second kind of classical presence that opposed to heroic conventions of monarchy a radical tradition derived from the Classical Republicans of Rome. This influence helped to subvert the high classical, conservative tradition of Dryden and Pope and opened the door to the secular, pragmatic, vernacular political verse of Defoe. The main cultural issues of Britain's revolutionary period were to be found in the conflicts between poetry for the privileged and sub-verse aimed at the people.

After the organization of the material into chapters the next step was to enter hundreds of pages of printed material on computer disks. Shah Karim, graduate student in economics and computer wizard, managed in an astonishingly short time to put the material on disks in the mainframe computer at Yale and then to move it to Macintosh disks which I could edit. My debt to the Macintosh and Microsoft Word is only exceeded by my debt to him.

To Nancy Woodington of the Yale Press, long an associate and friend, I am indebted for meticulous and rigorous editing from which the style and structure of the book have greatly benefited. Ellen Graham has given the manuscript the kind of incisive and wise editorial supervision that any author would hope for.

My friends Robert Newman and the Reverend Dr. Joseph Bishop have read and commented on versions of the book, and I owe them deep thanks for coping with its esoteric aspects and enthusiastically supporting the enterprise. After an association that began nearly a half-century ago, my dear friend Maynard Mack encouraged me to pursue a venture whose results he will see for the first time when he reads these lines.

Some old debts should here be acknowledged for the first time: to T. S. Eliot for his encouraging letter on an article, "The *Odyssey* and the Western World," in which I first set forth views I still share with Chapman about the evolutionary character of Odysseus; to E. M. Forster for correspondence and conversations in which he sometimes dwelt on Chapman's un-Homeric lapses; and to Dudley Fitts for his enthusiastic reading of *Homeric Renaissance: The* Odyssey *of George Chapman*.

Introduction

The period that extends from the Homeric translations of George Chapman (1611–15) to Pope's final version of the *Dunciad* (1743) constitutes the great age of English classicism. The influence of major Greek and Latin poets was pervasive, varied, and vital. As living presences Homer, Virgil, Ovid, and Horace were inseparable from the great poetic monuments of the period created by Milton, Marvell, Dryden, and Pope. This book explores the manifold ways in which the tradition was expressed in some of the most distinguished poetry of the age. It also explores many factors that contributed to the subversion and decline of the tradition and were fully manifested in its disestablishment, as witnessed by the anticlassical satires that began to appear in the 1660s and attracted wide popularity in the numerous editions of *Poems on Affairs of State.* The success of this huge body of subversive poems clearly contributed to "the gloom of the Tory satirists," who found in this aspect of the revolt of the Moderns against the Ancients a sign of cultural disaster.

If Chapman may be seen as raising the curtain of ignorance that had hidden Homeric epic from all but a small handful of Greek scholars in England, Pope, in his last major poem, was to witness its descent as "Universal Darkness buries all." The somber pathos of Pope's *all* clearly includes the comprehensive vision of *Paradise Lost,* a poem that he assimilated with such intelligence and imagination that it seems reasonable to mark the end of the Age of Milton with the death of Pope.

To offer an account of major seventeenth-century English poetry without reference to Donne, Jonson, Herbert, or Herrick may seem an irregular undertaking. Jonson's neo-Latin epigrams and elegies did not establish a strong English tradition and have been brilliantly analyzed in some recent studies. Herbert, practicing, like Donne, a vernacular, intimate, spontaneous style, eschewed classical traditions in a poetry even more introspective than Donne's. Herrick adapted minor Latin modes, and Donne, in Carew's brilliant elegy, had "exiled the goodly train of gods and goddesses" that had frequented the lyrics of Elizabethan and Jacobean poets.

Classical presences in the poetry of our period must be distinguished from the Elizabethan neoclassicism Donne rejected. Ovid supplied this neoclassicism with erotic themes and a host of prosodic and rhetorical "turns" to adorn lyrics. Unlike Milton, Marvell, Dryden, and Pope, Marlowe and Chapman (in his original poems) were not exploring archetypal epic depths or adapting them to their heroic and mock-heroic poems.

The Restoration revolt against epic traditions had a sociopolitical and religious basis supported by the competing tradition of the "Classical Republicans." As the character and conduct of Charles II and James II could not sustain the claims of divine right and heroic values, even defenders of the regime like Dryden had to assimilate some of their criticism, and the epic tradition was deflected in the direction of mock-epic. The efflorescence of mock-epic as *the* Augustan mode also had a lot to do with Milton's heroic achievement in writing the ultimate epic poem, and a major Miltonic influence was to be mock-heroic elements included in *Paradise Lost* and found in the *Iliad* as well.

A major development of the period that accompanied the diversion of epic vision into the ironic modalities of mock-epic was the revolutionary preoccupation with a secular realism, in part founded on the new science of the Royal Society established in 1660. Experimental science, Thomas Sprat wrote, required a "close, naked and plain style." In all writing he sought to curtail "volubility of phrase" and "tricks of style" in "bringing all things as near the mathematical plainness as they can, and preferring the language of Artizans, Countrymen, and Merchants before that of Wits and Scholars."[1]

Defoe supplies prime examples of this style both in his prose fictions and his vernacular poems like *The True-Born Englishman*. Robinson Crusoe and Moll Flanders bring a kind of bookkeeper mentality to their experiences. Values are quantified. The ingenuities of the virtuoso, more calculating than his picaresque precursors, supplant established and inherited virtues. The concept of a heroic tradition is dismissed at the end of *The True-Born English-man* in "down-right English," a bastard language that mirrors the genealogical mélange:

> Then let us boast our ancestors no more,
> Or deeds of heroes done in days of yore,
> In latent records of the ages past,
> Behind the rear of time, in long oblivion placed.
> For if our virtues must in lines descend,
> The merit with the families would end,
> And intermixtures would most fatal grow,
> For vice would be hereditary too;
> The tainted blood would of necessity
> Involuntary wickedness convey.   [1191–1200]

The authority of this "poetry of statement" exemplifies Sprat's program. Defoe, in fact, has assumed the argument of Dryden's satanic Achitophel, who attempts to persuade Absalom to challenge the principle of legitimate succession to the monarchy:

> All sorts of men, by my successful arts,
> Abhorring kings, estrange their altered hearts

> From David's rule, and 'tis the common cry,
> "Religion, Commonwealth, and liberty!"
> If you, as champion of the common good,
> Add to their arms a chief of royal blood,
> What may not Israel hope? and what applause
> Might such a general gain by such a cause?
> Not barren praise alone, that gaudy flow'r,
> Fair only to the sight, but solid pow'r;
> And nobler is a limited command,
> Giv'n by the love of all thy native land,
> Than a successive title, long and dark,
> Drawn from the mouldy rolls of Noah's Ark.   [289–302]

In a "naked, close and plain way of speaking" Defoe promulgates an attitude that, like Dryden's tempter, derides tradition and the figurative language essential to its full poetic realization and consigns them to oblivion. If, for Homer and Milton, memory was mother of the Muses and an essential constituent of heroic identity, for Defoe memory and the values preserved in long-established institutions were obstacles to truth conceived as empirical. Having cut himself loose from the traditional coordinates of value, Defoe here qualified himself for the *Dunciad*'s Lethean "wonders of th' oblivious Lake."

Clearly the rejection of belief in a heroic tradition, derived from epic, enshrined in a hereditary monarchy, and supported by a figurative style, opened the way for a Settle or a Defoe to subvert the conservative, cyclical views of history that lie at the heart of Dryden's and Pope's epistemology. Poetically, the shift is reflected in the descent from Dryden's and Pope's graceful and witty neoclassical correctness to Defoe's confessed artlessness: "I have . . . strove rather to make the thoughts explicit, than the poem correct."[2] Defoe here comes close to the declarative moral didacticism of Chapman's *Odyssey* without, of course, sharing Chapman's values.

Yet another major development in the poetry of the period is the shift from the introspective intimacy of lyric to a predominantly public, rhetorical mode exemplified par excellence in Marvell's career. That so little distinguished lyric poetry was written after the Restoration suggests, in Maynard Mack's memorable phrase, that the "contours of personal experience" ceased to be a primary poetic concern. The new neoclassicism of Dryden and the realistic mode of opposition satire alike reflect a preoccupation with social contexts that effectively excluded the lyric mode. In part this change marked a reaction against what had come to be regarded as idiosyncratic and even subversive, the "private spirit" of sectarian enthusiasm and the virtuosity of metaphysical extravagance. If Donne's characteristic ritual gesture was to shut the door on society to protect his little world of two, the new social mode of Dryden, in its ingratiating manner, opened the doors to a consensus about the nature of experience whose sources can be traced in part to the formal and formulaic qualities of Homer and the congeniality of Horace's *Sermones*. Donne's flamboyant individualism was now taboo. "Innovation," political or poetic, was now seen as "the blow of Fate."

As an elegy on the death of classicism, the *Dunciad* was to arraign the self-preoccupied ambitions of the Dunces expressed in the ephemeral commercial novelties of operatic mélanges and Cibberian dramatic spectacles, the myopia of virtuoso collectors, the venality of Walpole, the pedantry of Bentley, the Hanoverian succession where "Dunce the Second reigns like Dunce the First," and the hostility of Defoe to classical and political tradition as combining to extinguish the "holy Light, offspring of Heav'n first-born" that Milton had inherited from the Bible and from the example of Homer and Virgil.

CHAPTER ONE

Chapman's Renaissance Homer

"The archetypal Ulysses offered a wider foundation for later development than any other figure of Greek mythology, thanks to Homer's far-reaching conception of his character and exploits."[1] The opening statement from W. B. Stanford's vivid exploration of *The Ulysses Theme* may serve both as an encouragement and a warning to intepreters of Homer's most complex character. The extraordinary fascination Odysseus has exercised on Western civilization from Homer to Joyce has found expression in an equally extraordinary range of interpretations. The unsurpassed versatility of Homer's *anér polútropos* (man of many turns, or, in Joyce's phrase, "allround man") is demonstrated, for example, in the metamorphoses he has undergone in such figures as Pindar's plausible cheat, the cynical tempter of Neoptolemus in *Philoctetes,* Plutarch's Stoic, Dante's insatiate and damned adventurer, Shakespeare's statesman, Tennyson's pursuer of ever-receding horizons, and Joyce's bourgeois Dubliner, to mention some of the better-known ones. All these reincarnations have something of Homer's hero in them, yet how full of contradictions is the composite portrait they present! The vehemence with which Odysseus' supporters and detractors have advanced their insights into this polytropic figure suggest how strong and personal an interest he has elicited over a hundred generations. Such vehemence comes as no surprise, however, to anyone who has followed the critical battles over Falstaff and Hamlet, for Odysseus stands high among those great characters of literature with whom we feel we must come to terms, perhaps because they embody so much of what we sometimes wish, sometimes fear, to be.

Joyce's preference for Odysseus as an archetypal man—husband, father, son, lover, fabulous voyager, beggar, king, formidable warrior and master of patience, and, most of all, as a culture hero whose experiences incorporated and transformed the intellectual and ethical values of the Western world—is supported by Stanford's conclusion:

With one exception every portrait of Ulysses described in the previous chapters has been incomplete. Homer alone presented the whole man—the wise king, the loving husband and father, the eloquent and resourceful *politique,* the courageous wanderer, the goddess-beloved hero, the yearning exile, the deviser of many ruses and diguises, the triumphant avenger, the grandson of Autolycus and the favorite of Athene. Subsequent writers in the tradition usually selected one, or a related group, of these roles to suit their personal inclinations or artistic purposes.[2]

In the nonliterate world that Homer shared with his hero, memory was the sine qua non of personal identity and coherent purpose. Most of the temptations and obstacles encountered by Odysseus and his men threaten their identity by threatening their memory of home. Of all those who sailed from Troy, Odysseus alone succeeds in keeping alive his manifold dedication to Ithaca and, above all, to Penelope, his equal in resourcefulness and in love. Any true interpretation or translation of the *Odyssey* must give full recognition to the depth, power, and richness of this all-pervading motive of getting home as the symbolic and narrative goal of the Odyssey.[3] Chapman emphasized it in his version of the opening lines:

> The Man (O Muse!) informe, who many a way
> Wound with his wisdom to his wished stay.[4]

Chapman's translations of Homer's epics—the first complete translations into English verse—provide a point of departure for an examination of classical presences in the seventeenth century. Despite their eccentricities and the burden of often mistaken Renaissance Greco-Latin scholarship under which they labor, these versions were extremely influential in a period when few Englishmen knew enough Greek to cope with the originals.

Chapman's Homeric translations have received widespread attention from poets, critics, and scholars. While there has been much general comment on their style and some analysis of particular features, no study both comprehensive and specific enough to do justice to the subject has so far appeared. The remarks of Pope, Lamb, Coleridge, and Swinburne, as well as more recent articles on their ethical character by such scholars as the distinguished editor of Chapman's poems, Phyllis Bartlett, have been extremely valuable. Yet Chapman's translations make large claims not only as interpretations of Homer but as English epics. This is especially true of his *Odyssey,* a poem which demands a full study of ethical structure and poetic texture in relation to Homer and within the framework of Renaissance classicism.

We can see a classic only through our own eyes, however much our vision is broadened by anthropology, history, and philology; the best we can do even with a poem like the *Odyssey,* which has spoken so compellingly to all ages, is to find the fullest equivalents in our own experience for the experiences which it presents. This is shown clearly in analyzing different translations, and nowhere more clearly than by a comparison of the two most famous English versions: only a century after Chapman's fiery Elizabethan epic Pope's version appeared in the cool accents of the Augustan Age. The translator, no matter how faithful, neither can nor should try to avoid contemporary idiom, and idiom is plainly one of the most influential delineators of character. Bentley's familiar objection to Pope's *Iliad* ("A pithy poem, Mr. P., but don't call it Homer") can be made with equal truth against all translations.

One critic has observed that Chapman "probably believed that he was inspired by the soul of Homer."[5] Although the observation referred primarily to Chapman's vision of Homer in "The Teares of Peace," there is much other evidence that Chapman believed himself to possess a special insight into Homer's works. In his dedication of the *Odyssey* Chapman promised his patron no less a gift than "Homer, three thousand yeares dead, now reviv'd."[6] His notes, especially in the *Iliad,* resound with scathing criticisms of earlier translators and scholars, while his introductory comments to the different translations reflect a proprietary attitude devoid of humility except when he contemplates the greatness of his original.

Chapman's claim to a peculiar insight into Homer's meaning has usually met with amusement or indifference among his critics, who have concentrated on perceived eccentricities of his style or on his frequent departures from Homer's literal sense—often with the implicit idea of showing the preposterousness of his claim. Important twentieth-century studies have been devoted to showing the ways in which Chapman allegedly read into Homer alien ideas and philosophies in order to express his private conceptions of Odysseus. Thus Donald Smalley claims that in the *Odyssey* Chapman found "his own destined task of presenting to the modern world Homer's creation of the faultless man,"[7] while Phyllis Bartlett declares that "Chapman's Ulysses is first and foremost a pious man"[8] and that Chapman has made him perfect "through an injection in his veins of a natural stoicism."[9]

Such assertions raise issues of central importance about Chapman's translation. Is his Ulysses in fact pious and stoical? In what ways are Chapman's alterations of and additions to Homer's literal sense departures from Homer's meaning and his conception of the hero's character?

F. L. Schoell has shown Chapman's extraordinary debt in his tragedies and original poems to certain important Renaissance editions of the classics.[10] Time and again whole speeches are revealed as verbatim translations from the text or commentaries of these books. The degree of this influence, especially in Chapman's debt to editions of the Stoics in his original work, has led some of Schoell's successors to infer corresponding influences in his *Odyssey*. Bartlett draws such a conclusion:

For the past thirty years scholars have been increasingly interested in Chapman's debt to the Stoics. Professor F. L. Schoell, who proved that Chapman knew Epictetus through the Latin version of Wolfius (1563, 1593), observed that the years 1610–1612 were the period in Chapman's life when he "n'a pas su résister à l'attrait du beau stoicisme d'Epictète, tout parfumé de sagesse antique, et pourtant, par quelques côtés si proche du christianisme" [he could not resist the attraction of the lovely Stoicism of Epictetus, everywhere redolent of ancient wisdom, and moreover in some ways so close to Christianity]. This period may well be extended through 1615, for the translation of the *Odyssey* shows clearly the fascination that stoical doctrine continued to hold for him.

Schoell demonstrated the influence of Epictetus on Chapman's poems and plays by comparing them exhaustively with the *Discourses* and *Encheiridion* in the editions of Wolfius.[11] Many long passages in Chapman were shown to be taken directly from these books. Bartlett does not, however, indicate a single borrowing of this sort in the *Odyssey*. I have compared all Chapman's interpolations and alterations having the faintest aura of Stoicism about them with Epictetus and with the commentary of Wolfius without finding any traces of borrowing or even of recognizable influence. Considering the liberties he took in translating the *Odyssey*, may we not assume that, had he wished to make a Stoic version, his translation would show the kind of specific indebtedness which we find throughout *The Revenge of Bussy d'Ambois?* Unquestionably the self-restraint which Ulysses gradually develops toward the end of his ordeals has certain affinities with elements in the Stoic philosophy as represented by the *Discourses* and *Encheiridion* and by Plutarch's *Moralia*, but Ulysses' self-restraint is nothing like the Stoic's detachment from the world. Instead, it is a prerequisite to his attaining the rewards which he seeks in the world—his wife, his son, his home, and his kingdom.

Chapman's Ulysses is not the product of any particular philosophical or religious view. By the time Chapman translated the *Odyssey*, Epictetus' philosophy, "si proche du christianisme," had mingled with Neoplatonic, Platonic, humanistic, and Christian ideas in a characteristic Renaissance mélange. Chapman must have made a conscious effort not to interpret Homer in terms of any particular creed, for there are no borrowings from any other philosophical sources like those which Schoell demonstrates so fully in the original dramatic work. Wherever Chapman departed from Homer's meaning I have sought such borrowings in the books with which he has been shown to be familiar—Xylander's *Plutarch*, Ficino's *Plato* and his *Commentary* on Plato's *Symposium*,[12] Natalis Comes's *Mythologiae*,[13] and Erasmus' *Adagia*[14]—but I have not found a single unequivocal example like the dozens in the poems and plays.

While Chapman showed himself unusually independent of philosophical sources in the *Odyssey*, there are two important works of continental humanists which he used constantly, the *Homer* of Johannes Spondanus (Jean de Sponde)[15] and the Greek-Latin *Lexicon* of Johannes Scapula.[16] Spondanus prints alongside the Greek the word-for-word Latin translation in hexameters by Andreas Divus, and he also includes extensive commentaries which are often concerned, in the orthodox Renaissance way, with the moral implications of the poems. Frequently these are pious half-truths of a kind all too common in the history of Homeric interpretation, which see Homer's characters and incidents in the simple blacks and whites of moral exempla, but now and then there are flashes of real insight. Chapman used Spondanus' commentaries with discrimination, although, as Schoell has suggested, his debt to this volume was very great:

The name of Spondanus, let us hasten to add, has often been cited à propos of the Homeric commentaries of Chapman, first by T. Warton, then by Regel, Lohff, and J. E. Sandys.

And it would have been truly surprising had they not cited it, for Chapman twenty or thirty times has the name of Spondanus at the tip of his pen. But, strangely enough, no one, to our knowledge, has thought of examining closely the voluminous *Homer* of Jean de Sponde and studying what Chapman truly owes for his translation to the explanations of Sponde; for his *Commentaries* to the *Commentaries* of Sponde; for his Homeric epistles and his "Homeric critique" to the Homeric prolegomena of Sponde. [Schoell, p. 163; translation mine]

Nor, one might add, has anyone investigated the relation between Chapman's vocabulary and the Latin translation in Spondanus. Schoell's demonstration of the influence of Spondanus on the actual text of Chapman's *Odyssey* is limited to one long and very illuminating speech of Nausicaa in book VI. Wherever there was a possible borrowing I have examined both the Latin translation and the commentaries, and this search has been highly rewarding. Much of Chapman's Latinate diction is derived from this text, while many important passages in his translation incorporate ideas and even whole sentences from the commentaries, especially where Spondanus' remarks conform to Chapman's general interpretation of the poem.

The *Lexicon* of Johannes Scapula also had a dual influence on Chapman's *Odyssey*. Stylistically, it is responsible for some of Chapman's compound epithets, which are often grotesque, sometimes especially so, because of the lexicographer's faulty etymology. In larger matters of interpretation, Chapman occasionally finds in Scapula a not-always-dependable authority for giving explicit moral interpretation to a passage. Despite Schoell's statement (p. 157) that Chapman "did not translate a single Greek verse without verifying the sense of one or several words in his dictionary," his borrowings from Scapula are by no means as common as from Spondanus. Finally, it should be noted that the influence of these books, while wide, is in the main local, for we cannot ascribe to them fundamental influences on Chapman's conception of the *Odyssey*. He used them to implement a view he formed independently of any special source.

Chapman's distinctive style as a translator of Homer has received much more attention over the years than the equally distinctive ways in which he interpreted the themes of Homer's epics. With varying degrees of enthusiasm, Chapman's critics have singled out the originality of his manner for discussion. Pope, whom Millar McClure considers "very penetrating upon Chapman's methods of translation," concludes:

In a word, the Nature of the Man may account for his whole Performance; for he appears from his Preface and Remarks to have been of an arrogant Turn, and an Enthusiast in Poetry. . . . But that which is to be allowed him, and which very much contributed to cover his Defects, is a daring fiery Spirit that animates his Translation, which is something like what one imagines *Homer* himself might have written before he arriv'd to Years of Discretion.[17]

In pointing out the idiosyncratic and enthusiastic character of Chapman's performance, Pope has hit the mark. On this score I would like to emphasize that in translating Homer Chapman was a pioneer without a predecessor in the poetics of English epic to help him. His versions understandably fluctuate between eccentricity and great poetic power. For our purposes not the least of his contributions was in discovering and revealing truly Homeric archetypal patterns in Odysseus' long voyage home.

The nineteenth-century critic R. H. Horne, while deploring "the licentious spirit of English translations . . . purporting to be from Homer," likewise testified to the Homeric quality of Chapman's version, which he found to be "a paraphrase by a kindred spirit" and which he preferred to Pope's "paraphrase in his own spirit."[18] Havelock Ellis thought Chapman had embodied the character of the age in his "slowly-evolved translation of Homer . . . with its unflagging energy and spirit" and made it "the crowning achievement of Elizabethan Humanism."[19] The emphasis on the individuality of Chapman's style occurs over and over again, but a curious fact about these and other critical remarks is that they are directed at Chapman's translations collectively, as though the differences between them were stylistically insignificant. In fact, however, his Odyssey is as different from his version in fourteeners of the Iliad as it is from other versions of the Odyssey. Yet there is a pronounced tendency among critics to base generalizations about the style of Chapman's Homer on the Iliad, where Chapman's "ballad-manner" was condemned, though Chapman abandoned this verse-form in subsequent translations.[20] Hallett Smith continues the curious practice in his book Elizabethan Poetry when he fails to make any critical distinction between the Iliad and the Odyssey.[21] The glowing exception among Chapman's critics is Coleridge, who had little use for the Iliad, but found the Odyssey "as truly an original poem as the Faerie Queene."[22]

Originality may seem a dubious asset in the translation of a great and ancient epic poem, and for a long time there was widespread conviction among scholars that the excellence of a translation depended on its literalness. This view reached its fullest expression in Chapman's nineteenth-century critic, H. M. Regel:

Today we call that translation of a foreign poet true that reproduces the original line for line, and if possible word for word and in the same meter. We consider this the only admissible and practicable way to translate. But for Chapman, as for most of the earlier translators, it was of principal importance to reproduce the content of his author, the proper meaning of the verses, not the same words; he wanted to produce the same impression on his readers that the original had made on *him*.[23]

Here Regel, in supposing that there are English or German words which are "the same as" Greek words and that they can reproduce the effect of the original language, is committing the fallacy of interlingual identity. The assumption is that the real meaning of the passage inheres in the denotations of words, and that series of words whose denotations are similar to those of the original, in the same meter as the original, will reproduce the meaning of the original. This assumption overlooks entirely the distinctive idiom of each language and tends to regard words as building blocks rather than as living cells. The same false assumption lies behind Matthew Arnold's argument for English hexameters:

Applied to Homer, this meter affords to the translator the immense support of keeping him more nearly than any other meter to Homer's movement; and, since a poet's movement makes so large a part of his general effect, and to reproduce this general effect is at once the translator's indispensable business and so difficult for him, it is a great thing to have this part of your model's general effect already given you in your meter, instead of having to get it entirely for yourself.[24]

Arnold, like Regel, shows an unjustified confidence in the power of superficial resemblances to convey a significant part of the total experience of a poem into another language. Dactylic hexameters are adapted to the structure of Homer's Greek, but are completely alien to the rhetoric, rhythms, and accents of English. If there are fundamental resemblances between translation and original, the same meter may, in Arnold's words, help to reproduce the general effect of the original, provided that the meter used is as natural to the new language as to the old. On this score it may be noted that Chapman is least "Homeric" when he doggedly imitates Homer's compound epithets, which are as grotesque in English as they are natural in Greek. The general effect of any translation is due to the interaction of many elements which we designate by such words as *plot, theme, rhetoric, tone, rhythm, metaphor,* and *symbol.* Until the translator comprehends the living organism composed of these elements, the translation, however literal, will be spurious. Diction has always been a major stumbling-block to translating Homer or Virgil. Ezra Pound made an illuminating point on this score in a letter to W. H. D. Rouse about his translation of book II of the *Odyssey:*

NO, NO, Doc: here you are backslidin' on all your highly respectable principles and slinging in licherary langwidg and puttin' your sentences all out of whack.

'Odysseus' boy jumped out of bed as rednailed, etc. appeared thru the dawn mist', or whatever; and if he reached for his six-shooter before puttin' on his boots, *that* is a point to be made, as highly illustrative of the era. A guards officer wdn't.

But I reckon in Idaho in the 80's Blue Dick or Curly might have.

And as for his feet, they ought to be well-kept, or elegant or patrician, otherwise they slide into book-talk.

Tain't what a man says, but wot he *means* that the traducer has got to bring over. The implication of the word.

As fer them feet [presumably Telemachus' "lissom feet" in Rouse], the blighter had been usin' cold cream, the bloomin' Bloomsbury knutt.[25]

Chapman was fully aware that no amount of literal fidelity would capture the meaning of Homer. His criteria of translation are mostly set forth in his preface to the *Iliad,* where he scoffs at those who

> affect
> Their word-for-word traductions (where they lose
>   The free grace of their naturall Dialect
> And shame their Authors with a forced Glose).[26]

He recognized the crucial principle that a certain license was needed because of fundamental differences between Greek and English:

> For even as different a production
>   Aske Greek and English, since, as they in sounds
> And letters shunne one forme and vision,
>   So have their sense and elegancie bounds
>
> In their distinguisht natures, and require
>   Onely a judgment to make both consent
> In sense and elocution, and aspire
>   As well to reach the spirit that was spent
> In his example, as with arte to pierce
>   His Grammar and etymologie of words.[27]

The translator has a double responsibility. He must be faithful to the meaning of the original, but he must also be faithful to the nature of his own language. If he writes of Telemachus' "lissom feet," he has failed in both responsibilities. "The line and rhythm of the ideal poetic translation, the ideal reproduction, ought after all to be as indigenous as its language."[28] If the translation is not a poem it fails to imitate the most important aspect of the original. Chapman recognized this, and he possessed a vision of the profound relevance to himself and his age of the poem he was translating. We cannot evaluate the original style of Chapman's translation until we have grasped this vision and tested it by the essential meanings of Homer's poem. Only then can we judge whether or not his highly individualized speeches, varied pace and tone, changing rhythms, rhetorical inversions, and metaphorical language violate the spirit and meaning of the original, or whether he created with the resources native to his language a poem faithful to Homer because of its originality.

The explicit moral comments and the patterns of moral symbolism in Chapman's translation provide a background of values against which the major episodes of the poem are enacted. They constitute a relatively simple system, and if they alone represented Chapman's elucidation of the allegory of the *Odyssey,* one would have to admit that the allegory was as static and obvious as the contention between C. S. Lewis's *Patientia* and *Ira.* Most of the characters immediately concerned in this pattern, it should be noticed, are minor figures such as the suitors and Ulysses' sailors. They are the ruck of men who fall for the grosser temptations when moral sanctions unsupported by physical force are ineffective deterrents, and they lack the faith or discipline or imagination to deny themselves temporary gratification in exchange for a greater good in the future. The major characters—Ulysses, Athene, Telemachus, Penelope,

Eumaeus, Nausicaa, and Arete—are distinguished by loyalty to the future or to some high principle. The suitors and Ulysses' sailors are mostly bound to the temporal cycle of present satisfaction of present impulses, but these other characters, being committed to high or distant goals, are capable of hope and growth and change. The former act only in a limited way, because they repeat their characteristic actions over and over. Hence Ulysses' companions, with the exception of Eurylochus and poor Elpenor, are almost entirely undifferentiated. Since they are dominated by a few basic impulses, Chapman can treat them, quite properly, as mere personae.

It is the other characters who give direction and movement to the poem. Either they obey some moral principle which guides their conduct in the face of various obstacles or temptations, or they are seeking something beyond the present and above the anarchy of sensation and impulse. These characters, accordingly, produce the dynamic, evolutionary movement of the *Odyssey,* for they have the capacity to analyze experience and to act accordingly.

Chapman has underlined this principle of growth at various points in his translation, but most conspicuously, as one would expect, in the case of Ulysses. He makes clear the association between developments in the story and developments in the hero himself. The general line of growth can best be seen from three important speeches where Ulysses reflects in an unusually analytical manner on the nature of his experiences. Through all three speeches there runs a single theme—man's relation with the gods—and each marks an important step in Ulysses' growing self-knowledge, as he gradually discovers the proper limits of human power, intelligence, and freedom.

In Homer the first speech, which occurs in book X, is a simple statement of the navigational predicament in which Ulysses and his company find themselves on Circe's island. They have lost their geographical bearings. Although they can tell direction from the sun, they do not know in which quarter Ithaca lies. Ulysses is trying to convince his men of the need to ask directions, but they are reluctant to do so because of the fear of strangers which their recent encounters with Polyphemus and the Laestrygonians have given them: "Hear my words, comrades, for all your misery. O friends, we do not know where the darkness is nor where the dawn, nor where the sun, which gives light to men, goes beneath the earth, nor where it rises. Let us now consider whether there is any device left us. As for me, I do not think that there is" (X, 189–93). By his last two sentences Ulysses means only that their own resources are inadequate for finding the way home and that they must therefore take the risk of asking the inhabitants. Chapman turns this statement of fact into an analysis of the limitations of human knowledge and the need for God's help:

> Now, friends,
> Affoord unpassionate eare, though ill Fate lends
> So good cause to your passion. No man knowes
> The reason whence and how the darknesse growes,
> The reason how the Morne is thus begunne,

> The reason how the Man-enlightening Sunne
> Dives under earth, the reason how againe
> He reres his golden head. Those counsailes, then,
> That passe our comprehension, we must leave
> To him that knowes their causes; and receave
> Direction from him in our acts, as farre
> As he shall please to make them regular,
> And stoope them to our reason. In our state
> What then behoves us? Can we estimate,
> With all our counsailes, where we are, or know
> (Without instruction past our owne skils) how
> (Put off from hence) to stere our course the more?
> I thinke we can not. We must then explore
> These parts for information.   [X, 241–59]

In a marginal note Chapman, perhaps drawing on Aeneas' opening speech in the *Aeneid,* observes that "the whole end of this counsaile was to perswade his souldiers to explore those parts: which he knew would prove a most unpleasing motion to them, for their fellowes' terrible entertainment with Antiphas, and Polypheme, and therefore he prepares the little he hath to say with this long circumstance, implying a necessitie of that service, and necessary resolution to adde the triall of their event to other adventures." But Chapman's rendering also marks a change of view in Ulysses, who heretofore had often relied with calamitous results on his own judgment and reason. The implications of his speech are far more extensive than the practical point with which he concludes it. This is as much a self-revealing soliloquy as an argument: in the very process of explaining the present difficulty the hero suddenly realizes the inadequacy of all human devices. As a preface to Ulysses' encounter with Circe, who dwells on this island, it is a strangely prophetic speech, not only because the unexpected intervention of Hermes preserves him from her spells, but especially because through Circe he acquires the "instruction past his own skils" to reach Ithaca. Chapman's alterations illuminate this moment as a new phase in Ulysses' self-knowledge and in his relations with the gods. Having abandoned his old attitude of self-sufficiency, the hero is now prepared to put himself under Circe's direction and take the trip to the underworld which is an essential preliminary to his ultimate return to Ithaca.

The second speech, as Chapman has altered it, is even more self-revealing and also marks a new stage in Ulysses' development. The occasion is his arrival in Ithaca, where he meets Athene, whom he has not seen in ten years, disguised as a shepherd. In Homer he explains his failure to recognize the goddess as follows:

It is hard, goddess, for a mortal to know thee at sight, however wise he may be, for thou takest whatever shape thou wilt. But this I know well, that formerly thou wast kind to me, while we sons of the Achaians fought in Troy. But when we had sacked the towering city of Priam and had sailed away, and a god had scattered the Achaians, never since then did I see thee, daughter of Zeus, nor know thee to board my ship to ward off sorrow from me. But ever bearing a divided heart in my breast I wandered, until the gods freed me from evil, when, in the rich land of the Phaeacians, thou didst encourage me and thy self lead me to the city.   [XIII, 312–23][29]

The fact that he now recognizes Athene in the maiden who helped him among the Phaeacians is, perhaps, Homer's way of suggesting Odysseus' new insight. But the hero's gratitude expressed in the last part of this passage is tempered by the somewhat querulous tone in which he tells how Athene failed to help him over such a long period. Chapman uses this implied questioning of divine justice as the basis for an insertion of eight lines in which Ulysses charges that his sufferings were undeserved:

> Goddesse (said he) unjust men and unwise,
> That author injuries and vanities,
> By vanities and wrongs should rather be
> Bound to this ill-abearing destiny,
> Than just and wise men. What delight hath heaven,
> That lives unhurt it selfe, to suffer given
> Up to all domage those poore few that strive
> To imitate it, and like the Deities live?   [XIII, 452–59]

This is similar to Athene's own defense of her protégé before the Olympian council which was referred to earlier:

> But that *Ithacus*
> (Thus never meriting) should suffer thus,
> I deeply suffer. His more pious mind
> Divides him from these fortunes.   [I, 79–82]

Ulysses makes his complaint in response to the difficulties which Athene has warned him he has yet to face at home. Here, as Smalley has pointed out, "Though Athene does not reply directly to this question, Chapman renders the answer obvious in other parts of his translation. Heaven does not obviate man's difficulties. The purpose of divine grace is rather to steel man's soul to bear all ills without deviating from its proper course."[30] Homer also answers the question when Zeus, in response to Athene's remarks, after admitting Ulysses' wisdom and solicitous attention to sacrifices, stipulates the following conditions for his release from Calypso's island and return to Ithaca: "Hermes, since thou art our messenger, declare now to the fair-haired nymph our fixed resolve, the return of stout-hearted Odysseus, that he may go without the conveyance either of the gods or of mortals, but after woeful suffering, on the twentienth day shall approach Scheria on a wellbound raft" (V, 29–34). The return of Ulysses cannot be accomplished, therefore, by a simple act of divine intervention. Despite the approval of Zeus, the hero must confront his problems as a man, and (like Jesus in *Paradise Regained*) he must solve them within the limitations of his humanity. As we shall see, his own strength and will

prove inadequate, and he reaches the Phaeacian shore with the aid of a
sea-nymph and through prayers to the river-god. But this assistance must
plainly be distinguished from the sort of divine intervention which Zeus has
in mind. In the present scene Chapman, by making Ulysses proclaim his
virtuousness and question the justice of his sufferings, suggests further
answers.

In Chapman the second part of this speech is an extensive development of
the first sentence in the Homeric passage, in which Ulysses remarks on the
difficulty of recognizing Athene because of her numerous disguises:

> But where you wonder that I know you not
> Through all your changes, that skill is not got
> By sleight or Art, since thy most hard-hit face
> Is still distinguisht by thy free-given grace;
> And therefore truly to acknowledge thee
> In thy encounters is a maistery
> In men most knowing. For to all men thou
> Tak'st severall likenesses. All men thinke they know
> Thee in their wits. But, since thy seeming view
> Appears to all, and yet thy truth to few,
> Through all thy changes to discern thee right
> Asks chief Love to thee, and inspired light.   [XIII, 460–71]

We find here again the theme of the limitations of human knowlege. But
Ulysses restates it now with a different emphasis: Man cannot know divinity
through his own intelligence ("sleight or Art") but only through "free-given
grace." Without grace man, in his pride of knowledge, often thinks he knows
but is deceived: "all men thinke they know thee in their wits." The operation
of grace in man distinguishes divine truth from misleading appearances. This
is another important revelation for the hero. The very fact that he has recognized Athene, however tardily, indicates a new stage in his development.

In the last and most important part of the speech Ulysses unconsciously
reveals the reason for his having been so long deprived of Athene's aid. Here
there is also a direct but equally unconscious refutation of his opening
complaint:

> But this I surely know, that some years past
> I have beene often with thy presence grac'st.
> All time the sonnes of *Greece* wag'd warre at *Troy;*
> But when Fates full houre let our swords enjoy
> Oure vowes in sack of *Priams* lofty Towne,
> Oure Ships all boorded, and when God had blowne
> Oure Fleete in sunder, I could never see
> The seede of *Jove,* nor once distinguish thee
> Boording my Ship to take one woe from me;
> But onely in my proper spirit involv'd
> Err'd here and there, quite slaine, till heaven dissolv'd

> Me and my ill; which chanc't not till thy grace
> By open speech confirm'd me, in a place
> Fruitfull of people, where, in person, thou
> Didst give me guide and all their City show,
> And that was the renown'd *Phaeacian* earth.   [XIII, 472–87]

Comparison with the original will show that Chapman has elaborated its meaning considerably. "But ever bearing a divided heart in my breast I wandered, until the gods freed me from evil" becomes "But onely in my proper spirit involv'd, / Err'd here and there, quite slaine, till heaven dissolv'd / Me and my ill." This treats Odysseus' separation from Athene, which Homer is content to leave unexplained, as a state of spiritual isolation. Chapman merely states what is strongly implied in Homer, for he treats Odysseus' *dedaïgmenon hētor*—his "divided heart"—as a subjective spiritual condition, and thus makes his hero more self-analytical than Homer's. The complaints at the beginning of Ulysses' speech in Chapman find a more specific answer here. Until the sack of Troy he had enjoyed Athene's favor; his troubles probably began when he took a leading part in the destruction of the sacred citadel referred to in the opening lines:

> The Man (O Muse) informe, that many a way
> Wound with his wisedome to his wished stay;
> That wanderd wondrous farre, when He the towne
> Of sacred *Troy* had sackt and shiverd downe.   [I, 1–4]

There are two answers, general and particular, to Ulysses' complaints. As a general rule man's sufferings are not proportioned to his deserts. But Ulysses has not been as wise or just as he claims. In Chapman the connection between his actions at the fall of Troy and his subsequent separation from Athene is somewhat clearer than it is in Homer, where the facts are presented without the strong implication that they are related as cause and effect. Homer does, however, mention in book V how Odysseus and other Achaeans on the way from Troy "sinned against Athene," and he goes on to tell how the goddess "sent them an evil wind and long waves. There all his other noble comrades died, but the wind and waves brought him hither [to Ogygia]" (108–11). Homer never specifies the nature of this offense. Even in Chapman Ulysses is only vaguely aware of the connection between his actions and his separation from Athene, a connection which is nevertheless revealed to the reader. Since that moment, he tells Athene, he never saw her come to his aid in trouble, as she used to do. The intimacy between the man and his divine patroness has been interrupted by some offense on his part. The separation has cost him years of suffering during which he has been thrown on his own merely human resources: "But onely in my proper spirit involv'd / Err'd here and there, quite slaine. . . ." In these lines Chapman enunciates the state of mind which fell upon Ulysses after Troy. *Proper* here means "belonging to oneself." A distinction is implied between the individual human spirit and the divine spirit. The former by itself is ultimately ineffectual: "involv'd," enveloped and entangled thus, Ulysses "err'd," went astray both figuratively and geographically. Involved in the sense of wound suggests the futility of these wanderings. One should also note the religious terminology which Chapman uses to represent the spiritual nature of the hero's experience: "grac'st," "spirit," "heav'n," and "confirm'd." Homer is rarely as explicit about such inner, spiritual developments, yet all of Chapman's version is based on the implications of the original speech.

In the last half of the poem, after the old intimacy with Athene is reestablished, Ulysses is able to analyze his offense in terms of principles valid for the entire poem and enunciated at the outset, as we have seen, by Zeus. The chief instance of this is the hero's warning to Amphinomus, the best of the suitors, to save himself from the coming vengeance by quitting the company of the suitors while there is time. In Homer it is Ulysses' most self-critical speech, and Bartlett calls it "the one speech in Homer which most nearly justifies Chapman's interpretation of Ulysses."[31] Though Ulysses does not mention here the specific offenses he has committed, we must remember that he is bound, for the time being, to conceal his identity. After some introductory remarks praising Amphinomus' father as a just man, he says:

Earth nourishes nothing feebler than man of all creatures that breathe and move. For he thinks that he will never suffer in times to come, as long as the gods make him prosperous and his knees are unbowed, but when the blessed gods decree him sorrow, he bears it reluctantly but with a steadfast heart. For the spirit of man on earth is such as the day which the father of gods and men brings upon him. I, too, once hoped to prosper, but, yielding to my might and strength, did many wicked deeds, trusting in my father and brothers. Therefore, let no man be lawless, but let him keep in silence whatever gifts the gods may give.   [XVIII, 130–42]

The heart of this argument is that power is fortuitous and does not confer any exemptions from the rule of justice and fair play. It is the strongest statement for the principle of law, as distinguished from the anarchy of force, in Homer's poem, a principle which Homer sees as the divinely sanctioned basis of society. Chapman relates this part of the speech to Zeus's opening statement, quoted earlier, that man can avoid certain catastrophes by using his reason and by acting with due regard to the consequences of his actions:

> Of all things breathing, or that creepe on earth,
> Nought is more wretched than a humane Birth.
> Bless'd men thinke never they can cursed be,
> While any power lasts to move a knee.
> But when the blest Gods make them feele that smart,
> That fled their Faith so, as they had no hart
> They beare their sufferings, and what wel they might
> Have cleerly shun'd, they then meet in despight.
> The Minde of Man flyes stil out of his way,
> Unless God guide and prompt it every day.   [XVIII, 188–97]

The final couplet emphasizes the insufficiency of intelligence alone as a guide.

In the rest of the speech, in Chapman as in Homer, Ulysses applies the preceding generalities to himself:

> I thought me once a blessed man with men,
> And fashion'd me to all so counted then,
> Did all injustice like them, what for Lust,
> Or any pleasure, never so unjust,
> I could by powre or violence obtaine,
> And gave them both in all their powres the raigne:
> Bold of my Fathers and my Brothers still;
> While which held good, my Arts seem'd never ill.
> And thus is none held simply good or bad,
> But as his will is either mist, or had.
> All goods Gods gifts man cals, how ere he gets them,
> And so takes all, what price so ere God sets them;
> Saies nought how ill they come, nor will controule
> That Ravine in him, though it cost his soule.   [XVIII, 198–211]

In his former prosperity, Ulysses says, he thought himself blessed and, taking only material success as his guide, used any means to achieve his desires. The point of Chapman's translation turns on the word *ólbios,* which means both "blessed" and "prosperous," and it is developed in the indictment of the pragmatic philosophy of success in the couplet: "And thus is none held simply good or bad, / But as his will is either mist, or had." The importance of acting according to absolute moral principles is strongly implied in both poems. The great significance of this particular speech, in Homer as well as in the translation, lies in the wrongs which Ulysses confesses. He had set up his own will as the good and pursued it ruthlessly. Now he is at last in a position to assert what suffering has taught him. With the fulfillment of self-knowledge through an insight into his personal experiences the hero assumes a public role as judge and restorer of Ithacan society.

These self-analytical passages are landmarks in Ulysses' evolution. Now let us turn to some of the main episodes to see how Chapman has embodied this general concept in the texture of his poem.

Ulysses' sojourn in Phaeacia presents an important stage in this evolution. It terminates a decade of wandering in a fabulous world. It comes at the end of countless exhausting and terrifying struggles against hostile forces of nature. It is the hero's first encounter in twenty years with normal society in peacetime. Finally, it marks a turning-point in the process by which the hero has been relentlessly stripped of his fleet, his sailors, his booty, his weapons, and even his clothes. He reaches Phaeacia naked and nearly drowned; he leaves loaded with gifts, sleeping tranquilly in a magical ship which accomplishes in a single night the voyage home which he has been trying to make for ten years.

While Phaeacia is important as a setting for Ulysses' account of his adventures, his arrival and first experiences in that country provide Chapman with material rich in inner meaning. As the hero hauls himself out of the water and stumbles ashore, Chapman emphasizes the contrast between his physical exhaustion and the enduring vitality of his spirit. At first Ulysses' fatigue, which verges on death, is described in a magnificent passage:

> Then forth he came, his both knees faltring, both
> His strong hands hanging downe, and all with froth
> His cheeks and nosthrils flowing, voice and breath
> Spent to all use; and downe he sunke to Death.
> The sea had soakt his heart through: all his vaines
> His toiles had rackt t'a labouring womans paines.
> Dead wearie was he.   [V, 608–14]

The striking image at the end is not in the original: "And he let his two knees bend and his strong hands fall, for his spirit was crushed by the sea. And all his flesh was swollen, and the sea water flowed in streams up through his mouth and nostrils. So he lay breathless and speechless, scarcely strong enough to move, for terrible weariness had come upon him" (V, 453–57). From Chapman's gloss it is evident that he mistook one of the verbs in the Homeric passage for the aorist of another.[32]

Now Ulysses revives enough to move from the shore to a thick grove, where he covers himself with leaves and falls asleep. His decision to face in the woods the possible attacks of wild beasts rather than endure any longer "the seas chill breath, / And vegetant dewes" (V, 628–29) gives Chapman a chance to have the hero state a principle which it has taken him a long time to learn. For years he had tried to outwit or circumvent the hostility of the sea. Circe, for example, had warned him of fixed and inescapable losses which he must suffer in passing Charybdis, but Ulysses rebelled none the less:

> This Neede she told me of my losse, when I
> Desir'd to know if that *Necessitie*
> (When I had scap't *Charybdis* outrages)
> My powres might not revenge, though not redresse?
> She answerd: O unhappy! art thou yet
> Enflam'd with warre, and thirst to drinke thy swet?
> Not to the Gods give up both Armes and will?
> She deathlesse is, and that immortall ill
> Grave, harsh, outragious, not to be subdu'd,
> That men must suffer till they be renew'd.
> Nor lives there any virtue that can flie
> The vicious outrage of her crueltie.
> Shouldst thou put Armes on, and approch the Rocke,
> I fear six more must expiate the shocke.
> Six heads six men aske still.   [XII, 173–87]

Although Chapman has introduced here a few Christian overtones, as in "renew'd" in the sense of "redeemed" and in "expiate," his translation follows the original quite closely.[33] Thus, even in Homer, Ulysses displays on this occasion a spirit admirable from one point of view, but deplorable from another. When Circe speaks to him of yielding to the gods, she is not thinking only of Scylla, as Spondanus notes: "But Circe answers that this ordeal is to be overcome only by patience, because it is inflicted by the gods, whom it is not given to mortals to resist. Whence it seems to have a double inference about the gods: even of Jove himself, by whose will these things occur: hence also of Charybdis, or Scylla, whom she recognizes as gods." Circe clearly has in mind Ulysses' general attitude toward the gods and not merely his present hostility toward Scylla. Despite the warning, the hero does not restrain himself in the crisis, for as his ship threads the strait between the monsters,

> . . . then even I forgot to shunne the harme
> *Circe* forewarnd, who willd I should not arme,
> nor shew my selfe to *Scylla,* lest in vaine
> I ventur'd life. Yet could not I containe,
> But arm'd at all parts and two lances tooke.
> [XII, 336–40; cf. *Odyssey* XII, 226–30]

The principle uttered by Ulysses as he staggers ashore in Scheria shows that he has at last learned the lesson Circe tried to teach him. He has been saved from certain death only through his submissive prayer to the god of the river, who made his landing possible (V, 599–603; cf. *Odyssey* V, 445–50). Now that his rebellious, self-reliant spirit has finally been chastened, Chapman marks his newly acquired wisdom, as he leaves the shore to shelter in the woods, by adding this couplet to his reflections: "But he that fights with heaven, or with the sea, / To Indiscretion addes Impietie" (V, 642–43, p. 85). By this interpolation Chapman calls the reader's attention to a major revolution in Ulysses' outlook and prepares us for his glorification of the hero as the epitome of virtue in the final lines of the book, as Ulysses lies down in his bed of leaves:

> Patient *Ulysses* joyd that ever day
> Shewd such a shelter. In the midst he lay,
> Store of leaves heaping high on every side.
> And as in some out-field a man doth hide
> A kindld brand to keepe the seed of fire,
> No neighbour dwelling neare, and his desire
> Serv'd with self store he else would aske of none,
> But of his fore-spent sparks rakes the ashes on:
> So this out-place Ulysses thus receives;
> And thus nak't vertues seed lies hid in leaves.   [V, 658–67]

Except in two places this follows the sense of the original closely. Chapman has turned Ulysses the much-enduring—*polútlas*—into the patient Ulysses and has added the last line to extend the wonderful Homeric simile into an image of the hero's rebirth. Here is the original for purposes of comparison: "And the divine Odysseus, who had endured much, saw it and was glad and lay down in the midst, heaping the fallen leaves over himself. And just as a man hides a brand beneath the dark embers in an outlying farm, a man who has no neighbors, and so saves the seed of fire, that he may not have to kindle it from some other source, so Odysseus covered himself with leaves" (V, 486–91). Chapman's last line is translated almost literally from Spondanus' commentary on the simile: "Sic noster Ulysses, quasi semen aliquod virtutis sub istis foliis reconditur"[34] (Thus our Ulysses, as the seed of virtue, is hidden beneath those leaves). Chapman thereby stresses the meaning of the hero's condition—he is stripped of everything but virtue: the pangs of suffering have brought forth the naked child of virtue, in an extension of the earlier image—"all his vaines / His toiles had rackt t'a labouring womans paines." Chapman provides an effective but not over-obtrusive symbol of Ulysses' spiritual rebirth. We now have the essential, the "absolute" Ulysses.

Chapman continues to develop allegorically the distinction between the hero's miserable bodily condition and his spiritual vitality through the entire sixth book. One of the most significant places is Nausicaa's speech rebuking her companions for running away at their first sight of Ulysses: "Stand, my maidens. Where are you fleeing at the mere sight of a man? Surely you do not think that he is an enemy? There is no living mortal who shall come to the land of the Phaeacians as an enemy, for we are very dear to the immortals" (VI, 199–203). This is but the germ of the speech Chapman gives to the Princess:

> Give stay both to your feet and fright;
> Why thus disperse ye, for a mans meere sight?
> Esteeme you him a *Cyclop,* that long since
> Made use to prey upon our Citizens?
> This man no moist man is (nor watrish thing
> That's ever flitting, ever ravishing
> All it can compasse and, like it, doth range
> In rape of women, never staid in change).
> This man is truly manly, wise, and staid,
> In soule more rich, the more to sense decaid;
> Who nor will do, nor suffer to be done,
> Acts leud and abject, nor can such a one
> Greete the *Phaeacians* with a mind envious:
> Deare to the Gods they are, and he is pious.   [VI, 307–20]

From the fifth through the eighth lines this passage translates the Homeric phrase *dieròs brotós,* which simply means "living mortal." In his note to the passage, Chapman embroiders the faulty definition of *dierós* in Scapula's lexicon, which is "humidus, madidus, cui humiditas inest. . . . Apud Hom. *dieròs brotós,* cui vitalis quaedam humiditas inest"[35] (humid, liquid, that in which humidity exists. . . .). Chapman glosses the phrase thus: "cui vitalis vel sensualis humiditas inest. A *rhéo,* ut dicatur quasi *rhotós,* . . . quod nihil sit magis fluxum quam homo"[36] (in which there is a vital or sensual humor.

From *rhéo*, as it might be called *rhotós*, . . . because nothing is more changeable than man). Spondanus' Latin version of the Homeric phrase, *humidus homo*,[37] agrees with Scapula's definition, and both provide Chapman with an excellent opportunity for developing extensive symbolic meanings, far beyond those in the original. This particular part of the translation is grotesque, but in the context of the water symbolism which Chapman uses throughout the poem, as we have seen, "moist" and "watrish" imply flux, "humor," and instability of character. The use of "staid" reinforces these associations. Ulysses has achieved "stay," spiritual if not geographical. Another instance of Scapula's pervading influence is found in the four lines beginning with "this man is truly manly, wise, and staid," as Schoell notes.[38] The lines "who nor will do, nor suffer to be done, / Acts leud and abject" are shown to be a close translation of part of Scapula's definition of *anér*, "man," (= male) which stands in the same relation to another Greek word for man (= human), *ánthropos*, as *vir* does to *homo*. Scapula's definition makes the distinction: "Dicuntur etiam aliquando *ándres* quicunque aliquid dignum vero vel dicunt vel faciunt: & non esse andres, qui servile quidpiam et abiectum facere sustinent"[39] (Whoever truly does or says anything worthy is called an *anér*, and they are not *ándres* who can bear anything servile or abject). Chapman quotes part of this note without acknowledgment,[40] and takes the opportunity to make Nausicaa declare within the poem the virtue of the hero, who is truly "manly" in contrast to the common run of people. The distinction between the two sorts of men is, however, found in Homer's use of *anér* and *ánthropos*, as Geddes notes: "It is also to be noted that *aner* in Iliad is not so pre-eminent where all or most at least are *ándres*, while the *anér* of Odyssey stands out alone, as it were, among *ánthropoi*, which last word has an ampler range, and comes much more to the front in Odyssey as the ordinary designation of Man."[41]

Finally, Chapman pursues the distinction between Ulysses' physical decrepitude and his spiritual vitality by reading a moral meaning into Scapula's purely physiological definition, "cui vitalis vel sensualis humiditas inest," in the line "In soule more rich, the more to sense decaid." The speech as a whole is one of Chapman's most liberal and extreme elaborations of meanings he felt were implied in the context of the original. He had a perfect right to emphasize that Ulysses had become a virtuous and civilized man, but his way of doing it gives Nausicaa an extravagant degree of insight. This emphasis comes at the right time, but ineptly. Although the translation is based on mistaken authorities, it is consistent with the fundamental meaning of Ulysses' experiences as Chapman sees them, and its roots extend far through the poem in Chapman's patterns of symbolism.

In this book a corresponding alteration occurs in Chapman's treatment of the bath which Ulysses takes after his meeting with Nausicaa. Without any immediate warrant in the original he ascribes mysterious powers to the pool where the princess and her companions have been doing the laundry:

> Whose waters were so pure they would not staine,
> But still ran faire forth, and did more remaine
> Apt to purge staines for that purg'd staine within,
> Which, by the waters pure store was not seen.   [VI, 120–23]

Homer merely says that "abundant water welled up from beneath and flowed over to cleanse garments however dirty they might be" (VI, 86–87). As a description of wash-water Chapman's lines are unbearably quaint, and his style here is abominable, but the strange efficacy he imputes to the pool is not so far-fetched, I think as it at first appears to be. While in Homer there is not the slightest hint of a ritual purgation, right after the bath Odysseus undergoes a miraculous rejuvenation:

With the water from the river noble Odysseus washed from his skin the brine which covered his back and broad shoulders, and from his head he wiped the scurf of the unresting sea. But when he had washed his whole body and had anointed himself with oil and had put on the clothes which the maiden had given him, then Athene the daughter of Zeus made him taller and stronger to look upon, and from his head she made the locks flow in curls like the hyacinth. Just as a skillful craftsman whom Hephaestus and Pallas have taught all kinds of artistry overlays silver with gold and creates a work that is very graceful, so did the goddess endow his head and shoulders with added beauty. Then he went off and sat on the shore of the sea, radiant with grace and comeliness.   [VI, 224–37]

Chapman gives to this transformation a spiritual character in the phrase "When worke sets forth / A worthy soule to bodies of such worth":

> He clensd his broad soil'd shoulders, backe and head
> Yet never tam'd. But now had fome and weed
> Knit in the faire curles, which dissolv'd, and he
> Slickt with sweet oile, the sweet charitie
> The untoucht virgin shewd in his attire
> He cloth'd him with. Then *Pallas* put a fire,
> More than before, into his sparkling eies,
> His late soile set off by his soone fresh guise
> His locks (clensd) curl'd the more, and matcht (in power
> To please an eye) the *Hyacinthian* flower.
> And as a workman, that can well combine
> Silver and gold, and make both strive to shine,
> As being by *Vulcan* and *Minerva* too
> Taught how farre either may be urg'd to go
> In strife of eminence, when worke sets forth
> A worthy soule to bodies of such worth,
> No thought reproving th' act in any place,
> Nor *Art* no debt to *Natures* liveliest grace:
> So *Pallas* wrought in him a grace as great,
> From head to shoulders, and ashore did seate
> His goodly presence.   [VI, 356–76]

In Homer this miraculous transformation is a rite marking the conclusion both of Odysseus' struggle with the sea and his alienation from Athene. Chapman, following Homer's implications, endows it with a specifically spiritual emphasis couched in a tortuous style.

In the seventh and eighth books our attention turns from Odysseus' final ordeal as an *isolato* to his introduction into Phaeacian culture. This part of the story may well be regarded as his reintroduction into community values. At their center stands Queen Arete, whose name ("she who is prayed to") shows the devotion she inspires as ruler, wife, mother, and housewife. She shares with Penelope the discernment to recognize her handiwork in Odysseus' garments, and Odysseus is enjoined by Nausicaa and Athene to address himself first to her rather than to Alcinoüs. Athene describes her as follows:

> She may boast
> More honor of him [Alcinoüs] than the honor'd most
> Of any wife in earth can of her Lord,
> How many more soever Realmes affoord,
> That keepe house under husbands. Yet no more
> Her husband honors her than her blest store
> Of gracious children. All the Citie cast
> Eyes on her as a Goddesse, and give taste
> Of their affections to her in their praires,
> Still as she decks the streets; for all affaires
> Wrapt in contention she dissolves to men.
> Whom she affects, she wants no mind to deigne
> Goodnesse enough. If her heart stand inclin'd
> To your dispatch, hope all you wish to find,
> Your friends, your longing family, and all
> That can within your most affections fall.   [VII, 89–104]

Ulysses' supplication to this woman symbolizes his rededication to community and family. Like his meeting with Nausicaa, it contrasts with his erotic involvement with the seductive goddesses Circe and Calypso. Areté, indeed, represents the principles of *xenía* and *thémis,* to whose definition and reestablishment the whole *Odyssey* is devoted, violated by Helen and Clytemnestra. Homer embodies these values in his great women—Areté, Nausicaa, Penelope, and Eurycleia—and accordingly, as D. S. Margoliouth has written, "If the germ of the *Iliad* is the Praise of Man, that of the *Odyssey* is the Praise of a Woman."[42]

As the milieu in which Ulysses relates all his adventures since he sacked the temples of Troy, Scheria is a standard by which his former conduct is implicitly judged. From its perspective Ulysses reviews both the Trojan War and his subsequent wanderings through the fabulous world of the Lotophagoi, the Cyclopes, Aeolus, the Laestrygonians, Circe, Hades, the Sirens, Scylla and Charybdis, the Oxen of the Sun, and Calypso.

Chapman exploits fully the opportunities offered by the interaction of Ulysses' narrative with this context by making additions that illuminate the allegorical experience. The emotional breakdown the hero suffers just before he begins his long tale is especially interesting. After the customary days and nights as an unidentified stranger, the time has come to make himself known to his hosts. The most impressive introduction he can imagine is to have Demodocus sing of his most brilliant military exploit—the stratagem of the wooden horse and the sack of Troy. Yet as the psalmist says, "An horse is a vain thing for safety; neither shall he deliver any by his great strength" (33:17). Demodocus complies with the request, but Ulysses, instead of indulging in expected sentiments of pride and nostalgia, is surprised by other feelings. Homer presents the hero's unexpected reaction in the most important simile in the *Odyssey:*

This was the song the famous minstrel sang. But Odysseus' heart was melted, and tears wet his cheeks beneath his eyelids. And as a woman wails and flings herself about her dear husband who has fallen in defense of his city and his people, seeking to ward off the pitiless day from his town and his children, and, as she sees him dying and gasping for breath, clings to him and shrieks, while men behind her hit her back and shoulders and lead her off to slavery and toil and sorrow, while her fair cheeks are wasted with most pitiful grief, so did Odysseus let fall tears full of pity.

[VIII, 521–31]

Homer's similes often range beyond the points of comparison, but this one seems unusually relevant to its dramatic situation. Odysseus, as he hears Demodocus relate his triumph, weeps with pity. His sudden identification with a victim of war, whose plight is in every way like that foreseen by Andromache, marks a transcendence of the monocular heroic vision. The heroic code is suddenly seen from a truer perspective. Chapman, always ready to affirm the power of poetry to kindle the imagination, amplifies the opening of the Homeric passage:

> This the divine Expressor did so give
> Both act and passion that he made it live,
> And to *Ulysses* facts did breathe a fire
> So deadly quickning that it did inspire
> Old death with life, and renderd life so sweet
> And passionate, that all there felt it fleet;
> Which made him pitie his own crueltie
> And put into that ruth so pure an eie
> Of human frailtie, that to see a man
> Could so revive from Death, yet no way can
> Defend from Death, his owne quicke powres it made
> Feele there deaths horrors, and he felt life fade.
> In teares his feeling braine swet, for in things
> That move past utterance, tears ope all their springs.
> Nor are there in the Powres that all life beares,
> More true interpreters of all then teares.   [VIII, 708–23]

Chapman's exalted conception of the office of great poetry presented vigorously in this passage includes the characteristic details of divine inspiration, of the power of poetry to achieve a reality more real than life, and of its power to engage the deepest emotions. As a representation of Ulysses' new emotional and psychological state it is equally noteworthy. For the first time a great emotion overwhelms his normally analytical and calculating mind. Hereafter Ulysses will conceive of himself primarily as a member of the human race, not as a leading member of the aristocrary of warriors.

Following this outburst Ulysses is ready to begin his long narrative. Many of the episodes go far toward defining the lack of humanity and self-discipline which he has finally overcome, and consequently Chapman, like centuries of Homeric scholars and critics, sees them as moral allegories. Unlike his predecessors', however, Chapman's allegorical treatment of Ulysses is evolutionary and dynamic.

The first episode Ulysses describes contrasts strikingly with the emotional revolution he has just experienced, and it measures the extent of this revolution. He first speaks of himself as "known among all men for my wiles"—*polúmetis*—instead of using the epithet, in which he used to take such pride, of "city-sacker"—*ptolíporthos*. Then, bluntly, and without attempting in any way to extenuate his actions, he begins. Chapman follows the original very closely:

> From *Ilion* ill winds cast me on the Coast
> The *Cicons* hold, where I emploid mine hoast
> For *Ismarus,* a Citie built just by
> My place of landing, of which *Victory*
> Made me expugner. I depeopl'd it,
> Slue all the men and did their wives remit
> With much spoile taken, which we did divide,
> That none might need his part.   [IX, 71–78]

Odysseus gives no specific motive for attacking Ismarus, although the Cicones were allies of the Trojans. By omitting this fact Homer seems to have aimed at producing an effect of unextenuated genocide and plunder cited by Grotius in *De Jure Belli ac Pacis* (1515) as the first recorded violation of the Laws of Nations. Chapman underlines its cool brutality by his abstractions. "I sacked the city" becomes "a Citie . . . of which *Victory* made me expugner." "I depeopl'd it," Chapman's interpolation, also contributes to the sense of detachment, as does his rhetorical equalizing of wives and booty. In both the original and the translation Ulysses' scrupulous concern for a fair division of the spoils contrasts wryly with his indifference to the horrors inflicted on the Cicones.

The mission at Ismarus fails, eventually, because Odysseus' men disobeyed his orders. Just a case of postwar demoralization, perhaps, although his leadership seems to have fallen off since he turned back, single-handed,

the panicking, home-bent troops on the beaches at Troy. My suspicion that
this disastrous finale, which plunges the voyagers into a fabulous world of
alienation, is not due simply to bad discipline is strengthened by the fact that
in other, fictitious raids which he relates to Eumaeus (XIV, 257–84) and to
Antinoüs (XVII, 415–44) the consequences are also disastrous, and Odysseus
takes pains to dissociate himself from the hubris that led his men to kill and
plunder. In these accounts he may only be damning his soldiers for their
rashness, but he is also apparently trying to make a good impression by
disclaiming piratical intentions which, especially in the presence of Eumaeus,
who had been enslaved by Taphian pirates, would not have ingratiated him
with his listeners.

After the brief adventure with the Lotus-Eaters, Ulysses' insatiable curi-
osity draws him and a small band into the very cave of the Cyclops Polyphemus. This major episode reverses the situation at Ismarus, with the balance of
power against the hero at the start, but conflict nevertheless issuing in a
victory for the victims. Chapman skillfully highlights the reciprocating ironies in Homer. Ulysses prefaces his story with a description of the unsociable,
primitive, yet oddly idyllic life of the Cyclopes:

>   a race
> Of proud-liv'd loiterers, that never sow,
> Nor put a plant in earth, nor use a plow,
> But trust in God for all things, and their earth,
> (Unsowne, unplowd) gives every of-spring birth
> That other lands have: Wheate and Barley, Vines
> That beare in goodly grapes delicious wines,
> And *Jove* sends showres for all. No counsels there,
> Nor counsellers, nor lawes, but all men beare
> Their heads aloft on mountaines, and those steepe,
> And on their tops too: and there houses keepe
> In vaultie caves, their housholds governd all
> By each mans law, imposde in severall,
> Nor wife nor child awd but as he thinks good,
> None for another caring.   [IX, 167–81][43]

The Cyclopes live in the state of nature, in political anarchy and social
isolation, each one's will being law. The extreme contrast between their way
of life and that of the Phaeacians is emphasized by the addition of the
following details, where Chapman follows Homer closely:

> Nor place the neighbour *Cyclops* their delights
> In brave vermilion prow-deckt ships, nor wrights
> Usefull and skilfull in such works as need
> Perfection to those trafficks that exceed
> Their naturall confines. . . .   [IX, 193–97][44]

Ulysses then tells how his landing party disembarks on a neighboring deserted
island and feasts abundantly on wild goats and on the wine they took from the

Cicones. Then the hero leaves the bulk of his forces and sets out with a picked band to discover

> what men
> The neighbour Ile held, if of rude disdaine,
> Churlish and tyrannous, or minds bewraid
> Pious and hospitable. [IX, 253–56][45]

The narrator is here, perhaps, playing on the sympathies of his audience, who have, as he knows, ineradicable memories of the brutality of the Cyclopes and of their barbarous ways. He then describes the gift he brought.

> I tooke besides along
> A goat-skin flagon of wine, blacke and strong,
> That *Maro* did present, *Evantheus* sonne,
> And Priest to *Phoebus,* who had mansion
> In *Thracian Ismarus* (the towne I tooke).
> He gave it me, since I (with reverence strooke
> Of his grave place, his wife and childrens good)
> Freed all of violence. [IX, 279–86][46]

This is a close translation, even to "with reverence strooke," which translates *hazómenai.* The reverent behavior is strangely inconsistent with his otherwise untempered aggressiveness. The allusion to the attack on Ismarus, coming on the heels of Ulysses' declared intention of finding out whether the Cyclopes are churlish or hospitable, acts, both in Homer and in Chapman, as a reminder that the hero was at the time scarcely in a sound position to judge, and that he had no reason to expect kindness at the hands of strangers in view of the treatment strangers had received from him. Chapman goes on to indicate how superficial are Ulysses' civilized pretenses by making him recoil in fastidious horror at the monster's provincialism and inhumanity. In Homer he remarks: "My proud spirit had a foreboding that presently a man would come to me endowed with great strength, a savage knowing nothing of justice or law" (IX, 213–15). Chapman's Ulysses assumes an air of fastidious distaste.

> [I] long'd to see this heape of fortitude,
> That so illiterate was and upland rude
> That lawes divine nor humane he had learned. [IX, 307–09]

Throughout the encounter with Polyphemus Ulysses' manner oscillates between abject humility, with earnest invocations of the laws of hospitality, and swaggering arrogance. A fine ironic effect is achieved in the Cyclops' unexpected question when he discovers the little group cowering in his cave, and in Ulysses' answer: "Strangers, who are you? Whence are you sailing over the paths of the sea? Is it on some business, or do you wander at random over the sea, risking your lives and bringing evil to men of other lands?"[47] The savage monster asks the emissaries of civilization essentially the same question that they intended to ask him. Chapman points up this strange turnabout by making Polyphemus enquire piously about the state of their souls. He ascribes a second, anachronistic sense to the Greek *psuchai* by translating it both as "lives" and "souls."

As we consider Ulysses' answer, in which Chapman follows Homer very closely, we may begin to wonder whether the question was as outrageous as it first seemed:

> Erring *Grecians* we
> From *Troy* were turning homewards, but by force
> Of adverse winds, in far-diverted course,
> Such unknowne waies tooke, and on rude seas tost,
> (As *Jove* decreed) are cast upon this Coast.
> Of *Agamemnon* (famous *Atreus* sonne)
> We boast our selves the souldiers, who hath wonne
> Renowme that reacheth heaven, to overthrow
> So great a Citie, and to ruine so,
> So many nations.   [IX, 362–71][48]

By the happy ambiguity of "erring" (derived by Scapula's *erravi* from Homer's *apoplangthéntes*), Chapman suggests the moral as well as geographical strayings of Ulysses and his men. The answer is intended to deny the imputation of piracy, yet it unconsciously reveals, in the light of the military action against the Cicones and the wrecking of the sacred Trojan citadels, that the distinction between war and piracy is sometimes very small.

This introduction is scarcely calculated to arouse Polyphemus' hospitable feelings, nor is the threatening tone of Ulysses' appeal likely to win him over:

> We suppliants are, and hospitable *Jove*
> Poures wreake on all whom praires want powre to move,
> And with their plagues together will provide
> That humble guests shall have their wants supplide.   [IX, 377–80][49]

Chapman points up the inconsistency in Ulysses' behavior by adding the word "humble." His assumed humility lasts only until he escapes from Polyphemus' cave and, figuring that he is at a safe distance from the blinded monster, shouts this boast: "Then I spoke to the Cyclops with mocking words: 'Cyclops, that man was no weakling after all, whose friends you planned to devour brutally in your hollow cave. Surely your evil deeds were to fall on your own house. Therefore Zeus and the other gods have taken vengeance on you'" (IX, 474–79). Chapman changes this to make Ulysses proclaim a general principle of just and humane conduct which he himself repeatedly violated. The speech suggests a lack of self-knowledge in the speaker:

> I staid our ores and this insultance usde:
> *Cyclop!* thou shouldst not have so much abusde
> Thy monstrous forces to oppose their least
> Against a man immartiall, and a guest,

> And eate his fellowes: thou mightst know there were
> Some ils behind (rude swaine) for thee to beare,
> That feard not to devoure thy guests, and breake
> All lawes of humanes: *Jove* sends therefore wreake,
> And all the Gods, by me.   [IX, 635–43]

In view of the way in which he introduced himself to Polyphemus, Ulysses' designation of himself as "a man immartiall" is a glaring inconsistency. His arrogance is heightened by the assumption that he is the agent of divine vengeance. The worst, however, is yet to come. Having narrowly escaped death for himself and his men from a great rock which the blinded monster hurls in the direction of this taunt, Ulysses, once the boat is at a supposedly safe distance, shouts a second insult. Chapman inserts a prefatory remark full of unconscious irony:

> But I gave way
> To that wrath which so long I held deprest,
> (By great *Necessitie* conquerd) in my brest.   [IX, 670–72]

This just after his lack of self-control has come close to destroying the whole company. It is strange that one critic should cite this as an example of Ulysses' Stoic submission to necessity.

Chapman continues to emphasize the moral significance of Ulysses' behavior in this adventure by enlarging on Polyphemus' reply to the hero's second boast that Polyphemus' father, Poseidon, will be unable to restore his son's vision. The Cyclops says, "*Augur Telemus* / . . . said all this deed"

> Should this event take, author'd by the hand
> Of one *Ulysses,* who I thought was mand
> With great and goodly personage, and bore
> A vertue answerable, and this shore
> Should shake with weight of such a conqueror;
> When now a weakling came, a dwarfie thing,
> A thing of nothing, who yet wit did bring
> That brought supply to all, and with his wine
> Put out the flame where all my light did shine.   [IX, 687–95][50]

"And bore / A vertue answerable" is Chapman's addition. While "vertue" here undoubtedly has for its primary meaning the obsolete sense of "strength," its moral sense is surely relevant. Thus the "savage monster" reveals the moral shortcomings of the hero, who has completely failed to understand the meaning of his adventure.

The relatively few additions which Chapman has introduced into the episode do not alter its fundamental meaning. They emphasize the inadequacy of Ulysses' pseudocivilized assumptions, which conceal from him his own savage predilections. They show with sardonic humor the inconsistency of his appeals to the sanctions of civilized principles with his sacrilege, slaughter, and plunder at Troy and Ismarus. It would be as great a mistake, Chapman's reading of the episode shows, to postulate in Homer an uncritical approval of his hero's every action as it would be to assume that carnage and crime were blandly accepted and endorsed by a "primitive" poet who knew nothing better. In Polyphemus, Homer confronts Ulysses with a fantastic image of the spirit which led him to sack the temples of Troy and to depeople the town of Ismarus. When the savage-looking Odysseus emerged from the underbrush Nausicaa had asked her frightened companions the rhetorical question, "Surely you don't think he is an enemy?" (VI, 200). Yet one is bound to wonder whether events would have justified her confidence if Odysseus' first stop after Troy had been Scheria instead of Ismarus. Chapman had marked the hero's victory over the Cyclopean spirit that so aggravated his troubles in his translation of her question: "Esteeme you him a *Cyclop,* that long since / Made use to prey upon our citizens?" (VI, 309–10).

In Homer, Ulysses' experiences with Circe contain more allegorical features than his encounter with Polyphemus. Circe is a goddess whose potions transform Ulysses' men into beasts in form though not in mind. Ulysses is preserved by the intervention of Hermes and the gift of an antidote, and Circe is herself transformed from a dangerous sorceress to a friend, hostess, and guide of the wayfarers. In this adventure the danger is disguised, and the hero's escape from it does not depend on clever strategy. Polyphemus had an unexpected streak of tenderness toward his favorite ram, but Circe is a much more inhuman figure, beautiful, sinister, yet, if properly approached, helpful. Although Ulysses succumbed to arrogance in his conflict with Polyphemus, he survives the temptations of Circe unharmed and with new power.

This adventure has provided the most fertile field of all for allegorical interpreters of Homer. Comes summarizes his view of it in part as follows: "And as I shall say in conclusion, through this fable the ancients wished to signify that a man in every fortune should govern himself moderately and confront all difficulties unconquered, while the rest of the multitude like the lightest little boat are carried here and there by the waves, and the inconstancy of the winds drives them anywhere: for the companions of Ulysses were changed into beasts, while he remained unconquered because of his wisdom."[51] Chapman, in his general conception of the *Odyssey,* uses the basic symbol of man's moral infirmity and spiritual confusion "like a merest cockleshell borne here and there by the waves" which Comes uses here, but, as we have seen, he does not regard Ulysses as untroubled by such faults, while Comes always does. Heraclitus also emphasizes Ulysses' temperance, in interpreting the intervention of Hermes as the victory of wisdom and self-control over the anger he felt on hearing of his comrades' fate: "He is the counsellor who stands by Ulysses as he approaches Circe. At first the hero is inspired by passion and grief because of what he has learned and is carried away without judgment. But in a little while, as these emotions burn themselves out, he seeks to escape by the use of prudence, whence Hermes of the golden rod happens to meet him." The moly Hermes gives Odysseus Heraclitus considers to be wisdom.[52] These examples are quite typical of traditional interpretations of the Homeric myth. Pope goes even further in the elucidation of certain details: "The flower of *Moly* is white and sweet; this denotes that the fruits of instruction are sweet, agreeable, and nourishing; *Mercury* gives this plant; this intimates that all instruction is the gift of Heaven: *Mercury* brings it not with him, but gathers it from the place where he stands, to show that Wisdom is not confin'd to places, but that everywhere it may be found, if Heaven vouchsafes to discover it, and we are disposed to receive and follow it."[53] Thus in all times and all places the Circe episode has been read as a moral allegory of the triumph of wisdom.

Why has this episode been chosen above all as a leading example of allegory? The adventure, by its very nature, requires that it be read as allegory, for taken on the literal level as a fabulous experience it has little meaning. What then would be Circe's motive for transforming men into beasts? Why would Ulysses be singled out for a purely fortuitous gift of the wonderful antidote? Where is the interest in the tale if the hero saves himself and frees his companions simply by the accidental possession of such a gift?

Chapman allies himself with a long tradition in explicitly translating the episode as an allegory in which the hero's temperance in the face of temptations to sensuality makes him immune to the brutalization which his companions suffer. The main feature of Chapman's treatment of the allegory in this episode is his emphasis on what he takes to be the inner realities, especially the various aspects of Ulysses' character, to which elements in the action correspond. While Hermes (in Homer) emphasizes the efficacy of the moly— "She will mix a potion for you and put drugs in your food, but even so she shall not bewitch you, for the powerful herb that I shall give you will not permit it" (X, 290–92)—in Chapman he stresses just as much Ulysses' powers of resistance. Here we observe the first steps in the subjectivization of Homer's myth:

> With a festivall
> Sheele first receive thee, but will spice thy bread
> With flowrie poysons; yet unaltered
> Shall thy firme forme be, for this remedy
> Stands most approv'd gainst all her Sorcery.   [X, 386–90]

As Chapman here uses it, the word "forme" comes to mean much more than mere physical shape. It acquires some of the Renaissance associations of order as the essence of reality and truth. It becomes the essence of manliness when Hermes warns that Circe will try to destroy Ulysses, "by stripping thee of forme, and faculties." This translates "that, when she has stripped thee, she may render thee a weakling and unmanned" (X, 301).

When Ulysses has drunk Circe's potion without being affected, she exclaims: "No man has ever withstood this charm, once he had drunk it and it had passed the barrier of his teeth. The heart in thy breast cannot be charmed.

Surely thou art Odysseus, the resourceful man, who Argeiphontes of the golden wand always told me would come from Troy in a swift black ship" (X, 327–32). Chapman shifts this tribute to the hero's intellect into a recognition of his moral fibre:

> Never drunke any this cup but he mournd
> In other likenesse, if it once had past
> The ivorie bounders of his tongue and taste.
> All but thy selfe are brutishly declind:
> Thy breast holds firme yet, and unchang'd thy mind.
> Thou canst be therefore none else but the man
> Of many virtues *Ithacensian,*
> Deepe-soul'd *Ulysses,* who I oft was told,
> By that slie God that beares the rod of gold
> Was to arrive here in retreat from *Troy.*   [X, 436–45]

Thus Homer's hero "of many devices" becomes Chapman's "Man / of many virtues . . . / Deepe-soul'd *Ulysses.*"

The elaborate preparations which are now made to entertain the hero give Chapman an opportunity to emphasize, by a small but important addition, the virtues of a ritualistic approach to pleasure. Homer, when Ulysses first enters Circe's dwelling, and then when he has subdued the goddess with his sword, describes how the hero was seated in a beautiful chair and "beneath was a foot-stool" (X, 315, 367). Chapman repeats the detail just as simply the first time, but the second time tells how, ceremonially, a servant "did with silkes the foot-pace consecrate" (X, 466).

Even so Ulysses will not partake until he has discharged his duties to his comrades. The issue in this episode is not abstinence but temperance, for later he eats well, drinks deep, and then sleeps with the goddess. Here foresight is as much involved as self-control. For the first time in the course of his adventures Ulysses does not plunge blindly into the encounter, or, perhaps more precisely, for the first time he assures the security of his comrades as well as of himself before committing himself to a new adventure. As usual, Homer expresses the hero's new sagacity in terms of divine intervention, but the intervention of Hermes is accompanied by and corresponds to inner developments. Chapman indicates Ulysses' new restraint in a quaintly-worded interpolation:

> She wisht my taste emploid; but not a word
> Would my eares taste of taste; my mind had food
> That must digest; eye meate would do me good.   [X, 482–84][54]

The translator heightens the tone of moral responsibility in lines that strike the note of redemption in the theme of the return. Originally the hero merely says: "Circe, what just man could bear to taste food or drink before he had set free his comrades and seen them with his own eyes?" (X, 383–85). Chapman translates this thus:

> O *Circe!* (I replied) what man is he,
> Awd with the rights of true humanitie,
> That dares taste food or wine before he sees
> His friends redeem'd from their deformities?   [X, 494–97]

"Redeems" translates *lúsasthai* "set free," and Chapman apparently found this suggestion in the Latin version, where the word is *redimantur*.[55]

From an analysis of these major episodes we are able to form a view of Chapman's allegorical approach, reflected in the body of the translation. He shares the time-honored view of the hero's fabulous adventures as representations of the dangers with which passions threaten both the individual and society as a whole, but in seeing Ulysses as involved in and threatened by these struggles and not placed above them by any absolute virtue, Chapman's translation is not only more dramatic than others but is in much closer harmony with Homer. His more flexible view permits faithfulness to the spirit of the original and to the facts of human experience. Thus Ulysses, like most, is proof against temptations of one sort while greatly disturbed by others. In the raid on Ismarus we see him gripped by the predatory and unreflecting spirit which, the poem suggests, has brought civilization to the brink of chaos. In the encounter with Polyphemus we find the warrior's code examined satirically and see how the hero's humility, born of peril, vanishes with it. In the Circe episode Ulysses' men are enslaved and degraded by sensual pleasures, pleasures which, by exercise of moderation, their leader shows can be made to serve rather than enslave. Over this ten-year period of Ulysses' life, Chapman has underlined his spiritual evolution from the prisoner of his own will and desires into one who, having conquered himself, has finally the power to conquer his nihilistic foes and restore justice and order to Ithaca.

To complete this analysis of Chapman's handling of the allegory in the *Odyssey* it would be fitting to conclude with his treatment of Ulysses' final glorification by Athene. This occurs after he has killed the suitors and purged his palace in book XXIII, and Homer here uses exactly the same simile by which the hero's earlier transformation in Phaeacia was described: "Just as a skillful craftsman whom Hephaestus and Pallas have taught all kinds of artistry overlays silver with gold, and the work he creates is very graceful, so did the goddess endow his head and shoulders with added beauty." Smalley says of this passage: "Chapman could hardly fail to recognize an ethical significance in these lines, portraying, as they do, the glorification of the 'absolute man,' triumphant at last over his woes in the 'sea of life'; and indeed he did his best with his opportunity. The relationship between 'power infused' [divine wisdom] and 'acquisition' [Ulysses' wisdom] is symbolized in a striking figure."[56]

Here is Chapman's version of this passage:

> Looke how a skilfull Artizan, well seene
> In all arts metalline as having beene
> Taught by *Minerva* and the God of fire,
> Doth gold and silver mix so, that entire
> They keepe their selfe distinction, and yet so,
> That to the silver from the gold doth flow
> A much more artificiall luster than his owne,
> And thereby to the gold it selfe is growne
> A greater glory then if wrought alone,
> Both being stuck off by eithers mixtion:
> So did *Minerva* hers and his combine;
> He more in Her, She more in Him did shine.   [XXIII, 233–44]

Several points might be added to Smalley's remarks on this passage. For one thing, Chapman has preserved the distinction between Ulysses' wisdom and the divine wisdom of Minerva—"They keepe their selfe distinction." This reinforces his emphasis on the fact that the hero has won "his wished stay" partly through his own wisdom and partly through the operation of divine aid, and it marks the judgment and self-control he has so strenuously achieved through his own efforts. The simile thus preserves the balance so central to the poem between man's moral responsibility and divine immanence in human affairs. Second, while the transformation does without doubt portray the "glorification of the 'absolute man,' " it symbolizes more specifically, within the context of Chapman's poem, the culmination of the process whereby Ulysses is informed and fashioned into an absolute man. This glorious transformation marks the final victory of his true form over the deforming passions which have so long beset him. Chapman accepted and brought into the translation the suggestion hesitantly advanced by Spondanus: "Nisi etiam Poeta velit pristinae illi Herois formam hanc a Minerva Novam infundi, ille penitus latente haec tantum appareat: quod fortasse ratione non caret"[57] (Unless the poet wished that the new form poured on the hero by Minerva should appear as latent: because he is not lacking in reason). Finally, Chapman has emphasized in this transformation the themes of spiritual illumination and union with the divine in his vigorous description of the partnership of human wisdom and divine grace: "He more in Her, She more in Him did shine." The line seems to echo the words of the Anglican Communion service: "that we may evermore dwell in Him and He in us."

CHAPTER TWO

Pretexts and Subtexts in Milton's Renaissance Homer

Milton, like Chapman, knew the great Renaissance edition of Homer by Spondanus as well as the *Thesaurus* of Henri Estienne (Henricus Stephanus). His other main Homeric source was Eustathius' *Commentary,* which exceeds in bulk the *Iliad* and the *Odyssey.*[1] Thanks to the Homeric allusions in *Paradise Lost* compiled in the index to the Columbia Milton, we can readily see that here was no casual acquaintance, but an intimate, profound, and extensive knowledge of the *Iliad* and the *Odyssey.* Milton had read Greek from an early age and, as we can tell from his marginalia on Euripides as well as his allusions to Homer, had achieved a mastery of the language and literature that was extremely rare in seventeenth-century England.

In many ways the final and greatest flowering of the Renaissance in England, *Paradise Lost* in one important respect represents a major departure from the epic tradition of the Renaissance, especially in its unallegorical and anti-allegorical nature. From post-Homeric times through the Middle Ages and well into the late Renaissance in England, allegory dominated critical views about how heroic poetry had been composed and how it must be read. The notion that the epic poem served to convey mystically truths concealed from the vulgar had been for over twenty centuries a critical commonplace. Spenser's "good discipline clowdilly enwrapped in Allegoricall devises" is like Chapman's suggestion that wherever the narrative seems fantastic or impossible we must dive for allegorical meaning: "if the Bodie (being the letter, or historie) seems fictive, and beyond Possibilitie to bring into Act, the sence then and Allegorie (which is the Soule) is to be sought which intends a more eminent expressure of Vertue, for her lovelinesse, and of Vice for her uglinesse, in their severall effects, going beyond the life than any Art within life can possibly delineate."[2]

J. W. H. Atkins has shown how the allegorical interpretation of Homer began in the sixth century B.C. with Theagenes and Anaxagoras as a defense against charges of impiety and immorality, the most famous of which was to be Plato's attack on the poets in the *Republic.* Atkins implies that there was something casuistical in this reaction: "Philosophy, which had led the attack, provided also the main line of defence. Already among philosophers the idea had obtained currency that the earlier poets in their myths had concealed profound wisdom in enigmatic and symbolic fashion; and that by means of an allegorical interpretation it was possible to arrive at the real significance of the myths concerned."[3] According to Domenico Comparetti, Homer bore the brunt of this approach:

Allegory was applied by the ancients to mythology generally and to the language of the poets particularly, as these latter formed, in the absence of a religious code, the only written authority for the common faith. . . . For those who were anxious to find documentary authority for the common beliefs, no other writers could have the weight of Homer, whether on account of his prehistoric antiquity or the marvellous power of his genius or the character and national importance of his poems.[4]

In the Christian era pagan authors continued to be read (there was no orthodox literature, except the Bible, of equal quality and interest), and the allegorical approach continued to preserve it from censure. Ovid was an especially interesting case, as Davis Harding has shown,[5] because it was believed that in his accounts of the creation of the world in the *Metamorphoses* he had in some way had access to a version of Genesis. In this way Ovid became moralisé. But there were impieties in Homer that no scriptural authority could explain away, such as the seduction of Zeus by Hera in *Iliad* XIV. Pope summed up the attempts to save this passage by an allegorical approach:

In the next place, if we have recourse to Allegory (which softens and reconciles everything) it may be imagin'd that by the Congress of *Jupiter* and *Juno,* is meant the mingling of the *Aether* and the *Air* (which are generally said to be signify'd by these two Deities). The Ancients believ'd the *Aether* to be Igneous, and that by its kind influence upon the Air it was the Cause of all Vegetation: putting forth her Flowers immediately upon this Congress.

Paradise Lost is founded on a wholly different conception of truth from that embodied in the allegorical tradition. Throughout the poem Milton insists on the reality of the events he is telling, as distinguished from the feigned truths of his epic predecessors. As Basil Willey puts it, the fact that Milton "was able to believe in his own subject matter as 'real' as well as 'typical' was due . . . to his sharing of Protestant confidence in the authority of Scripture. That he did so believe in his own high argument is evident . . . from the fact that the poem as a whole does not read like allegory."[6]

The one major exception to this statement is Satan's much-discussed encounter at Hell's gates with Sin and Death. Sin, in her monstrous Spenserian features, is a throwback to the mode Milton rejected. Ultimately, like Spenser's Error, she is compounded of self-contradiction, and has no intrinsic power. Death has only a shadowy reality suggested by a succession of negatives:

> The other shape,
> If shape it might be call'd that shape had none
> Distinguishable in member, joint, or limb,
> Or substance might be call'd that shadow seem'd,
> For each seem'd either; black it stood as Night,
> Fierce as ten Furies, terrible as Hell,

> And shook a dreadful Dart; what seem'd his head
> The likeness of a Kingly Crown had on.   [II, 666–74]

Sin exists, the primordial sin having been committed at the moment of Satan's revolt, but Death is all seeming, shadow without shape or substance, since he has not yet found his mortal prey. The unstable ontological character of Sin and the insubstantiality of Death reflect their status before the Fall, which will fulfill their existential claims, but Milton in using the allegorical mode is suggesting that in the long run they are unreal. More than that, the passage at Hell's gate employs allegory to expose its own insufficiencies, and this motive is thoroughly in accord with Milton's representation of Hell, whose physical torments are much less real than its psychological ones, expressed in Satan's anguished soliloquies:

> Me miserable! which way shall I fly
> Infinite wrath, and infinite despair?
> Which way I fly is Hell; myself am Hell;
> And in the lowest deep a lower deep
> Still threat'ning to devour me opens wide,
> To which the Hell I suffer seems a Heav'n.   [IV, 73–78]

"The hateful siege of contraries" so appallingly and movingly expressed in Satan exemplifies Milton's epic focus on the human mind and heart as the crucial arena of conflict.

Oddly enough Milton's "materialism" puts him much closer to Homer than to most of the intervening epic writers, including Virgil, Ovid, Ariosto, Tasso, and Spenser. Milton's world has a solidity of specification that we certainly do not find in these others, not even in Virgil, whose apparently solid world is occasionally shaken by the most extravagant kinds of magic (the metamorphosis of Aeneas's ships, or the attack by the Harpies, or the strange wonders of the bleeding cornel plant into which Polydorus has been transformed). Perhaps Homer's gods are more solidly anthropomorphic than those of subsequent epic writers; at any rate Homer's immortals exhibit a degree of realism and psychological verisimilitude that brings us very close to Milton. The predominant pattern of allusions in *Paradise Lost* is Homeric, and Milton himself, in chapter 4 of *Christian Doctrine,* suggested that the issue of *Paradise Lost,* man's freedom and his moral responsibility, is also the central issue of the *Odyssey:*

Whoever has paid attention to what has been urged, will easily perceive that the difficulties respecting this doctrine have arisen from want of making the proper distinction between the punishment of hardening the heart and the decree of reprobation; according to Prov. xix. 3. "the foolishness of man perverteth his way, and his heart fretteth against Jehovah." For such things do in effect impugn the justice of God, however vehemently they may disclaim the intention; and might justly be reproved in the words of the heathen Homer:

> . . . they perish'd self-destroy'd
> By their own fault.

And again, in the person of Jupiter:

> Perverse mankind! whose wills, created free,
> Charge all their woes on absolute decree:
> All to the dooming gods their guilt translate,
> And follies are miscall'd the crimes of fate.

The implications of this reference at the center of Milton's discussion of man's free will and moral responsibility are momentous. Milton saw the *Odyssey* as a theodicy, justifying the ways of God to men, and in this he followed Spondanus, who observed of the words of Zeus quoted by Milton, "This passage is elegant and worthy not only of a Gentile but of a Christian man. Under the guise of Jove's speech the poet declares that the cause of the evils which befell men is not to be traced to God but to the iniquities and dishonesties in man himself."[7] Zeus's words occur at the divine conclave with which the action of the *Odyssey* begins. Such an allusion also shows that Milton was much less systematically antiheroic than studies of Milton's antiheroic attitudes suggest. The balance needs to be redressed to permit us to see the many ways in which Milton adapted the heroic tradition to express or enhance various moral and spiritual values at the heart of *Paradise Lost*. This has been done for Ovid and Virgil by Davis Harding and others, but the Miltonic view of Homer requires fuller and more precise exploration.

We turn now to a prime example of Milton's imaginative adaptation of classical texts. At the heart of what may be the most famous extended simile in English, Milton introduces, in an epic voluntary, the fatal heroine of *Paradise Lost* and the *locus amoenissimus* she and her uxorious mate will soon be compelled to leave, having tasted—she under the seductions of the grisly king of the underworld and he out of despair at the prospect of life without her— the fruit of that forbidden tree.

The simile's twenty lines offer with apparently dégagé opulence a succession of Sicilian, Middle Eastern, and African paradises that cannot "strive" with this true biblical Eden. Like so many of the major similes in *Paradise Lost,* it is a "dissimile"—what Widmer calls a dismissive simile[8]—a trope developed from Homer in which characters and places, often of exotic and legendary power, are invoked only to be discarded as false or inferior by comparison with Milton's true mythical version. The strategy of expanding the differential ratios of the simile beyond its referential ones is to a large extent dictated by the poet's compelling need throughout *Paradise Lost* to establish the unique truth of his epic in contrast to the impositions of his precursors. The need is all the greater in view of the poem's central event— Eve's rash acceptance of Satan's false myth for God's true one. Thus, in his crucial introduction of our "grand parents," Milton repeatedly denies the beauty of countless pagan paradises in comparison with Eden, while tacitly employing their strong legendary associations to enhance and embellish its incomparble perfections:

> Not that fair field
> Of *Enna,* where *Proserpin* gath'ring flow'rs
> Herself a fairer Flow'r by gloomy *Dis*
> Was gather'd, which cost *Ceres* all that pain
> To seek her through the world; nor that sweet Grove
> Of *Daphne* by *Orontes* and th' inspir'd
> *Castalian* Spring might with this Paradise
> Of *Eden* strive; nor that *Nyseian* Isle
> Girt with the River *Triton,* where old *Cham,*
> Whom Gentiles *Ammon* call and *Lybian Jove,*
> Hid *Amalthea* and her Florid Son,
> Young *Bacchus,* from his Stepdame *Rhea's* eye;
> Nor where *Abassin* Kings thir issue Guard,
> Mount *Amara,* though this by some suppos'd
> True Paradise under th' *Ethiop* Line
> By *Nilus* head, enclos'd with shining Rock,
> A whole day's journey high, but wide remote
> From this *Assyrian* Garden, where the Fiend
> Saw undelighted all delight, all kind
> Of living Creatures new to sight and strange. . . .   [IV, 268–87]

The sentence runs on for another twenty-two lines to describe Adam and Eve for the first time in the poem. The lines quoted, as is well known, are based on Ovid's account of the rape of Proserpina in the *Metamorphoses* and *Fasti* and also draw on Claudian's epic *De Raptu Proserpinae.* Enna, Proserpin, and Dis are sufficient to mark the false Hesperian fable from Sicily that Milton dismisses before enumerating and discarding various oriental paradises as inferior to his Eden. The passage may also draw on Milton's familiarity with other accounts of the fable in Comes, in Sandys's commentary on the *Metamorphoses,* in Apollodorus, and in Pausanias. He probably would have known allusions in the *Helen* of Euripides and surely would have recognized references to Persephone and Demeter in the culminating episode of *Oedipus at Colonus,* one of the models for *Samson Agonistes.* Unlike Chapman, who had to use Latin versions to translate Homer, Milton's mastery of Greek would have made him equal to the task of reading the original version of the tale of Persephone in the Homeric *Hymn to Demeter,* the only version that brings together nearly all the allusions to the archetypal myth in his simile.

Yet his choice of a late and degenerate Latin version of the myth as pretext artfully conceals the vital, pristine subtext in the pseudo-Homeric hymn that was transcribed at about the time when the *Iliad* and the *Odyssey* attained their final written form in the eighth century B.C., more than seven centuries before Ovid. The ghostly presence of the ancient text, with its rich etiological resonances not to be found in the versions of Ovid and Claudian Milton conceals and dismembers, and the ghostly presence of the hymn helps to endow the great simile of *Paradise Lost* with a force and poignancy that has reverberated in the imaginations of generations of readers.[9]

Before I consider how Milton may have known—or may have reconstituted—the details of this crucial subtext, when the only manuscript we know today was catalogued in Moscow in 1777, let us examine some of the ways in which the *Hymn to Demeter* makes its presence felt in Milton's simile. Here are the opening lines, as modified from the translation of G. Evelyn White.

Now shall I sing of rich-haired Demeter, a holy goddess, and of her slim-ankled daughter whom Aïdoneus seized as a gift from Zeus the Thunderer, who sees all, while she played with the buxom daughters of Ocean, far from Demeter of the golden blade, bearer of rich fruit, gathering flowers in a soft meadow—roses, crocuses, lovely violets, irises, hyacinths, and the narcissus Earth made flourish as a bait for the flowerlike girl, as Zeus willed, to please the Host of the Many—a gleaming wonder that awed all who saw it whether men or gods. From its root a hundred blossoms grew; they smelled so sweet that all wide heaven above and all the earth and the briny swell of the sea smiled with delight. Amazed, the girl stretched out both her hands to grasp the lovely toy. Wide earth gaped there, in the Plain of Nysa, and the Host of the Many, with his deathless horses, sprang on her, the Son of Kronos, the Lord of Many Names.

He caught her up in his golden chariot and bore her off lamenting, against her will. She cried out aloud, calling her father, the Son of Kronos, who is supreme and powerful. Neither god nor mortal heard her cries, nor did the rich-fruited olive tree; only gentle Hecate, the bright-coifed daughter of Persaeus, heard the girl from her cave, and the Lord Helios, bright Son of Hyperion, as she cried to her father, son of Kronos, but he was aloof, sitting apart from the gods, in his temple, where many pray, accepting their sweet offerings. And so the many-named Son of Kronos, Ruler and Host of Legions, by the will of Zeus, her father's own brother, was carrying her off against her wishes with his immortal horses. As long as the goddess still saw earth and starry heaven and the flowing sea filled with fish, and the sun's rays, and hoped still to see her dear mother and the tribes of immortals, hope calmed her great mind for all her grief . . . , and the mountain ridges and the depths of the sea echoed her immortal voice, and her queenly mother heard her.

A bitter pang seized her heart, and with her hands she tore the veils that covered her lovely hair, and throwing the dark cloak from her shoulders, she flew like a bird over land and sea, seeking. But no one, divine or mortal, would tell her the truth, nor would the birds of omen. For nine days queenly Deo wandered over the earth with torches in her hands so grieved that she never tasted ambrosia or sweet nectar, nor did she bathe. But when the tenth dawn came, Hecate, bearing a torch, met her and told her the news:

"Lady Demeter, bringer of seasons and rich gifts, what heavenly god or what mortal has seized Persephone and grieved your heart? I heard a voice, but saw not who it was. But let me tell you briefly all I know."

Thus spoke Hecate. The daughter of rich-haired Rhea did not answer, but sped off with her, holding torches in her hands, and they came to Helios, the seer of gods and men, and stood before his horses, and the bright goddess asked:

"Helios, you at least should respect me, goddess as I am, if ever by word or deed I have cheered your heart. Through the barren air I heard the loud cry of the girl I bore, the sweet scion of my body, lovely in form, as of one seized violently, but I didn't see her with my eyes. But you, who look over all the earth and sea from the bright heavens with your brilliant glance, tell me truly of my dear child, if you have seen her anywhere, what god or mortal has violently seized her against her will and mine and so fled?"[10]

The pathos of the search that "cost Ceres all that pain" depends partly on the functional limitations the bereaved mother suffers, as most of the Olympians do, despite their divinity. That she could hear her daughter's cry without seeing what was happening to her makes Demeter's passionate grief all the more poignant, especially in contrast to Zeus' omiscient detachment, which is much like that of Milton's God, who

> From the pure Empyrean where he sits
> High Thron'd above all highth, bent down his eye,
> His own works and their works at once to view.   [III, 57–59]

Obviously Milton's orientation to the Middle East rather than to Ovid's Sicily or to the hymn's Attica as the fons et origo of his true myth of Creation was determined by his Old Testament sources—Genesis especially. Enna, in the center of Sicily, a halfway point in the westward movement of empire and culture, was by his standards a scene fabulous and corrupt, a ground of pagan delusions to be readily and firmly rejected—even while he used some of the Ovidian legend's associations to enhance his own. The Attic original, however, contributes even more to the proleptic intimations of the seduction of Eve and goes far beyond the later versions in intimating that the heroine's apparently fatal experience is a sort of felix culpa.[11]

Ovid's most complete version, in the Metamorphoses, is set in a thematic context of erotic love that reduces the archetypal myth of Proserpina's loss and recovery to an Olympian social comedy, entertaining but doggedly inconsequential, while the Hymn to Demeter accounts for the birth of agriculture and achieves a vision of the interdependence of life and death that forms the etiological model for the oldest, the longest-lasting, and the most influential cult of religious mystery in the pre-Christian West. The Eleusinian mysteries were vital enough to be regarded by Clement and other church fathers as challenging the hegemony of Christianity. Originating before the Trojan War, Eleusis thrived even under Roman occupation, until Alaric's hordes and Christian monks destroyed it in the fifth century.

The rape of Proserpina/Persephone at Enna/Eleusis by Dis/Hades as she is gathering flowers, and her unwilling trip to the underworld, where she becomes consort of the lord of death, are proleptic of Eve's seduction/abduction by Satan, the father of death, after she has tasted a forbidden fruit that may bind her to the realm of mortality forever. Eve, a fertility figure (mother of mankind) like Persephone/Proserpina, has wedded herself and all her progeny to mortality. In the Old Testament version of the myth, she replicates her own seduction by seducing Adam into tasting the forbidden fruit, thereby altering the role of innocent Persephone, and, in an ultimate betrayal, seducing Adam into assuming, with her, the deadly function of multiplying death.

Most of these elements of the myth appear in the opening lines of the *Hymn to Demeter* (1–73). For "that fair field of Enna," which Milton borrows from Ovid, the hymn specifies the *Núsion pedíon* (17), the Plain of Nysa, located between Eleusis and Athens, where Persephone was abducted by the "Lord of Many Names," a euphemism. In the Miltonic passage, Nysa (an element in the name of Dionysus), is transferred to "that Nyseian Isle," where "Amalthea's florid son," Dionysus, following one of many legends, was born. The originating myths about Dionysus or Bacchus are manifold, but all the myths concur in his being twice-born: Zeus concealed the infant in his thigh, according to one version, to protect him from "stepdame Rhea." In some versions of the Eleusinian myth Bacchus/Dionysus appears under the name Iacchus, the god of wine who functions in the myth as the child of Persephone and Pluto and, in the ritual, as the leader of the procession from Athens to Eleusis, while Rhea is entirely benign. Milton had no choice, if he followed the *Hymn to Demeter,* but to make the Nyseian isle of the Middle East Bacchus's birthplace, despite the multitude of places where he was supposed to have been born and reborn. Yet it is impossible to exaggerate the importance of the Attic plain of Nysa as the area in which the vine, like grain, was perhaps first cultivated.

Other exotic places Milton picks up and discards are "*Daphne* by *Orontes,*" and "th' inspir'd *Castalian* Spring." Daphne, with its "sweet grove," about two-thirds of the twenty-kilometer journey from Athens to Eleusis along the Sacred Way, was a famous stopping point for the Eleusinian procession. As for other key landmarks, the Castalian spring Milton mentions is a shadow of the prototype at Delphi, within easy walking distance, as Oedipus to his horror discovered, of nearby Corinth.

These, therefore, are the links between Milton's *Enna* simile and the *Hymn to Demeter*. Milton mentions and discards Enna, Proserpina, Dis, and Ceres as constituents in a myth that lacks the beauty and verity of his own. The name of the sacred area where Persephone was carried off is relegated to an island in a Middle Eastern river, the alleged birthplace and hiding place of Dionysus, who is a major figure in the Eleusis myth. The sacred grove of Daphne, again relegated to the Levant by Milton and his sources, is originally the main place of sojourn between Athens and Eleusis for the initiates in their progression along the Sacred Way. The famous Castalian Springs of Delphi, which play a major role in the mythical landscape of Eleusis and Delphi, Milton also relocates (as he must, following his Old Testament geography) in Mesopotamia. The divine child, whose birth is held to have been the climax of the *epopteía* at Eleusis, born, according to some accounts, of Zeus and a mortal mother, but immortalized by his second birth, is huddled off to concealment in what is now Tunis and there kept effectually out of play. But Dionysus/Iacchus was ritually reborn at Eleusis as the son of Persephone and Pluto/Dis, and he is, by implication, a type of Christ.

If we now add the major links between Ovid's version of the Proserpina story and Milton's simile, we find that, combined with the hymn, it supplies a rich background myth that influences and enhances Milton's poem. Milton prefaces his golden age account of Eden with the lines,

> The Birds thir choir apply; airs, vernal airs,
> Breathing the smell of field and grove, attune
> The trembling leaves, while Universal *Pan*
> Knit with the *Graces* and the *Hours* in dance
> Led on th' Eternal Spring.   [IV, 264–68]

This is a deft adaptation of the lines with which Ovid introduces the story of Proserpina in *Metamorphoses* V:

> Haud procul Hennaeis lacus est a moenibus altae,
> nomine Pergus, aquae: non illo plura Caystros
> carmina cycnorum labentibus audit in undis.
> silva coronat aquas cingens latus omne suisque
> frondibus ut velo Phoebeos submovet ictus;
> frigora dant rami, tyrios humus umida flores:
> perpetuum ver est.[12]

[Not far from Henna's high walls there is a deep pool of water, Pergus by name. Not Caÿster on its gliding waters hears more songs of swans than does this pool. A wood crowns the height around its waters on every side, and with its foliage as with an awning keeps off the sun's hot rays. The branches afford a pleasing coolness, and the well-watered ground bears bright-coloured flowers. There spring is everlasting.]

Bird song, the chiaroscuro of sun and leaves, and, most of all, Ovid's *perpetuum ver* contribute to Milton's synaesthetic, vital, and static "eternal spring," although Ovid could never have reached the deep implications of Milton's eternal cycle of fecundity. While it would be too much to claim that the Homeric hymn had reawakened in Milton the mythological motifs latent in Ovid's belated version, the comparison of the Ovidian passage with its counterpart in *Paradise Lost* suggests some of the ways in which Milton was revitalizing a myth that had become decorative and vulgar.

A similar Miltonic adaptation from the *Hymn to Demeter,* which also occurs shortly before the *Enna* simile, offers another example:

> As when to them who sail
> Beyond the *Cape of Hope,* and now are past
> *Mozambic,* off at Sea North-East winds blow
> *Sabaean* Odors from the spicy shore
> Of *Araby* the blest, with such delay

> Well pleas'd they slack thir course, and many a League
> Cheer'd with the grateful smell old *Ocean* smiles.   [IV, 159–65]

Looking back at the opening lines of the hymn, we find that Persephone, playing with the daughters of Ocean, is captivated by a narcissus whose fragrance makes heaven and earth and "even the briny swellings of Ocean smile" (14). In both cases the innocent harmonies of man and nature are broken by a fatal fruit or flower, and Milton's familiar tone toward "old *Ocean*" mimics the insouciance of the destined victim.

Unlike Eve, however, this victim is innocent. As she collects the flowers of the narcissus (not included in Ovid), Persephone reaches both her hands out toward the *dólos* (lure, bait) that the earth (personified as Gaea) has fostered, as Zeus willed. In her distracted delight, she is overtaken by Dis/Pluto, who catches her up with passion (*dilectaque raptu* [V, 395]) and takes her off to the underworld as his bride.

As subtext, the hymn's elaborate account of the *nárkissos* as the *dólos* that distracts Persephone and makes her vulnerable to the sudden onslaught of Aïdoneus is deeply significant. Like Eve she is amazed and stretches out her hands to the bait (15–16). And as she does so, the earth gapes or splits open and Death claims her:

> So saying, her rash hand in evil hour
> Forth reaching to the Fruit, she pluck'd, she eat:
> Earth felt the wound.   [IX, 780–82]

Unlike Persephone, Eve's rash plucking is the fruit of her narcissism. The fruit she has taken from the tree of knowledge, later called "the bait of *Eve* / Us'd by the Tempter" (X, 551–52), functions symbolically as both the *dólos* of the narcissus and the pomegranate seeds that Persephone swallows beneath the earth (in the hymn, secretly given her by Hades) that confirm her commitment to the underworld. The pomegranate, as Richardson notes, "was symbolical of blood and death, but also of fertility and marriage" (*Hymn to Demeter*, p. 276). Clearly the *pomum* element of pomegranate would associate Eve's apple with Persephone's fruit, while the distinction between the young flower goddess who eats seeds (*grana*), and the mother who presides over the fruiting stage would be preserved.

George Sandys, whose commentary Milton knew, claimed that the younger goddess's Latin name, *Proserpina*, is derived from *proserpo* (to creep forth), which would be appropriate to her presiding over the germinal stage in which shoots appear from seeds. As he observes, "*Ceres* as we have said, is taken for corne: her *Proserpina* for the fertility of the seed, which of creeping forth is so called: begotten by *Jove*, that is by the aetheriall virtue and clemency; when corrupting and dying (for even that which groweth dies before it be quickened)." He almost makes the figurative connection between the serpentine Proserpina and Eve in a further comment: "But *Proserpina*

having eaten seven graines of Pomegrannet (a fatal liquorishness, which re-
tains her in Hell; as the Apple thrust Evah out of Paradise whereunto it ·is
held to have a relation) . . . her hopes were made frustrate."[13] Sandys is
commenting on the following passage:

> frigora dant rami, tyrios humus umida flores:
> perpetuum ver est. quo dum Proserpina luco
> ludit et aut violas aut candida lilia capit
> dumque puellari studio calathosque sinumque
> inplet et aequales certat superare legendo
> paene simul visa est dilectaque raptaque Diti.   [V, 390–95]

[The branches afford a pleasing coolness, and the well-watered ground bears bright-
colored flowers. There spring is everlasting. Within the grove Proserpina was playing,
and gathering violets or white lilies. And while with girlish eagerness she was filling
her basket and her bosom, and striving to surpass her mates in gathering, almost in
one act did Pluto see and love and carry her away.]

Sandys's comment reminds one of Eve's capacity to play the serpent, a role she
learns instantly from Satan in book IX, and one signalized by Adam's devastating rejection of her in book X: "Out of my sight, thou Serpent, that name
best / Befits thee with him leagu'd, thyself as false / And hateful" (867–69).
The Latin name of the young goddess enables Milton to suggest proleptically
the serpentine rhetoric and "covert guile" (II, 41) she will employ on Adam.
Of course the predominant impression of Milton's Eve/Proserpina juxtaposition is one of feminine innocence and faith and beauty unwittingly reaching
out for a beguiling bait while Death lurks close by. The impression is reinforced by the powerful affection that binds mother and daughter and drives
Ceres to seek the vanished Proserpina through the world (and through the
underworld), a quest, as has often been observed, that anticipates Christ's
redemptive role.[14] Through its derivation, the name *Proserpina* can also remind us that Eve's act, though its consequences are mortal, will—like Proserpina's—entwine the forces of destruction and renewal. In one forbidden fruit
Milton combines the *dólos* of the ambiguous narcissus and the equally ambiguous pomegranate seeds that bind Proserpina/Persephone to an annual sojourn
with Death as her husband. Like the narcissus, the apple is an emblem of the
narcissism that motivates Eve's rebellious act; like the narcissus, its fragrance
is almost irresistible:

> Meanwhile the hour of Noon drew on, and wak'd
> An eager appetite, rais'd by the smell
> So savory of the Fruit, which with desire,
> Inclinable now grown to touch or taste,
> Solicited her longing eye.   [IX, 739–43]

The hymn's narcissus, the narcotic and deadly properties of which are indicated by its inclusion in the wreath Pluto wears, according to Comes,[15] is "die

verhängnisvolle Todesblume" in the words of Franz Bömer's commentary on the *Metamorphoses*. But as he also points out, it forms the garlands "worn by the mother and daughter," presumably Demeter and Persephone, in *Oedipus at Colonus*, 1. 682.[16] The motifs of the narcissus's beauty, intoxicating and some-times deadly power, narcissistic symbolism, and fragrance are combined with "the smell / So savory" (from *sapor,* derived, like *sapientia,* from *sapio*) of pomegranate and apple as Eve "Greedily . . . ingorg'd without restraint, / And knew not eating Death" (IX, 791–94). "Knew not eating Death" puns on the latent paradox that from the *sapor* of this fruit Eve not only fails to acquire more *sapientia;* its mortal taste is devouring her as she devours it.

Like Persephone, Eve is the victim of fraud, but while Persephone was the innocent victim of Pluto's guile, Eve participated willingly in the solicita-tions of "the spirited sly snake." Ovid's Proserpina wanders innocently through the underworld sampling the fruit:

> non ita fata sinunt, quoniam ieiunia virgo
> solverat et, cultis dum simplex errat in hortis,
> poenicum curva decerpserat arbore pomum
> sumptaque pallenti septem de cortice grana
> presserat ore suo, solusque ex omnibus illud
> Ascalaphus vidit.   [V, 534–39]

[Not so the Fates; for the girl had already broken her fast, and while, simple child that she was, she wandered in the trim gardens, she had plucked a purple pomegra-nate hanging from a bending bough, and peeling off the yellowish rind, she had eaten several of the seeds. The only one who saw the act was Ascalaphus.]

The fruit this tree bears, metaphorically speaking, is sterile. Ovid often empties old myths of their profounder attributes, and so here nothing would have come of Proserpina's indulgence if Ascalaphus (who has no other function in the story) had not seen her eat and blabbed about it.

Although Milton employs the associations of the Persephone/Proserpina myth chiefly to evoke the pathos that surrounds Eve and Eden in the intro-ductory simile, the redeeming aspects of the myth—especially in the Greek version—reverberate powerfully in the "true" fable of *Paradise Lost*. The redemptive role undertaken by Demeter/Ceres, while presented in Ovid as the resolution of a difficult social contretemps, is represented in the hymn as a profoundly mystical reconciliation of apparently irreconcilable oppositions that seem to lie at the heart of the human condition.

In order to see the reconciliation we must briefly survey the events that follow the rape of Persephone. After a fruitless ten days' search through the world, Demeter comes to the town of Eleusis disguised as an old woman. Here she is welcomed into the family of a leading citizen, Celeus, whose wife has given birth late in life to her first son, Demophöon. Demeter undertakes to nurse the child and, through secret rites involving the use of ambrosia and fire, plans to make the boy immortal, perhaps as a substitute for the goddess-daughter she has lost. When the mother learns of these strange practices and reclaims her child, Demeter berates her, discloses her divine nature, and demands that the Eleusinians build her a temple. Having learned that her husband, Zeus, had helped to plot the abduction of their daughter by Pluto, she retires into the temple for a year and imposes a total blight on the land. When Zeus is finally forced to make concessions, he and his wife agree that Persephone will spend a third of each year with her chthonic husband and the rest in the upper world. In response, Demeter provides the Eleusinian Triptolemus with her dragon-drawn chariot and a supply of seed sufficient to provide abundant harvests. This part of the myth celebrates both seasonal rhythms of growth and death (with the very important, if mistaken, idea that the seed "dies" before it germinates—a mistake shared by St. John and St. Paul) and the birth of agriculture, which first occurred, according to Greek legend, on the Nysion plain that extends from Eleusis eastward. Although the time division differs in various versions of the myth, the eight months correspond to the normal growing season in Attica and approximate the period of human gestation.

The climactic *epopteía* achieved in the vast *telestérion* at Eleusis seems to have involved a reenactment of Demeter's torchlit search for her daughter and a culminating pronouncement by the hierophant of the birth of the sacred boy: "The sublime one has borne a sacred boy, Brimo has given birth to Brimos."[17] In some versions Brimos is identified with the infant Bacchus, a connection that would reinforce the vinicultural and agricultural concerns of the myth. At any rate it is this aspect of the mystery, the birth of the sacred boy, that St. Paul, recognizing Pluto's alternate function as god of riches, converts into the *ploútos tou Chrístou,* the "unsearchable riches of Christ."[18] While Milton seems nowhere to suggest such a Christianization of the myth in *Paradise Lost,* his myth parallels that of the hymn in seeing the ultimate and restorative fruit as the divine child. It should also be emphasized that such an epiphany at Eleusis was accompanied by the initiates' sharing in a sacred drink, *ho kukeión,* whose mildly intoxicating qualities remind one of the communion wine, just as the blade of wheat that was displayed as in a monstrance obviously suggests the consecrated bread.[19]

We come now to the conclusion of the hymn and the reunion of Demeter and Persephone:

So then all day with one heart they cheered each other, and with many embraces relieved their grief in mutual joy.

Then bright-coifed Hecate approached them and often embraced Demeter's holy daughter, and thenceforth was her minister and companion.

And all-seeing, deep-thundering Zeus sent fair-haired Rhea as messenger to bring dark-robed Demeter back to the the immortals, and promised to give her whatever honors she chose among the deathless gods and agreed that the Maiden should spend a third of each circling year in the misty gloom and two-thirds with her mother and the other gods.

So he ordered, nor did the goddess disobey the message of Zeus. Swiftly she plunged from the peaks of Olympus and came to the Rharian Plain, once rich corn land, but now entirely barren, for it lay idle and leafless, because the white grain was hidden by the design of trim-ankled Demeter.

But afterwards, as spring came on, it was soon rippling with long ears of corn, its rich furrows laden with cut grain or with grain in sheaves. There she first alighted from the fruitless air. Gladly the goddesses looked at each other, and their hearts were cheered.   [434–58]

Rhea proceeds in Homeric fashion to repeat Zeus's message verbatim and then continues:

"But come now, my child, give way; don't be unrelentingly angry with the dark-clouded Son of Kronos, but rather increase the fruit that gives men life."

So she spoke, and fair-crowned Demeter did not disobey: she made fruit spring quick from the rich lands, and the wide earth was covered with leaves and flowers. Then she went to the kings who administer justice, Triptolemos and Polyxeinos and Diocles, the horse-driver, and mighty Eumolpus and Celeus and taught them all her mysteries—awful mysteries that no one may transgress or pry into or utter, for deep awe of the gods checks the voice.

Happy is he of earth-born men who has seen these mysteries, but the uninitiated, who has no part in them, never has the same good lot, once he is dead, down in the misty gloom.

Then when the bright goddess had taught them all, the three goddesses went to Olympus to the grave conclave, and there they dwell beside Zeus who rejoices in thunder, holy and wonderful goddesses. Blessed is he whom they freely love: soon do they send Plutus as guest in his great house, Plutus who gives wealth to mortal men.

But now, queen of Eleusis and sea-girt Paros and rocky Antron, lady, giver of good gifts, mistress of the seasons, queen Deo, may you and your daughter, lovely Persephone. for this song of mine cheer my heart, and now will I remember you and remember another song as well.   [467–95]

The adjudication of the central conflicts in the hymn is a sign of a peculiarly Attic genius for resolving in ways satisfactory to all the interested parties contesting claims that seem irreconcilable, in the course of which (as in the transformation of the Furies into Eumenides) major cultural advances are achieved. In the *Metamorphoses* the resolution is simply a recognition of contending interests. In the hymn the settlement, which on the surface appears to be a more or less arbitrary recognition of competing equities (the contending rights of Persephone, Demeter, and Pluto), gains its authority through the vital implications of the associated myth. Through its mystical vision, the apparent oppositions between mother and husband, underworld and upperworld, life and death, fertility and decay are seen as profoundly interdependent, and this vision of a divine *discordia concors* pervading the entire universe must have been close to the undisclosed *mysterion* at the heart of the ritual.

Briefly, these are the facets of the Demeter myth in *Paradise Lost*. The heroine is captured by the king of the underworld while she is preoccupied with flowers. She has moved away from her chief protector: Persephone from Demeter; Eve, the "fairest unsupported Flow'r, / From her best prop so far, and storm so nigh" (IX, 432–33), from Adam. Both flowerlike in their innocence and beauty, they are "gathered" in the act of gathering blossoms and fruit of strong sensuous appeal. At the crucial moment "earth feels the wound," as Milton puts it, or, as the hymn says, "the earth yawned there on the Nysion Plain" (*cháne de chthòn . . . Núsion àm pedíon*" [16–17]). The plucking of fruit or flower thus opens earth to the power of death, and harsh weather, drought, and blight ensue.

The abducted or seduced heroine has become the bride of Death—Persephone in fact and Eve figuratively. Adam sees this when he exclaims: "How art thou lost, how on a sudden lost, / Defac't, deflow'r'd, and now to Death devote?" (X, 900–01). Notwithstanding its alliterative excess, this statement associates Eve's experience with the kind of sexual violation suffered by Persephone. Persephone inadvertently binds herself to periodic sojourns in the underworld as bride of Death by having eaten a single seed of the deadly pomegranate, the death apple which has the same "mortal taste" as Eve's. Not only does the narcissus share with the forbidden fruit associations with narcissism and narcosis; both fair objects are referred to as "bait," and both strike their rash gazers with amazement. Persephone "*d'ára thambésas' oréxato chersìn am' ámpho*" ("in amazement put forth both her hands," 15); Eve's amazement is repeatedly emphasized in book IX, both before and after she eats the fruit, and most notably in the following passage:

> Lead then, said *Eve*. Hee leading swiftly roll'd
> In tangles, and made intricate seem straight,
> To mischief swift. Hope elevates, and joy
> Bright'ns his Crest, as when a wand'ring Fire,
> Compact of unctuous vapor, which the Night
> Condenses, and the cold invirons round,
> Kindl'd through agitation to a Flame,
> Which oft, they say, some evil Spirit attends
> Hovering and blazing with delusive Light,
> Misleads th' amaz'd Night-wanderer from his way
> To Bogs and Mires, and oft through Pond or Pool,
> There swallow'd up and lost, from succor far.   [IX, 631–41]

The simile constitutes a proleptic scenario of Eve's oblique physical and mental movements to the point where, like Persephone, she will be "swallow'd up and lost, from succor far." This simile implicitly refers to the possibly hallucinated visions "some belated Peasant sees, / Or dreams he sees" (I, 783–84) and confirms the impression that both Persephone and Eve are not only amazed but fooled. Milton may even be alluding to the hallucinogenic properties of the narcissus and the fruit of the tree of knowledge, both of them lusus naturae, in his description of Eve as "hight'n'd as with Wine, jocund and boon" (IX, 793).

At this point we should take note of a fundamental distinction between the ways in which the myths of these two divine comedies reach fulfillment. The innocent Persephone accepts an accommodation ultimately worked out by her mother and father (Demeter and Zeus) between the demands of death and life. Her strong attachment to her mother allows her to avoid or deny not only the claims of mortality but those of marriage and child-bearing, the last now ludicrously incompatible with her destined career as a fertility goddess like her revered mother. If abduction by Death and marriage to him are seen, understandably, as repellent, the match in the long run, as Helios remarks, is not such a bad one. Although queen of the dead, she nevertheless succeeds in producing life out of death both through her marriage and through her mysterious function as the divinity of the germinating seed. The marriage with Death converts her life from a perpetually unfruitful virginity into true fertility. The triptych of the three generations of women at the end of the poem—Rhea, Demeter, and Persephone—emphasizes major stages in the traditional life of a woman as bride, mother, and grandmother. Here we find a *seasonal* emphasis on the human life-cycle that, since these are immortals, is momentarily represented in a stasis that points to fulfillment rather than frustration. In this respect it is worth noting that Persephone and Demeter are virtually indistinguishable in such Eleusinian works of art as the Niinion tablet. The Demeter myth, far from celebrating abstemiousness, as the Genesis myth does, celebrates a growth in *techné* and wisdom in this world as a prelude to happiness in the next. If *thémis* is violated, as it obviously is in the conspiracy of Zeus and Pluto, the offense can be compensated for by arbitration, without anything like "the rigid satisfaction, death for death" that the justice of Milton's God requires. In fact the Eleusinian rites are remarkable for the virtual absence of blood sacrifices. Triptolemus, the Eleusinian agricultural hero, transformed from an Ares-like threefold warrior (tripolemos) to plougher of the triple furrow, left three commandments: "Honor your parents. Honor the gods with fruits. Spare the animals."[20]

Carl Kerényi, who, with George Mylonas, has done more than anyone else to elucidate the implications of Eleusinian myth and ritual, says that the cult was important "not only because people continued [after the fall of Greece] to come from every corner of the earth to be initiated, as they had in the days of the Emperor Hadrian, but also because the mysteries touched on something that was common to all people. They were connected," he continues,

not only with the Greek and Athenian existence, but with human existence in general. And Praetextus clearly stated just this: "*bios,* life," he declared, would become "unlivable (*abiotos*)" for the Greeks if the celebration were to cease. Beyond a doubt the Greeks are here contrasted with the Christians. The sharpness of the formulation of the significance of Eleusis, which has no parallel in earlier documents, springs from the conflict between Greek religion and Christian. Nonetheless, it suffices to give the mysteries a special significance for us, which goes beyond any concern for the history of religions. If life was unlivable for the Greeks without the annual celebration of Eleusis, it means that this celebration was a part not merely of non-Christian existence but also of Greek life, of the Greek form of existence; and this is another reason why it is of concern to us. Despite the enormous amount of literature devoted to them, the Eleusinian mysteries have not been studied from the standpoint of Greek existence, nor has Greek existence ever been considered in the light of Eleusis.[21]

That Praetextus, the proconsul of Greece, should have ignored the decree of the Emperor Valentinian ordering the termination of the Eleusinian observances is a further tribute to the power of the vision which attracted men and women throughout the civilized world to participate in them. Finally, it was the pale Galilean who conquered. As Kerényi remarks, "The men in dark garments who moved in with Alaric were monks."[22] It took more than monks and Visigoths to extinguish the light from Eleusis, however. Church fathers such as Clement of Alexandria, Tertullian, and Psellos probably knew only a debased version of Eleusis established in Egypt under the Ptolemies with a decidedly erotomorphic tone that failed utterly to suggest the unique character of the original, cosmogonic myth and the mysteries out of which it grew. Mysteries "thought to hold the world together"[23] were degraded into lewd performances that, according to Lactantius, represented theatrically, among other things, Persephone's coition with Zeus and Alexander's with Thaïs under the direction of an Eleusinian expatriate, derided in Dryden's *Alexander's Feast,* named Timotheus.

Like Praetextus, Milton seems to have preserved the mysteries, alluding to them only in their debased Latin versions, while deploying all the elements of the Greek original as a vital subtext for *Paradise Lost.* His art is the art that conceals art, as the involutions in the gesture of artful authorial diffidence that introduces the *Enna* simile shows:

> But rather to tell how, if Art could tell,
> How from that Sapphire Fount the crisped Brooks,
> Rolling on Orient Pearl and sands of Gold,
> With mazy error under pendant shades
> Ran Nectar, visiting each plant, and fed
> Flow'rs worthy of Paradise which not nice Art
> In Beds and curious Knots, but Nature boon
> Pour'd forth profuse on Hill and Dale and Plain.   [IV, 236–43]

So involuted is the passage from which this is taken that we may not notice that Milton fails to supply a verb to govern the infinitive *to tell.* This ornamental passage, which he slyly offers in his "Hesperian fable true," further conceals the latent archetype from Eleusis that transforms the simile into true gold. The Eleusinian subtext winds endlessly through the roots and branches of Milton's forbidden tree and, like that tree, will bear restorative fruit, implying by what Bagehot termed its "enhancing suggestion" the "essential gift" of "the ceremonies which no one may describe or utter." In dismissing

Eleusis by dismissing its Ovidian version, Milton was obeying the dictates of his Christian and monotheistic myth. As scholars like John Steadman have shown, he rejects classical models in an explicit way while reassimilating them selectively and tacitly.[24] The Enna simile may be the most significant example of artful innocence in *Paradise Lost*.

If Milton knew the entire myth of Demeter, internal evidence suggests very strongly that he knew it through the *Hymn to Demeter*, but no such knowledge has been documented. Is it therefore necessary to conclude, because we have only the text of the hymn that was found in Moscow in 1777, that he could not have seen a version during his Italian trip in 1638–39? What was found was once lost, and the interest in Eleusis and in the *Hymn to Demeter* in antiquity certainly implies that the poem existed in multiple copies. Or knowledge of the poem could have come to him from his friend Marvell's long sojourn in Moscow in 1663–65 as a member of the earl of Carlyle's diplomatic mission. In any event, however the myth of Demeter found its way into a consummately beautiful simile in *Paradise Lost,* we can only rejoice that it did.

In contrast to Chapman, who used every opportunity to explicate the archetypal patterns of Odysseus' quest and to interpolate sometimes heavy-handed comments on the moral and spiritual conflicts that lie behind his polytropic ordeals, in my judgment well-supported by Homer's epic in most cases, Milton's practice is to implicate his myth with enhancing suggestions from his classical and biblical models, thus preserving a deep sense of awe toward "those mysteries that no one may transgress, or pry into, or utter." Against Chapman's ebullient assertions of the rightness of his insights, Milton, conceived of his role in his epic undertakings as a profoundly religious encounter with the numinous.

CHAPTER THREE

Milton's Translation of Epic Conventions

No poet in the great tradition of Western epic has projected himself more fully into his poem than Milton in *Paradise Lost*. Where Homer, Virgil, Tasso, and Spenser left relatively few autobiographical traces in epics which seem to have aspired to a condition of anonymity, Milton, especially in the invocations to books I, III, VII, and IX, emphasizes the emotional, psychological, and spiritual circumstances in which he was composing his poem. Far from concealing traces of personality, Milton employed the tradition of divine inspiration to explore his role as instrument and collaborator of the heavenly muse. As a result, *Paradise Lost* is everywhere marked by the impress of his personality. Not only has Milton outdone his progenitors in magnitude and range of subject; he has also established for himself a unique epic role as man and poet. In "soaring above th' *Aonian* Mount" to "write of things invisible to mortal sight" and venturing thereby "to justify the ways of God to men" he not only extended the range of epic from eternity to eternity but affirmed simultaneously his paramount achievement as a quasi-divine poet of omniscience.[1]

The boldness of Milton's venture is the more remarkable in light of his subject, the original sin of aspiring to divine knowledge. The dangers for the poet of reenacting the sin in singing of it are manifold and obvious. Milton was clearly aware of them, and his autobiographical invocations dramatize the struggle to reconcile the grandeur of his aspirations to his condition as an inheritor of original sin and his obligations as a Christian. Not the least heroic aspect of Milton's venture is his identification with Satan. Far from being of the devil's party without knowing it, he elaborated the analogies between Satan's proud lust for preeminence and his own unmatched ambition as a poet. The hazards of his enterprise are continually evoked by references to soaring, to heights and depths, to rising and falling, references which everyone recognizes as dominant motifs in the poem.

Milton's unabashed projection of himself into his epic is one reason for the continuing discussion about the hero of the poem. In addition to the Satanists, there are critics who champion Adam, Eve, Adam and Eve, the Son, and even Abdiel. There are those who feel the poem has no hero, or that the role of hero is distributed among several characters. It has even been suggested that the real hero is the ideal reader, one of that "fit audience though few" for whom Milton was writing. Without examining these conflicting claims, I would like to explore the ways in which Milton qualifies as hero.

But first let us consider what distinguishes Milton from his predecessors in the role of poet and narrator. In the Homeric epics there is scarcely a trace of the conscious artist at work reflecting on the process of composition or the experience of divine inspiration. There is not even an "I" or a "me" in the *Iliad*'s invocation to represent the poet as a personality separate from the muse. The anonymous voice simply tells the muse to sing the wrath of Achilles. Traces of the poet's personality are so faint and few that scholars have leapt hungrily upon them, an example being the diffident remark at the beginning of the catalogue of the ships (II, 484) where the poet asks the muse to tell him the names of the captains of the Danaans and their lords, "for ye are goddesses and are at hand and know all things, whereas we hear but a rumor and know not anything" (485–86).[2] Almost the only other trace of Homer's personal involvement in the *Iliad* is his use of the vocative to address Patroclus just before his death.

Similar instances of this personal address in which the poet for a moment drops his customary anonymity to suggest emotional involvement with a character occur in the repeated references in the *Odyssey* to Eumaeus, the first loyal person Odysseus encounters on his return to Ithaca. The repeated *o subóte* (O swineherd!) I take to be an extraordinary tribute to a faithful servant whose fidelity to his long-absent lord is singled out for recognition.

The presence of Homer in the *Odyssey* is only slightly greater than in the *Iliad*. Instead of asking the muse to *sing* he asks her to *tell me*, and he permits himself to comment a little more frequently on characters and action: the sailors of Odysseus who ate the forbidden cattle of Apollo he calls "fools" and lays the blame for their destruction on their own "blind folly," a phrase which Zeus applies a few lines later to Aegisthus and Clytemnestra for the murder of Agamemnon. Thus even this exclamation of disapprobation may be construed as coming via the muse rather than as the poet's personal comment on the action.

In his prominent use of *I sing* at the beginning of the *Aeneid,* Virgil is a touch more self-assertive than Homer. It may be one significant indication of their spuriousness that four lines prefixed to the *Aeneid* in Suetonius but absent in all good manuscripts show an obtrusion of autobiographical detail unmatched by anything else in the poem:

> Ille ego, qui quondam gracili modulatus avena
> carmen et egressus silvis vicina coegi
> ut quamvis avido parerent arva colono,
> gratum opus agricolis; at nunc horrentia Martis
>
> [I am he who once tuned my song on a slender reed,
> then, leaving the woodland, constrained the neighboring
> fields to serve the husbandmen, however grasping—
> a work welcome to farmers: but now of Mars' bristling].

Even if spurious, the passage is enormously influential. Spenser incorporated it into the beginning of the *Faerie Queene* and used it as license to project himself into the poem in the pastoral figure of Colin Clout, and Milton, in starting *Paradise Regained* with his own version of these lines, also emphasized the self-conscious artistry of the Virgilian progression from eclogue to epic. Not only do the lines point to the steadily increasing presence of the poet in the poem, but they foreshadow the evolution of the epic tradition toward long autobiographical poems like *The Prelude* and quasi-epics like *Don Juan* in which the poet's personal reflections shoulder aside the exploits of the nominal hero. After Milton had exhausted the possibilities of true epic, the genre inevitably transformed itself into such egocentric works or moved in the direction of mock-heroic or the picaresque novel of ordinary life.

A steady increase in the poet's preoccupation with himself and with the process of poetic creation is evident from these examples. With this tendency toward self-projection and self-analysis in the epic tradition there appears a tendency to mingle the figure of the poet with the hero of the poem. Ultimately the disappearance of God from these Romantic avatars of the epic accelerates the process, which culminates in Wordsworth's egotistical sublime.

These contrary leanings—on the one hand toward the objective, formal, and impersonal and, on the other, toward the subjective, improvised, and autobiographical—are balanced in *Paradise Lost*. The theocentric force of Milton's myth is a primary factor in disciplining the egocentric tendencies of the poet's self-concern, but it is equally obvious from the vast number of failed religious epics that religious myth alone is no guarantee of such a balance. Milton's astonishing achievement in reconciling and harmonizing the inward drive of self-conscious authorship with the outward drive toward supernatural authority is finally attributable to the extraordinary candor, subtlety, and insight with which he dramatizes the interior workings of religious doubt and faith, of despair and hope, of egotism and selflessness, of pride and humility, in the meditative process of epic creation.

To achieve this harmony between the subjective and the objective Milton established a dialogue between the omniscient voice—in religious epic ipso facto divine or divinely inspired—and the voice of the limited, fallible, mortal poet. These voices correspond to and evolve from the omniscient, muse-inspired narrator of classical epic, whose purest example is found in the *Iliad,* and the delegated narrator whose knowledge of things, already limited by mortality, may be further impaired by pride, fraud, self-ignorance, or various ulterior motives. Satan is a prime example of the fallible voice trying to sound like the inspired, as in the ludicrous account he gives to Abdiel of diabolical self-sufficiency:

> That we were form'd then say'st thou? and the work
> Of secondary hands, by tasks transferr'd

From Father to his Son? strange point and new!
Doctrine which we would know whence learnt: who saw
When this creation was? remember'st thou
Thy making, while the Maker gave thee being?
We know no time when we were not as now;
Know none before us, self-begot, self-rais'd
By our own quick'ning power.   [V, 853–61][3]

The autogenous myth of Satan marks the extremest form of the egocentric
creator, in which ignorance (We know no time when we were not as now)
claims omniscience.

In writing the epic of everything Milton had to assume the omniscient
voice. In writing the epic of Man fallen he was also limited to the knowledge
available to fallen humanity. As the fallen poet with omniscient voice he had
recourse to the Homeric tradition of divine inspiration by the muse, but in
dramatizing his own plight as poet and man he projected a personality far
richer and more complex into the poem than did any of his predecessors.
Dante, no doubt, was a vital example of the poet as epic voyager in his own
poem, but the *Odyssey* provided Milton a more influential model for the role of
limited or delegated personal narrator. As the first epic beginning in medias
res and employing extensively the mode of delegated narrative, the *Odyssey* was
an even more crucial influence on *Paradise Lost* than it was on the *Aeneid*.
With its thematic concentration on the experiences of Man it provided an
equally important model for the reconciliation of the humanly individual with
the representative. For our purposes, however, the most important aspect of
the *Odyssey* is the use of the device of delegated narrative to permit the hero
himself to speak. In striking contrast to the *Iliad,* in which the hero's adventures are related by the omniscient voice, the psychological complexity of
Odysseus, as he pursues his *nostos,* requires that he tell us a great deal of his
own story. Poised between the losses of the past and the hope of redemption
in the future, Milton assumed the role of Odysseus on a cosmic scale:

Of Man's First Disobedience, and the Fruit
Of that Forbidden Tree, whose mortal taste
Brought Death into the World, and all our woe,
With loss of *Eden,* till one greater Man
Restore us, and regain the blissful Seat,
Sing Heav'nly Muse. . . .   [I, 1–6]

Virgil, of course, also imitated the in medias res structure of the *Odyssey* and
began his epic with the hero poised between the disasters and trials of the
past and the hope of the future—between ruined Troy and the voyage to
Latium where Troy would be restored—but he did not implicate himself in
the action in the way that Milton does. For Milton made the unusual claim
that the ultimate heroic act was to create his epic of the fall and the
promised redemption,

> sad task, yet argument
> Not less but more Heroic than the wrath
> Of stern *Achilles* on his Foe pursu'd
> Thrice Fugitive about *Troy* Wall; or rage
> Of *Turnus* for *Lavinia* disespous'd,
> Or *Neptune's* ire or *Juno's,* that so long
> Perplex'd the *Greek* and *Cytherea's* Son.   [IX, 13–19]

Not only is Milton's argument more heroic than those of Homer and Virgil, but his telling is a task more heroic than any imposed on Achilles, Turnus, Odysseus, or Aeneas.

The prominence Milton gives to his role as heroic creator tends to dissolve conventional distinctions of subjective and objective. It allows his epic to assume the form of an extended meditation in which the divine story and his own experiences interact, a form where his own feelings and experiences are mingled with, illustrate, and become a vital part of the story he is telling.[4] Something like this occurs in the *Odyssey* when the hero, suspended between years of war, shipwreck, and marvelous adventures and his imminent return home, recounts his experiences. While Homer's language is not nearly as reflective as Milton's, it is clear that Odysseus has somehow been prepared for his triumphant return to Ithaca by assimilating and relating his trials and adventures. In fact the good king Alcinoüs ventures to remark that the purpose of wars and other such tedious havoc is to provide material for good tales:

> But come, now, put it for me clearly, tell me
> the sea ways that you wandered, and the shores
> you touched; the cities, and the men therein,
> uncivilized, if such there were, and hostile,
> and those godfearing who had kindly manners.
> Tell me why you should grieve so terribly
> over the Argives and the fall of Troy.
> That was all gods' work, weaving ruin there
> so it should make a song for men to come!   [VIII, 574–82][5]

As he starts to tell his story, Odysseus begins with the epic singer's question about the disposition of his material: "What shall I / say first? What shall I keep until the end?" (IX, 14–15). Next comes the pious acknowledgment of suffering and mortality and *xenía:*

> The gods have tried me in a thousand ways.
> But first my name: let that be known to you,
> and if I pull away from pitiless death,
> friendship will bind us, though my land lies far.   [IX, 16–19]

Suffering, mortality, and love are the authenticating tokens of this heroic teller, as they are of Milton. They also share the excruciating torment of isolation, "from the cheerful ways of men / Cut off" (III, 46–47) and of alienation, "In darkness, and with dangers compast round, / And solitude" (VII, 27–28). Both win deliverance through the tales they tell.

While the emphasis of the Miltonic narrator on his Odyssean suffering and endurance is obvious, his Odyssean adventurousness and lust for knowledge may be less apparent. Nonetheless, at the opening of book III, the first reaction to the invocation, "Hail, holy light," is to impute the words to Satan, whom we have just seen at the end of book II "by dubious light" beholding "Far off th' empyreal Heav'n"—not to Milton. So powerful is Milton's kinesthetic evocation of Satan's prodigious flight from hell through chaos to the empyrean that his identity is temporarily merged with Satan's, and so is the reader's. This sympathetic identification is intensified by a key allusion to the *Odyssey* a few lines earlier:

> He ceas'd; and *Satan* stay'd not to reply,
> But glad that now his Sea should find a shore,
> With fresh alacrity and force renew'd
> Springs upward like a Pyramid of fire
> Into the wild expanse, and through the shock
> Of fighting Elements, on all sides round
> Environ'd wins his way; harder beset
> And more endanger'd, than when *Argo* pass'd
> Through *Bosporus* betwixt the justling Rocks:
> Or when *Ulysses* on the Larboard shunn'd
> *Charybdis,* and by th' other whirlpool steer'd.   [II, 1010–20]

The latent association of the heroic voyages of Satan and Milton from darkness and confinement ("on all sides round / Environ'd" anticipating "In darkness and with dangers compast round / In solitude") to deliverance and light is reinforced by the allusion to Jason and the Argonauts, but even more by the allusion to Odysseus threading Scylla and Charybdis on his homeward journey. The association is emphasized even more in the following lines from the invocation to book III addressed to holy Light:

> Thee I revisit now with bolder wing,
> Escap't the *Stygian* Pool, though long detain'd
> In that obscure sojourn, while in my flight
> Through outer and through middle darkness borne
> With other notes than to th' *Orphean* Lyre
> I sung of *Chaos* and *Eternal Night.*   [III, 13–18]

The complexity of Odysseus—rash and hubristic adventurer, insatiable seeker after knowledge, unprovoked slayer, on the one hand—wise, pious, much-enduring home-seeker, on the other—could embrace both the ruthless ambition of Satan and the consecrated ambition of Milton. As one critic puts it, "The explicit comparisons of poet and devil in *Paradise Lost* are intended by Milton to demonstrate an undeluded recognition of the satanic potential of his poetic act. Within the epic, ambition and presumption dog the poet in the form of satanic resemblances to his attempt to understand and give poetic shape to the pattern of God's ways with men."[6] Milton, building on the model of the *Odyssey* with its alternations of omniscient and delegated narrative, exploited and dramatized the dilemma of fallen and fallible man writing omnisciently about the Fall of Man.

A further aggravation of "the satanic potential of his poetic act" lies in Milton's peculiarly independent religious beliefs. While he took care in *Paradise Lost* to minimize disputed points of doctrine, a cursory acquaintance with his life shows him frequently at odds with fellow Protestants on many issues of belief and fashioning his own special faith. His aversion to institutionalized authority made him an arch example of the dilemmas which the schismatic tendencies of liberal Protestantism could create. The idea Milton shared widely with other Protestants was that divine guidance was to be sought within the individual soul by prayer and meditation on the Bible. Opportunities for mistakenly erecting one's own inclinations into manifestations of God's will are obvious and became a source of such polemical satire as *Hudibras* or of Dryden's attacks on "the fruits the private spirit brought." For Milton, as for many of his contemporaries, the dangers of falling into such heretical individualism in pursuit of inner light were compounded by his championing radical political freedom against constituted authority. Having narrowly escaped proscription at the Restoration for supporting the execution of Charles I, his voice in public affairs silenced, the blind poet was more isolated than ever, in double darkness bound. Whatever else it is, *Paradise Lost* is the instrument of Milton's deliverance, but unlike other great records of spiritual deliverance, it records the reassertion and consecration of the ego rather than its submission to external authority.

Of all Milton's biographers James Holly Hanford has traced most clearly and convincingly his development from a somewhat self-gratulatory champion of virtue, who could resort to vituperation and innuendo (as in his reply to Salmasius), into a more serene and magnanimous servant and mouthpiece of God. Speaking of the autobiographical passages in *Paradise Lost* Hanford observes: "The lineaments of this portrait are essentially the same, but there is a new depth in interpretation, a more complete confidence in execution. It is as if Milton, hitherto troubled by a weak desire for approbation from without, needed now no witness but all-judging Jove."[7] Milton's most creative period seems to have been inaugurated with the writing of the *Second Defense of the English People,* published in 1654, a passionate oration defending and celebrating the cause of liberty and affirming himself as its spokesman and champion. The pamphlet represents "the beginning of a new cycle of self-exaltation, which has followed as natural reaction from the depression of the preceding years."[8] There Milton, according to Hanford, "rouses himself, throws off the intimations of despair, and turns the great affliction which has come upon him into a final seal of consecration."[9] The mark of Milton's transition from the defensive self-exaltation of the earlier pamphlets with their touches of narcissism to a serener conviction of his destiny as poet and prophet is the transformation of his blindness from an affliction to a token of divine favor:

There is, as the apostle has remarked, a way to strength through weakness. Let me then be the most feeble creature alive, as long as that feebleness serves to invigorate the energies of my rational and immortal spirit; as long as in that obscurity, in which I am enveloped, the light of the divine presence more clearly shines, then, in proportion as I am weak, I shall be invincibly strong; and in proportion as I am blind, I shall more clearly see. O! that I may thus be perfected by feebleness and irradiated by obscurity! And, indeed, in my blindness, I enjoy in no inconsiderable degree the favor of the Deity, who regards me with more tenderness and compassion in proportion as I am able to behold nothing but himself.[10]

As Hanford says, "The importance of *The Second Defense* is that it exhibits the actual struggle which led Milton to his final victory."[11] In his two sonnets on his blindness and in *Paradise Lost* he now proceeded to give the world a poetic interpretation of that "deeper vision of spiritual truth which had begun to come upon him in his solitary communion with the Most High."[12]

At the heart of *Paradise Lost* is the familiar Christian formula that *humilitas* is the foundation stone of *sublimitas*. Milton differs from his predecessors, however, in the energy with which he explores and displays his humbled and exalted self. More than that, he outdistances all his poetic models in the subtlety and fidelity with which he explores his own devilish inclinations. The result is a drama of the mind in which the self is chastened and disciplined by affliction and is then exalted in the knowledge and love and service of God. Milton's lifelong fascination with temptations and trials, which lies at the heart of *Comus, Lycidas, Paradise Regained, Areopagitica,* and *Samson Agonistes,* as well as *Paradise Lost,* is always focused on the attractions and dangers of unbridled egotism. The young Milton treated the temptations of sensual self-indulgence in *Comus* and the lust for poetic fame in *Lycidas.* The mature Milton dealt with uxoriousness in Adam. But the great temptation which obsessed him in his later years was the lust for power, and it is this drive which provides the dangerous energy we find in "On His Blindness," in Eve and the Satan of *Paradise Lost,* and at the center of *Paradise Regained* and *Samson Agonistes.* Again and again Milton reverts to the Promethean motif of the hero in chains, of the heroic activist immobilized, transfixed, incarcerated—the Lady frozen in her chair by Comus's spell and unable to utter a sound, Satan on the burning lake, immured in darkness visible, the blind Samson, a prisoner "in double darkness bound," the Son of God balanced on a spire of the Temple. But these physical afflictions of immobilization and blindness are metaphors for even more painful and dangerous ones. Once Satan has " 'scap'd the dark Abyss," he discovers that wherever he goes he is his own prison:

> myself am Hell;
> And in the lowest deep a lower deep
> Still threat'ning to devour me opens wide,
> To which the Hell I suffer seems a Heav'n.   [IV, 75–78]

As Abdiel sternly reminds him:

> This is servitude,
> To serve th'unwise, or him who hath rebell'd
> Against his worthier, as thine now serve thee,
> Thyself not free, but to thyself enthrall'd.   [VI, 178–81]

After the Fall Adam's paroxysm of guilt and self-reproach sounds like Satan's: "O Conscience, into what Abyss of fears / And horrors hast thou driv'n me; out of which / I find no way, from deep to deeper plung'd!" (X, 842–44). The state of sinful self-imprisonment is often expressed in *Paradise Lost* as frenetic, restless, and futile movement. Milton employs the Virgilian implications of the maze of Daedalus and loads the key word error with the associations it has in the *Aeneid* as *inextricabilis error* or *irremediabilis error*. A little earlier in the speech from which I have just quoted Adam says: "All my evasions vain / And reasonings, though through Mazes, lead me still / But to my own conviction" (X, 829–31). While Adam's reason at least leads him to his own conviction, the first step toward his regeneration, the more philosophical devils get nowhere:

> (They) apart sat on a Hill retir'd,
> In thoughts more elevate, and reason'd high
> Of Providence, Foreknowledge, Will, and Fate,
> Fixt Fate, Free will, Foreknowledge absolute,
> And found no end, in wand'ring mazes lost.   [II, 557–61]

At the heart of Milton's conception of deliverance from such bondage is obedience to the will of God. Adam and Eve can perform this act of atonement, but the devils cannot. Adam and Eve

> forthwith to the place
> Repairing where he judg'd them prostrate fell
> Before him reverent, and both confess'd
> Humbly thir faults, and pardon begg'd, with tears
> Watering the ground, and with thir sighs the Air
> Frequenting, sent from hearts contrite, in sign
> Of sorrow unfeign'd and humiliation meek.   [X, 1098–1104]

In the psychodynamics of damnation, egotism prevents Satan from making the essential act of contrition, and he continues to be a prisoner of the ego:

> Hadst thou the same free Will and Power to stand?
> Thou hadst: who hast thou then or what to accuse,
> But Heav'n's free Love dealt equally to all?

> Be then his Love accurst, since love or hate,
> To me alike, it deals eternal woe.
> Nay curs'd be thou, since against his thy will
> Chose freely what it now so justly rues.
> Me miserable! which way shall I fly
> Infinite wrath, and infinite despair?
> Which way I fly is Hell.   [IV, 66–75]

It seems likely that Milton's disappointing political experiences as an unappreciated deliverer of the English people contributed profoundly to his preoccupation with the theme of the liberator in chains, while the schismatic tendencies of Protestant sects taught him to scrutinize the motives of political and religious leaders and to project the destructive ones in the character of Satan. The projection could never have attained the imaginative power and psychological subtlety it displays in *Paradise Lost* if Milton had not invested a lot of his own feelings in Satan or recognized vital aspects of Satan as potentially present in himself. Such self-knowledge permits Milton to become the spokesman of things invisible to mortal sight in *Paradise Lost* without a trace of the self-sufficiency, smugness, or priggishness found in some of his early accounts of himself and in the character of the Lady in *Comus*. It is his extraordinary combination of humility and soaring aspiration, in this poem tuned by an inner ear to the divine voice, that saves the poet from the ruinous pride of Satan and at the same time inspires him to sublimities that satanic pride could never reach. The collapse of Milton's hopes as spokesman for England's apocalyptic role can be seen as leading to a submission *ho kaíros,* to the working out of divine providence:

> Magnanimous Despair alone
> Could show me so divine a thing,
> Where feeble Hope could ne'er have flown
> But vainly flapt its Tinsel Wing.   [Marvell, *The Definition of Love*]

Milton's most confident and challenging assumption of the role of omniscient poet and prophet is found in the invocation to the poem. Here he not only glances ironically at Ariosto's proud declaration as he "pursues / Things unattempted yet in Prose or Rhyme," but he outdoes all epic predecessors in the boldness with which he associates himself explicitly with Moses (supposed author of Genesis) and implicitly with the author of the fourth gospel. In weaving elements from Homeric and Virgilian epic into his own, Milton is also claiming for himself not only a greater subject than theirs but a much more active part in the creation of the poem. The anonymity of Homer is blended with the comparative self-assertiveness of Virgil in such a way that the divine sources of inspiration and the poet's creative role are both raised to a higher power. The invocation for the muse's aid is in no way incompatible with the sturdy assertion in "my advent'rous song" and the breathtakingly confident clause that amplifies the phrase: "That with no middle flight intends to soar / Above th' *Aonian* Mount." Milton's limitations are acknowledged, but not in a humble petition for assistance. Although he refers in a later invocation to the spirit who "nightly dictates to him / Slumb'ring," here it almost seems as if Milton were himself the dictator:

> What in me is dark
> Illumine, what is low raise and support;
> That to the highth of this great Argument
> I may assert Eternal Providence,
> And justify the ways of God to men.   [I, 22–26]

Milton calls spirits from the vasty deep and knows that they will come; there is no separation between the omniscient voice and the voice of mortal limitation here. Instead, he views his limitations from the lofty perspective of the inspired Knower.

It is right that *Paradise Lost* should begin by displaying the poet in serene possession of his divine role. Milton's subsequent appearances in the poem are like autobiographical flashbacks by which we can trace his painful evolution toward this fully achieved and integrated persona. Since the perspective of this invocation is the most comprehensive of all—it includes everything, from the creation of the world to the Second Coming—it is appropriate that the poet manifest a personality to correspond. To the extent that *Paradise Lost* is concerned with Milton's own struggles and vicissitudes in writing it, his first appearance in the poem expresses the perfect fulfillment of his role as Christian epic poet.

The beginning in medias res does not conflict with this conception of the poet's dynamic evolution in the poem but rather enhances it. With this perspective, Milton can express a confidence based on a total view of the workings of providence. The promise of redemption is at the heart of this confidence. The poet's subsequent appearances in the poem, being really earlier in time, are not nearly so untroubled, and there we can pursue the dramatic conflict between his doubts as a fallible and limited person and his intimations of immortality. Thus *Paradise Lost*, like the *Odyssey*, begins with an omniscient survey of the story, which reassures us that everything will turn out all right in the end, and then, through a succession of dissolves, focuses on the plights of various actors, who are unaware, or only partly aware, of divine providence. Taking the example of Odysseus as narrator of his own experiences, Milton assumes for himself, in these later appearances in *Paradise Lost*, the role of an Odyssean adventurer on a mission of the spirit. In his new persona at the beginning of book I he combines the omniscience of Zeus with both the limited knowledge and the experiential wisdom Odysseus has acquired through his sufferings. Divine and mortal vision are there fused.

While the invocation of book I conveys a total vision of divine providence and introduces the entire poem, subsequent invocations show the more limited perspective characteristic of delegated narrative. They are also more

narrowly focused on the specific difficulties of the narrator's situation, dramatizing the tension between the aspiration to divine knowledge and the fear of
presumption or failure. The proem of book III is not written from the lofty
perspective of the opening invocation, but after the arduous terrors of an
ascent from hell. Its interrogatory mode suggests the extent to which Milton's
visionary confidence has been shaken by his imaginative participation in Satan's heroic voyage:

> Hail holy Light, offspring of Heav'n first-born,
> Or of th' Eternal Coeternal beam
> May I express thee unblam'd? since God is Light,
> And never but in unapproached Light
> Dwelt from Eternity, dwelt then in thee,
> Bright effluence of bright essence increate.
> Or hear'st thou rather pure Ethereal stream,
> Whose Fountain who shall tell?   [III, 1–8]

The tentative, faltering movement of this passage reflects the uneasiness of a
poet who, like Odysseus, Aeneas, Dante, or Guyon, has suffered the ordeal of
a descent to the underworld and a return to light. The uneasiness stems as
well from the uncertain quality of the light Milton is hailing; which may be
the ordinary light of day; or the "offspring of Heav'n first-born" on the first
day of the hexaemeron; or it may be a "Coeternal Beam" of the Eternal; or,
since God is light, it may even be God. In any case Milton approaches it with
none of the assurance with which he first hailed the muse, but with diffidence
and awe, as if he had only light enough to speculate about the light he is
addressing. He thus puts himself implicitly in the company of a succession of
fallen witnesses to the various lights which glimmer in a series of similes in
the first two books:

> the Moon, whose Orb
> Through Optic Glass the *Tuscan* Artist views
> At ev'ning from the top of *Fesole,*
> Or in *Valdarno,* to descry new Lands,
> Rivers, or Mountains in her spotty Globe.   [I, 287–91]

> As when the Sun new ris'n
> Looks through the Horizontal misty Air
> Shorn of his Beams, or from behind the Moon
> In dim eclipse disastrous twilight sheds
> On half the Nations, and with fear of change
> Perplexes Monarchs.   [I, 594–99]

> As when from mountain tops the dusky clouds
> Ascending, while the North wind sleeps, o'erspread
> Heav'n's cheerful face, the low'ring Element
> Scowls o'er the dark'n'd lantskip Snow, or Show'r;
> If chance the radiant Sun with farewell sweet

> Extend his ev'ning beam, the fields revive,
> The birds thir notes renew, and bleating herds
> Attest thir joy, that hill and valley rings.   [II, 488–95]

Blindness is a symbol for Milton's limitation as a visionary narrator, but it is also the affliction that spurs him to seek a truer source of enlightenment than the visiting sun. The invocation in book III, after its tentative opening, proceeds by a series of alternations between fears of presumption and dismay at his blindness to an increasingly resolute pursuit of the celestial light. Although the movement may be uncertain, it is persistent:

> Yet not the more
> Cease I to wander where the Muses haunt
> Clear Spring, or shady Grove, or sunny Hill,
> Smit with the love of sacred Song.   [III, 26–29]

While, as Leslie Brisman has suggested, "wander" here carries ominous overtones,[13] its main force is to convey the blind poet's erratic but dogged pursuit of the true source of inspiration, a pursuit which is for the moment rewarded, as shown by the inner peace of the concluding injunction.

> So much the rather thou *Celestial* Light
> Shine inward, and the mind through all her powers
> Irradiate, there plant eyes, all mist from thence
> Purge and disperse, that I may see and tell
> Of things invisible to mortal sight.   [III, 51–55]

The "advent'rous Song" Milton confidently proclaims in book I gives place, however, to the feeling of precariousness expressed in these lines from book III:

> Thee I revisit now with bolder wing,
> Escap't the *Stygian* Pool, though long detain'd
> In that obscure sojourn, while in my flight
> Through utter and through middle darkness borne
> With other notes than to th' *Orphean* Lyre
> I sung of *Chaos* and *Eternal Night*,
> Taught by the heav'nly Muse to venture down
> The dark descent, and up to reascend,
> Though hard and rare.   [III, 13–21]

This passage clearly alludes to Aeneas's ascent from the underworld, which the Sibyl tells him is arduous and difficult. But Milton's own descent to and return from the underworld is ultimately much more than a venture, with that word's associations of casual and perhaps foolhardy heroism. To the extent that he is imitating Aeneas (who was imitating Odysseus) Milton's hellish experience is a rite of passage, an initiation into the darker regions of the spirit. It is a temptation which goes beyond that of Guyon in the Cave of Mammon in that Milton's imagination actually responds to the enticing manifestation of demonic power. His concept of temptation has become infinitely more complex than it was in his earlier work because of an imaginative and (up to a point) sympathetic involvement in satanic heroism. The worst part of Milton's ordeal has been encountering the satanic part of himself, which is a necessary precondition to his emancipation from it.

In turning to the proem of book VII we find Milton even more intensely aware of the hazards of his epic enterprise. Where in book III he lays emphasis on the perils of the flight upward from the dark abyss, in book VII he is deeply troubled by the dangers of a descent to earth. Whether climbing or gliding, Milton displays none of the soaring confidence of the opening invocation. His address to Urania is filled with a deep sense of his own fallibility and vulnerability:

> Up led by thee
> Into the Heav'n of Heav'ns I have presum'd,
> An Earthly Guest, and drawn Empyreal Air,
> Thy temp'ring; with like safety guided down
> Return me to my Native Element:
> Lest from this flying Steed unrein'd, (as once
> *Bellerophon,* though from a lower Clime)
> Dismounted, on th' *Aleian* Field I fall
> Erroneous there to wander and forlorn.   [VII, 12–20]

The feeling is fearful, humble, and prayerful; flying here inspires Milton with dread. Although Antaeus-like he regains some strength by his renewed contact with the earth ("Standing on Earth, not rapt above the Pole") and by renewed confidence in the muse who visits his slumbers nightly, Milton ends this invocation with an agonized plea:

> But drive far off the barbarous dissonance
> Of *Bacchus* and his Revellers, the Race
> Of that wild Rout that tore the *Thracian* Bard
> In *Rhodope,* where Woods and Rocks had Ears
> To rapture, till the savage clamor drown'd
> Both Harp and Voice; nor could the Muse defend
> Her Son. So fail not thou, who thee implores:
> For thou art Heav'nly, shee an empty dream.   [VII, 32–39]

The whole proem to book VII should be seen as an imploring meditation on true guides and false ones, with the passage on Orpheus and Bacchus serving as an extraordinarily vivid composition of place. The tentative note on which it ends perfectly realizes the precariousness of Milton's heroic venture, while the vitality and beauty of Raphael's subsequent account of the creation is a confirmation of the poet's prayer for guidance.

As Milton tunes his notes to tragic in the last of his invocations, his voice becomes more authoritative and less personal, as if he shared the "distance and distaste / On the part of Heav'n / Now alienated." "Tragic" implies not only the catastrophe which Eve and Adam enact and suffer in books IX and X, but the essentially dramatic mode in which this portion of the story is presented. Now that the human protagonists are fully prepared for the encounter with temptation, the poet withdraws from the action and allows them to play out the tragedy. His introductory remarks have something of the detachment many readers have found in God's anticipatory comments on the fall in book III. Like him, Milton is forthright, precise, and succinct:

> I now must change
> Those Notes to Tragic; foul distrust, and breach
> Disloyal on the part of Man, revolt,
> And disobedience: On the part of Heav'n
> Now alienated, distance and distaste,
> Anger and just rebuke, and judgment giv'n,
> That brought into this World a world of woe,
> Sin and her shadow Death and Misery,
> Death's Harbinger. [IX, 5–13]

While Milton's presence is still felt in these books in occasional Virgilian expressions of disapproval or dismay, his resumption of the role of omniscient narrator after the delegated narrative of Raphael in the preceding four books brings the poem back to the predominantly objective and dramatic mode of the opening ones. The terse assurance of this proem, however, is quite different from the anguish and anxiety in the two preceding ones. Milton's role as epic creator is no longer threatened by the inner strife of fallibility and omniscience, although it is still contingent on his celestial patroness, "who deigns / Her nightly visitation unimplor'd, / And dictates to me slumb'ring, or inspires / Easy my unpremeditated Verse" (IX, 21–24).

Milton's passive stance as the muse's instrument is not only compatible with a new assurance in the supreme value of his argument, but marks his own deliverance from the heroic ordeals of Odysseus and Aeneas as he takes leave of the themes of classical epic in "*Neptune's* ire or *Juno's,* that so long / Perplex'd the *Greek* and *Cytherea's* Son." In dismissing the strenuous exploits of Odysseus, Milton implicitly leaves behind the heroic phase of his role as creator. He now looks on the risks of his venture with philosophical detachment:

> Mee of these
> Nor skill'd nor studious, higher Argument
> Remains, sufficient of itself to raise
> That name, unless an age too late, or cold
> Climate, or Years damp my intended wing
> Deprest; and much they may, if all be mine,
> Not hers who brings it nightly to my Ear. [IX, 41–47]

THE NEGATIVE WAY: PARADISE REGAINED

Despite the austere manner in which it seems to eschew the traditional mythic allusions of epic, *Paradise Regained*[14] can be seen as a deeply symbolic version of Joseph Campbell's "monomyth," an archetypal pattern in which the hero "ventures forth from the world of common day into a region of supernatural wonder"; then encounters and wins, with divine help, a victory over "fabulous forms"; and "comes back from this mysterious adventure with the power to bestow boons on his fellow man."[15]

Campbell's discussion is also relevant in showing how *Paradise Regained* ·can be read as combining elements of the fairy-tale hero with its primary emphasis on Jesus as the ultimate hero of myth: "Typically, the hero of the fairy tale achieves a domestic, microcosmic triumph, and the hero of myth a world-historical macrocosmic triumph: the former—the youngest or despised child who becomes the master of extraordinary powers—prevails over his personal oppressors, the latter brings back from his adventures the means for the regeneration of his society as a whole."[16] The domestic, microcosmic aspect of *Paradise Regained* is evident, inter alia, in the innocence and ignorance and youth of the hero. Although Jesus asserts, in his first meditations, his early aversion to "childish play" and dedication to "public good," he sets out without any idea of how he will fulfill the ultimate role of which he is, nevertheless, assured:

> To rescue *Israel* from the *Roman* yoke,
> Then to subdue and quell o'er all the earth
> Brute violence and proud Tyrannic pow'r,
> Till truth were freed and equity restor'd.   [I, 217–20][17]

His ignorance, lack of power, and submissiveness imply something like the initial weakness of the young would-be redeemer of folktale, as does his dependence on his mother, in the absence of his father, for what information he has about his mission:

> These growing thoughts my Mother soon perceiving,
> By words at times cast forth, inly rejoic'd,
> And said to me apart: High are thy thoughts,
> O Son, but nourish them and let them soar
> To what height sacred virtue and true worth
> Can raise them, though above example high;
> By matchless Deeds express thy matchless Sire.   [I, 227–33]

In his unannounced departure from home to undertake the inward adventure of self-discovery in the wilderness and in going back to his mother in the end—"he unobserv'd / Home to his mother's house private returned"—Jesus is tracing the monomyth in the private and domestic mode of the fairy tale. Both the "growing thoughts" she fosters and the single, approving theophany of the Father, who announces impersonally and laconically (according to Satan's report), "This is my son Belov'd, in him am pleas'd," sustain Jesus as he tries to fathom the perplexed question of his identity as "Son of God" (an identity Satan will also claim for himself). He never questions the public end to which his career is dedicated, only the means.

The uncertainty about Jesus' specific mission and the means to its accomplishment is compounded by Milton's resolute confinement of the action of *Paradise Regained* to his inner psychomachia. From the public point of view, represented mainly by his mother and his discomfited disciples, he achieves nothing. They are kept ignorant of the whole adventure. The negative way of his quest, through denial and privation, qualifies Jesus as more quintessentially "private" than any of his predecessors in privation, such as Odysseus or Guyon.

Thus the "adventures" of Milton's hero are microcosmic as far as the public is concerned, and readers alone are privileged to share the knowledge of the Son's secret quest. His actions, in the context of the epic tradition, are inactions; his return home at the end of the poem something less than an anticlimax—a return, apparently, to the status quo ante that appears to deflate the great expectations he had shared with his mother and to abrogate the implications of his Father's annuciation at the Jordan. It is interesting to try to imagine the homecoming scene:

> MOTHER: Where did you go?
> SON: Out.
> MOTHER: What did you do?
> SON: Nothing.

Perhaps one of the implied conditions of the Son's inward quest is that its successful achievement must remain a secret, shared only by God and Satan, until the proper time for the beginning of his active ministry comes round. Jesus, in the necessarily private mode of his experience, is deprived of the privilege of sharing his self-revelation. The austere manner in which the revelation is presented to us is counter to the rich celebratory style with which epic normally records heroic deeds. In any case, Milton achieves in *Paradise Regained* the ultimate instance of the heroism of inaction that had engaged him throughout his career: in *Comus, Upon His Blindness, Lycidas, Paradise Lost, Samson Agonistes,* and other works.

Paradise Regained is a fairy-tale version of the monomyth in other respects. Jesus in this story is, like many folklore heroes, the youngest son. He is, moreover, the youngest of three and thus enjoys that special position of apparent inferiority and real inner strength that third sons in fairy tales often occupy. As Son incarnate he is a figure distinctly different from and, for the time being, separate from the Son of *Paradise Lost,* the "Second Omnipotence" (VI, 684). Of this omnipotent, omniscient figure the Son incarnate of *Paradise Regained* knows little, since, like other mortals, he is in most respects confined to seeing the divine through a glass, darkly, Satan is not alone in regarding him as distinct and separate from that Son who with "his fierce thunder drove us to the deep" (I, 90) and shares his perplexity with his fellow devils:

> Who this is we must learn, for man he seems
> In all his lineaments, though in his face
> The glimpses of his Father's glory shine.   [I, 91–93]

The Son of *Paradise Regained* is likewise confined to knowledge of the Old Testament and, like Satan, to uncertain predictions about the future. In knowledge, then, the contestants are evenly matched, and Satan's uncertainty about the Son's identity is a demonic version of the Son's own uncertainty. The critical difference between them lies in Satan's compulsive and vain pursuit of knowledge about his opponent as distinct from the Son's imperturbable faith in the adequacy of whatever knowledge God vouchsafes him. On the eve of his ordeal he declares:

> And now by some strong motion I am led
> Into this Wilderness, to what intent
> I learn not yet; perhaps I need not know;
> For what concerns my knowledge God reveals.   [I, 291–94]

This calm resignation, unhesitatingly supported by faith, is reflected in Jesus' quiet, unempathic, laconic responses to Satan:

> Who brought me hither
> Will bring me hence, no other Guide I seek.   [I, 335–36]

> Why dost thou then suggest to me distrust,
> Knowing who I am, as I know who thou art?   [I, 355–56]

> Thy coming hither, though I know thy scope,
> I bid not or forbid; do as thou find'st
> Permission from above; thou canst not more.   [I, 494–96]

> They all had need, I as thou seest have none.   [II, 318]

> Thy pompous Delicacies I contemn,
> And count thy specious gifts no gifts but guiles.   [II, 390–91]

> Shall I seek glory then, as vain men seek
> Oft not deserv'd? I seek not mine, but his
> Who sent me, and thereby witness whence I am.   [III, 105–07]

> But what concerns it thee when I begin
> My everlasting Kingdom? Why art thou
> Solicitous? What moves thy inquisition?
> Know'st thou not that my rising is thy fall,
> And my promotion will be thy destruction?   [III, 198–202]

In all these instances Jesus counters Satan's attempts to goad him into action or to make him declare his messianic intentions with an intelligent brevity of speech that instantly exposes the fraudulent motive behind the temptation.

The encounters have their comic aspect, as the obsessed Satan, in Bergsonian fashion, repeats and repeats his vain gambits and suffers one pratfall after another. They dramatize the foredoomed failure of a lying and imprisoned intelligence to enthrall a free one. The effect is to keep Satan in a state of frantic uncertainty that reaches its highest pitch when Christ rejects the benefits of Greek philosophy with this devastating response,

> Think not but that I know these things: or think
> I know them not; not therefore am I short
> Of knowing what I ought: he who receives
> Light from above, from the fountain of light,
> No other doctrine needs, though granted true. [IV, 286–90]

The Son's gnomic utterances express essential truth unadorned, and his longer speeches, almost devoid of imagery and rhetorical complexity, also imply an innocence that can express itself artlessly. Against this artlessness Satan's more figurative and involuted style is powerless.

Satan's desire for knowledge of the Son is, as I have said, in the service of his compulsion to convert him from trust in God to a premature exercise of his destined messianic role. The "wiser" older brother, we might say, tries to subvert the secret strength of the younger, which is essentially beyond his comprehension. Such jealousy is a persistent element in folklore, as one sees in Cinderella and her older half-sisters, in Cordelia and her two evil older sisters, in Joseph and his brothers, and in many other cases. Satan's machinations are bound to fail, if only because he cannot dissociate knowledge from the corrupting, self-serving exercise of power, and is therefore incapable of recognizing the Word incarnate. As in *Comus* and *Samson Agonistes,* this hero is never seriously tempted, and the interest of his career lies elsewhere than in the drama of temptation. The suspenseless, virtually actionless nature of his encounter is characteristically Miltonic, implying that the human spirit is the arena where real action occurs. If there is a dramatic element in *Paradise Regained,* it can be found in the Son's gradual self-definition, culminating in a sudden, blinding, self-revelation. It can also be found, in Jung's terms, in the dramatized encounter between the Son, considered as self, and Satan, considered as ego. A similar relationship obtains when Cordelia is in conflict with Regan and Goneril. Although Satan and Regan and Goneril are older, they have never developed beyond the infantile ego, which can relate to others only in terms of its own drives, and therefore cannot comprehend that infinitely larger entity, the achieved self. Thus too, as in countless fairy tales, *As You Like It* among others, the despised and often dispossessed youngest child defeats his evil older brother, even though the older brother seems to have the power to arrange things pretty much as he likes. For Milton and Shakespeare worldly power is anatomized as weakness, and other-worldly weakness as the only real strength.

An even more important fairy-tale aspect of the relation of Jesus and

Satan is seen in the main model for *Paradise Regained,* the Book of Job. Whereas Satan proposes the testing of Job and has divine permission to afflict him in any way he wishes, the Father in *Paradise Regained* takes the initiative in offering Jesus to Satan as a subject for temptation. In both texts the Father withdraws during the trial of his favorite son, and Satan becomes his surrogate. In folklore terms this apparently harsh paternal behavior corresponds to that stage in the young hero's development at which the father is seen as an ogre. Job's wife and friends seem bent on persuading him to take such a view, but they fail. The idea, of course, never occurs to Jesus, because his faith is founded upon unshakable trust in the divine goodness. Job's God finally speaks to him, though incomprehensibly, out of the whirlwind, but the only direct communication Jesus has with the Father is the brief theophany at the Jordan. In view of Jesus' divine nature, that is sufficient. Unlike Job, the Son is given no rewards at the end of the poem, for he lacks nothing. The Son's final utterance on the pinnacle of the temple, "It is written, thou shalt not tempt the Lord thy God," is an impersonal declaration in the Father's words of the underlying truth which Satan has labored to destroy. As Jesus utters them, the words apply equally to himself and to Satan, but the accompanying miracle, which he does not anticipate, gives them a further and astounding application to himself. In refusing to tempt God, Jesus manifests the truth that he is God. Posed dizzily on the spire of the temple with, one would imagine, his arms outstretched to maintain his balance, the concluding ordeal of the Son is to symbolize the New Testament figure of the crucified Jesus triumphantly raised upon the apex of the Old Testament.

The presence of other elements of the monomyth in *Paradise Regained* may help shed light on the vexed question of the poem's genre. The opening lines that imitate through Spenser the discarded proem of the *Aeneid* imply, in the "Virgilian progression," Milton's adherence to a threefold poetic career— from pastoral, through georgic, to epic:

> I who erewhile the happy Garden sung
> By one man's disobedience lost, now sing
> Recover'd Paradise to all mankind,
> By one man's firm obedience fully tried
> Through all temptation and the Tempter foil'd
> In all his wiles, defeated and repuls't,
> And *Eden* rais'd in the waste Wilderness.   [I, 1–7]

"The happy Garden" emphasizes the pastoral aspects of *Paradise Lost,* but the prelapsarian labors of Adam and Eve in "lopping and propping" their garden and their arduous labors after the Fall reflect the georgic tradition, going back to Hesiod's *Works and Days* and summed up in the Virgilian phrase *labor improbus.* "The happy Garden," lost "by one man's disobedience," gives place, in *Paradise Regained,* to "the waste Wilderness," an inversion of Eden's "wilderness of sweets." Now, Milton seems to say, we come to the true epic, the recovery of Paradise "to all mankind" through the unmatched heroic achievement of "one man's firm obedience fully tried / Through all temptation" and the raising of Eden in compensation for its earlier razing.

Paradise Regained completes the central myth of loss and redemption projected in *Paradise Lost* from its very beginning and affirmed emphatically at its close in Michael's final promise to Adam of "a paradise within thee happier far." Once the enclosed garden of Eden is seen as an irrecoverable and local paradise, the way is open for Adam and Eve to take the first steps in the human saga that leads to the mission of Jesus in the wilderness. Like them he wanders, the verb suggesting resignation.

If *Paradise Regained* is construed in some ways as the culminating epic in Milton's career, we must try to understand why its style is so austere that it succeeds in excluding many of the features of epic: heroic action, divine interventions, allusiveness, sublimity of style, and figurative richness. The repression of these grand aspects of the traditional epic is clearly appropriate to the themes of privacy and deprivation that provide the thematic keynote to Jesus' ordeal. The negative way is reflected in the privation of this chastened style. The style also suggests the humility of Jesus and corresponds to the fairy-tale aspect of the solitary adventures of a little-known youth. Finally, by directing our attention toward the inner journey, a meditation in process, the austerity annuls the outer copiousness and richness of setting that are appropriate to the traditional epic. The polychromatic garden gives place to a monochromatic desert. The fecundity of Eden yields to the sterility of the Transjordanian wilderness. The total effect is to contract the infinite variety of *Paradise Lost* into a desolate and largely featureless milieu in which topographical features are almost entirely irrelevant.

The Son's forty-day journey differs from the voyages of Odysseus or Gilgamesh or Aeneas or Dante or Beowulf or Satan (in *Paradise Lost*) in having no geographical goal. His point of departure is the Jordan, where he was baptized, but the time is not specific:

> So they in Heav'n their Odes and Vigils tun'd.
> Meanwhile the Son of God, who yet some days
> Lodg'd in *Bethabara,* where *John* baptiz'd,
> Musing and much revolving in his breast,
> How best the mighty work he might begin
> Of Savior to mankind, and which way first
> Publish his Godlike office now mature,
> One day forth walk'd alone, the Spirit leading,
> And his deep thoughts, the better to converse
> With solitude, till far from track of men,
> Thought following thought, and step by step led on,
> He enter'd now the bordering Desert wild,
> And with dark shades and rocks environ'd round,
> His holy Meditations thus pursu'd.   [I, 182–95]

The many present participles contribute to the rapt, musing mood of this passage and suggest the passivity of the traveler. "One day" he walked forth alone: the temporal vagueness is augmented by the line "He enter'd now the bordering Desert wild." When is now? When he entered the desert. Temporal vagueness here suggests the "once upon a time" with which fairy tales begin, and it discounts the importance of chronology. In the forty days that follow, chronology is all but forgotten, and place, to the extent that it is described at all, does not mark progression in a journey; its notations are purely symbolic or for atmosphere, the Son's "holy meditations" being interrupted only by nightfall or by Satan's visitations. Such places, in most instances, are not located, being unconnected by time, movement, or geographical relation to any other places. It is inner time and place that matter, as Jesus meditates on the time and place and manner in which he may "first / Publish his Godlike office now mature," an event that does not occur in the poem and which constitutes a prelude to his destined career. His interior journey, then, has nothing to do with the times or places where events occur, except for the scene on the pinnacle of the temple. The passage, in its simplicity, may seem to anticipate the style of Wordsworth in one of his reflective excursions into the natural scene, except that it is quite devoid of Wordsworth's unceasing interest. Jesus' detachment from his milieu is another major manifestation of the intense inward focus of his experience.

Outwardly the emptiness and topographical bleakness of the wilderness reflect both the privacy and the privation of the hero's quest. Inwardly, it may serve in this case, as it often does in both fairy tale and myth, as "a free field for the projection of unconscious content."[18] In emptying himself of will and submitting to a blank and undifferentiated environment, in exposing himself to Satanic suggestion, Jesus also submits to the repertory of visions and ideas projected on that blankness by the satanic imagination. In his sharing of these visions, despite his resolute rejection of the implications Satan finds in them, must there not be, in Jesus' own imagination, a degree of participation? For him as well as for the tempter they have meaning and interest. Were he utterly indifferent to them, the whole experience would be meaningless, and he would not be moved, as he sometimes is, to make extended analytical rejections of the motives for action Satan fallaciously claims for them. In response to Satan's argument that it is the Son's urgent duty to seize "Occasion's forelock" and assert himself as Messiah, Jesus defines his role with compelling cogency and force:

> All things are best fulfill'd in their due time,
> And time there is for all things, Truth hath said:
> If of my reign Prophetic Writ hath told
> That it shall never end, so when begin
> The Father in his purpose hath decreed,
> He in whose hand all times and seasons roll.

> What if he hath decreed that I shall first
> Be tried in humble state, and things adverse,
> By tribulations, injuries, insults,
> Contempts, and scorns, and snares, and violence,
> Suffering, abstaining, quietly expecting
> Without distrust or doubt, that he may know
> What I can suffer, how obey? who best
> Can suffer, best can do, best reign, who first
> Well hath obey'd; just trial e'er I merit
> My exaltation without change or end. [III, 182–97]

Repeatedly Satan projects a colorful and animated image of one culture or another, crammed with exotic names and compelling details. He is a geographer and historian, the custodian of limited time and place, as God is of eternity and omnipresence. Invariably, however, Jesus nonsuits his gambit by rejecting the temptation to seize the time and place for the beginning of his career, and his language is as insistently abstract as Satan's is specific. Despite its austerity, however, the Son's style has a sinuous, interconnected clarity and an intellectual tightness whose sublime simplicity cancels Satan's virtuosity. Since Satan has intimations of his doom, and since the Son's reign will be eternal, Satan's point of view is confined to specific historical opportunities which the Son can serenely refute. Offers of power, of fancied strange delights, and threats of violence cannot shake his twofold piety as Son of God and Son of Man.

At key moments in the poem the wilderness through which the Son wanders is presented as a maze or labyrinth. And so it must seem to one fixated on time, space, and goal, like Satan:

> The way he came not having mark'd, return
> Was difficult, by human steps untrod;
> And he still on was led, but with such thoughts
> Accompani'd of things past and to come
> Lodg'd in his Breast, as well might recommend
> Such solitude before choicest Society. [I, 297–302]

Dwelling among untrodden ways, this second Adam tests his progenitor's admission to the independent-minded Eve that "solitude is sometimes best society" (*Paradise Lost* IX, 249); unlike Eve, who is "amazed" by the physical and rhetorical involutions of the Serpent, the Son, with providence his guide, never questions the validity of the route he follows. Though isolated and physically disoriented in the wasteland, Jesus nonetheless proves Satan's vain boast in *Paradise Lost* that "the mind is its own place" in the calm confidence he evinces: "Who brought me hither / Will bring me hence, no other Guide I seek" (I, 335–36), and he reminds Satan of his ghastly discovery that he is "never more in Hell than when in Heaven" (*Paradise Lost* I, 420). "Oracles are ceast," he declares and continues:

> And thou no more with Pomp and Sacrifice
> Shall be inquir'd at *Delphos* or elsewhere,
> At least in vain, for they shall find thee mute.
> God hath now sent his living Oracle
> Into the World to teach his final will,
> And sends his Spirit of Truth henceforth to dwell
> In pious Hearts, an inward Oracle
> To all truth requisite for men to know.   [I, 457–64]

In dismissing oracles like Delphos, Jesus is differentiating himself from a long line of epic heroes whose rites of passage require a guided visit in pursuit of visionary or oracular knowledge in the underworld, as Odysseus visits Tiresias; Aeneas, the Sibyl and the spirit of Anchises; as Dante traverses Hell with Virgil; or as Guyon descends to the cave of Mammon. In the wilderness Jesus enacts the double role of the heroic seeker of truth and the source of "all truth requisite for men to know." Place again is displaced, and the ancient identification of Delphi as the navel of the world is replaced with the Christian revelation of the oracle within. Thus Jesus' rite of passage is distinguished from all others in being a descent into the truth within himself, the individuation there achieved being independent of the time or place where it occurs. His enunciation of this truth exposes Satan's essential unreality:

> To whom our Saviour with unalter'd brow.
> Thy coming hither, though I know thy scope,
> I bid not or forbid; do as thou find'st
> Permission from above; thou canst not more.
>   He added not; and Satan, bowing low
> His grey dissimulation, disappear'd
> Into thin Air diffus'd; for now began
> Night with her sullen wing to double-shade
> The Desert; Fowls in thir clay nests were couch't;
> And now wild Beasts came forth the woods to roam.   [I, 493–502]

These lines, which end book I, typify a pervasive characteristic of Milton's wilderness setting. It is low, earthbound, and largely two-dimensional. There is one scene in heaven, two devilish consistories held somewhere in the air, and a brief apotheosis when Jesus is borne up by flights of angels from the pinnacle of the temple, but the earthbound milieu, eschewing the upward and downward sublimities of action in *Paradise Lost,* reflects the persistently humble vision of Jesus' via negativa, as well as the peripatetic meditative mode of his quest. In addition to this incidental observation, one might note the negative quality of the scene. Into this monochromatic landscape, doubly shaded at nightfall, the Prince of Hell, in Milton's brilliant phrase a "grey dissimulation . . . disappear'd / Into thin Air diffus'd," assuming, or being absorbed into, the insubstantiality of his new status as Prince of the Air. Even birds nest on the ground. What little energy is left in the waning light is transferred rather perfunctorily to unspecified wild beasts who now come "forth the woods to roam." We are witnessing them through the untroubled eye of the Son. All the conventional elements of romantic horror are here, as in countless scenes in Spenser's fairyland, or in Macbeth's spine-chilling "Light thickens, and the crow makes wing / To the rooky wood," but Milton somehow contrives to divest them of horror. The tone, like the scene, does not reflect but rather absorbs the horror, leaving the Savior "unalter'd."

That Jesus does not alter in response to any of the temptations again suggests that, unlike other heroes undergoing rites of passage, his individuation has already been achieved before the story begins. The self into which he descends at the outset of his meditations is perfect and fully formed. His ordeal is a matter of self-discovery rather than self-fulfillment.

The tempter, in the first encounter, according to Campbell's monomyth, may be seen as a "threshold guardian" on the borders of a zone of magnified power. Beyond him "is darkness, the unknown, and danger; just as beyond the parental watch is danger to the infant and beyond the protection of his society danger to the member of the tribe."[19] Jesus is capable of converting this zone of danger to beneficial uses, whereas a more conventional hero would jeopardize not only himself but his society, as does Eve in her solitary excursion. As threshold guardian and Prince of the Air, Satan has power over space and time, moving the Son of God up and down and around at will and simultaneously exchanging his gray dissimulation (reminiscent of Archimago) for a repertory of ephemeral identities that counterpoint the Son's unchanging self.

If Jesus has already achieved the fundamental goal of true selfhood before the events of *Paradise Regained* begin, the poem may seem to lack action, to amount to little more than a series of demonstrations of his spiritual perfection, with all the activity left to that energetic virtuoso Satan. On the other hand, the main action of the poem may, paradoxically, be a kind of inaction, Jesus' persistent determination to refrain from untimely or inappropriate deeds. If, according to Campbell, the fairy-tale hero "achieves a domestic, microcosmic triumph," this occurs in Jesus' private interior victory. If the hero of myth achieves "a world-wide macrocosmic triumph," this is the inevitable and undoubted consequence of Jesus' secret victory. The fact that Milton utterly ignores Jesus' active career indicates his conviction that it is the destined sequel to his ordeal in the desert.

The series of temptations must then be regarded as moments in a process of self-discovery. "Wand'ring the woody maze" for forty days of total deprivation, he undergoes the temptation to turn stones into food, the manifold temptations of the banquet (II, 302–405), the offer of wealth and political power to redeem Israel (II, 406–86), of glory (III, 1–144), of "zeal and duty" in assuming the throne of David (III, 145–250), of world empire (III, 251–443), of Roman "wealth and power, / Civility of Manners, Arts, and Arms, / And long Renown" (IV, 44–194), and the rich delights of Greek culture (IV,

195–366). Milton recapitulates major episodes in the epic tradition that he is radically revising, and Satan's attitude toward such achievements is quite orthodox, according to tradition. After Greece fails, "quite at a loss, for all his darts were spent" (IV, 366), Satan now turns to other strategies to shake his steadfast victim. Returning him to the wilderness ("What dost thou in this world?") he employs all the special effects in his repertory to harrass and disturb the Son with darkness, cold, ugly dreams, thunder, "fierce rain with lightning mixt, water with fire / In ruin reconcil'd," hurricane winds, "infernal ghosts and hellish furies," who howl, yell, and shriek and brandish fiery darts. But these Dantean apparitions are, like the dismal night of their occurrence and the impresario conducting them, "unsubstantial" (399). On the fair morning that ensues, the Son answers Satan's solicitous inquiries with a stroke of deflating sprezzatura, "Mee worse than wet thou find'st not" (IV, 486). Clearly there is dramatic interest in the interplay between Satan's versatile arts and the artlessness of the Son's rejoinders. Perhaps, on the other hand, the Son's artlessness is the art that conceals art in the spontaneous simplicity of truth.

   The last encounter with specious terrors and double darkness is a hyperbolic reprise of the first, and the two episodes bracket the seven temptations enumerated above—analogues, perhaps, for the seven deadly sins—isolating the visionary mode of Christ's ordeal in the wasteland from events in the "real" world that precede and follow them: the Son's baptism and his triumphant stand on the pinnacle of the temple.
   Incarnation has cut the Son off from all direct access to the Father (except for the epiphany at the Jordan), and the action of the poem consists, finally, of the gradual discovery, through essentially human resources, of the nature of his career as Son of God and savior of mankind. The climax on the temple spire is a culminating revelation of his divine identity, one in which the Logos moves beyond the realm of discursive language and debate to an almost wordless epiphanic mode. His rescue and succor by the angels is outside the framework of the action proper, and a nine-word coda brings him back to the point of his departure: "hee unobserv'd / Home to his Mother's house private return'd." Unlike other heroes of the monomyth, the hero of *Paradise Regained* undertakes a dark voyage in which space, time, direction, and destination are sublimely indifferent matters. In fact, that they are sublimely indifferent is essential to the successful completion of his quest. From a public standpoint, he has achieved nothing. From Milton's point of view of the via negativa as the essential way, he has fulfilled his quest so perfectly that not a trace of it can be discerned at the poem's end except by those who have the privilege of sharing Milton's vision.

Paradise Regained is an epic poem that radically modifies traditional aspects of epic. The career of the meditative hero, outwardly inactive, must be rendered in a style shorn to a large extent of those qualities that contribute to the grandeur of traditional epic: rich and elaborate imagery (there are almost no similes in the poem), classical allusion, rhetorical, metrical, and syntactical inversions, suspensions, and variations, and the sensuous sound patterns that have so much to do with the incantatory and sonorous effects of the *Aeneid* or *Paradise Lost.* The style is terse. Diction is chastened.

All such tendencies toward a lower and more austere style appear most conspicuously in the passages of narration and in the speeches of the Son. Since Satan's speeches are repeated invitations to regress into an inappropriate and outmoded course of heroic deeds, his language tends to be more conventionally epic. The temptations he offers recreate experiences and deeds that are central to earlier epic: prowess in battle, self-glorification, elaborate banquets, the advancement of an ethnic or national destiny, even the great philosophical and literary achievements of ancient Greece, which undergird so much of *Paradise Lost.* An outstanding example is Satan's animated account of Rome:

> Many a fair Edifice besides, more like
> Houses of Gods (so well I have dispos'd
> My Airy Microscope) thou mayst behold
> Outside and inside both, pillars and roofs
> Carv'd work, the hand of fam'd Artificers
> In Cedar, Marble, Ivory or Gold.
> Thence to the gates cast round thine eye, and see
> What conflux issuing forth or ent'ring in,
> Praetors, Proconsuls to thir Provinces
> Hasting or on return, in robes of State;
> Lictors and rods, the ensigns of thir power
> Legions and Cohorts, turms of horse and wings:
> Or Embassies from Regions far remote
> In various habits on the *Appian* road,
> Or on th' *Aemilian*, some from farthest South,
> *Syene,* and where the shadow both way falls,
> *Meroë, Nilotic* Isle, and more to West,
> The Realm of *Bocchus* to the *Blackmoor Sea.*   [IV, 55–72]

These eighteen lines are part of a sentence that extends to twenty-four lines and forms but a small portion of Satan's sinuous, variegated representation of Rome, geographical, political, and architectural. The epic emphasis on power, wealth, and culture, to which we can supply analogues in *Paradise Lost,* lacks, nevertheless, a point of view or a vision that can discern any real meaning behind all this busy detail. The accounts of Hell and Eden in *Paradise Lost* are unified by coherent values, but this vivid heterogeneity is devoid of insight. Satan can supply an engaging tableau of imperial Rome with a lot of going and coming, and he can indicate its greatness by a catalogue of exotic places it governs, but there is no inkling of any authentic purpose or principle underlying this inventory. "Fam'd Artificers" reminds us of Daedalus, but neither the most famous of ancient mythopoeic artists nor any artist or work of art is here. Rome is an ornamental and inchoate anthill rendered in a relentlessly materialistic mode. This fact is obviously related to the fact that everything Satan has to offer is specious, but it also suggests that, in the course of his degeneration, the heroic rebel has lost whatever appreciation of the heroic he once had. Jesus unerringly exposes the hollowness of the proffered vision:

> Embassies thou show'st
> From Nations far and nigh; what honor that,
> But tedious waste of time to sit and hear
> So many hollow compliments and lies,
> Outlandish flatteries?   [IV, 121–25]

Satan's speech has some of the momentum and cumulative power that is so evident in *Paradise Lost,* with "the sense variously drawn out from one verse into another," but the offer ends in anticlimax as he feebly concludes, "to me the power / Is given, and by that right I give it thee" (IV, 103–04). Since he cannot identify any recognizable value in the gift, he is easily put down by the laconic simplicity of Jesus' rejoinder.

Jesus' apparent inaction, "deeds above heroic / Though in secret done," is heroic conduct of a unique order, since on it depends not only the restoration or preservation of a nation but the opportunity for the salvation of all humanity. Only an achievement of this illimitable magnitude can cancel the consequences of the Fall. Unlike Adam and Eve, the hero of such an ordeal must achieve his triumph by resolutely denying himself any form of self-assertion, any impulse of the will that might lead him to exercise his power prematurely and to some limited end, like Achilles or Aeneas. The acts of Jesus are a disciplined and total obedience to the promptings of the spirit. With the rejection of traditional modes of heroic behavior, Milton must find a form and a style that adequately express the *via humilis* Jesus pursues. By blending the usual epic preoccupation with the sublime with the humbler mode of the fairy tale, the dualistic style of *Paradise Regained* is responsive both to the secret character of Jesus' ordeal and to its enormous implication for the human race. Jesus' experiences in the wilderness are folklore and romance, much influenced by Spenser, while their public consequences are celebrated in the sublime epic quality of the climactic epiphany and apotheosis.

The interaction of Satan's and Jesus' styles may be understood as a conflict between two modes of epic value, patterned, it may be, on the aggressive and self-assertive Achilles as contrasted with the much-enduring Odysseus. Whatever power he still has, no one has ever thought of Satan as the hero of this poem. Irrevocably lost, his vain hope is to subvert the power of the new hero through second-hand versions of old epic temptations. Ultimately the difference in their utterances goes beyond modes of action, values, and styles. Satan's speeches are self-defeating because they are solely governed by the egoistic compulsion toward personal power, and they mask only hollowness. Jesus' speeches are always in the service of belief in the transpersonal divine, and he speaks with the sublime simplicity of truth.

Since the hero of *Paradise Regained* is both man and God incarnate, his self-defining ordeal, though limited to a sense of divine destiny that is inscrutable and to a purely human wisdom supported by that sense of destiny, puts him in a different class of hero. Nonetheless, the privation of knowledge about his divine career places Jesus firmly among the other heroic figures whose rites of passage yield revelations that lead to the founding of a new society or the restoration of an old one. Thus *Paradise Regained,* in following the self-denying and self-fulfilling career of Odysseus and in rejecting systematically the collective, secular vision of the Roman empire, exemplifies strong affinities with the mythical via negativa of the *Odyssey* and the *Inferno* while rejecting implicitly both the philosophical individualism of later Greek culture and the collectivistic power-centered social principles of the *Aeneid.* In his final epic Milton succeeded brilliantly in producing a hero apparently stripped of heroic power, in the mode of the unestablished No Man of Homer's *Odyssey,* who exemplifies, through his total rejection of appeals to the ego and his profound, godlike, aversion to the exercise of godlike power toward inadequate ends, the essential reality of the achieved self.

Paradise Regained then appears to be a palinode of the *Aeneid* and a liberal, enfranchised version of the *Inferno.* For a variety of reasons Milton does not need the elaborate Augustinian and Thomistic categories of sin that are deployed so elaborately in the *Inferno.* While Milton's hero encounters more tempting versions of damnation than Dante can depict in his hideously stratified Hell, the Son of God, in his divine intuitions, his wise passiveness, his established self, is indifferent to the manifold modes of sin, except to the degree that Satan offers opportunities for him to violate his mission. Milton's Jesus, as God incarnate, exemplifies the *coincidentia oppositorum,* the union of opposites, that establish him as the ultimately heroic antihero.

CHAPTER FOUR

Andrew Marvell and the Virgilian Triad

The poetical career of Andrew Marvell exemplifies major generic, thematic, and stylistic concerns of seventeenth-century English poetry. From the remarkable lyrics, mostly in the pastoral mode, in which the metaphysical imagination of Donne and Herbert is disciplined by a Jonsonian formalism, he creates in *Upon Appleton House* a major poem in the georgic mode that serves as a transition from lyric introspection to commitment to a public career that climaxes in the heroic panegyric, *The First Anniversary of the Government under His Highness the Lord Protector.* The line of development exemplifies, on a small scale, the Virgilian progression from pastoral to georgic to epic. This evolution is enriched by Marvell's adaptation, in *An Horatian Ode upon Cromwell's Return from Ireland,* of a complex irony that captures the spirit of Horace. To extend the analogy of the Virgilian progression further, Marvell, after the collapse of the Protectorate, went on to write the first major mock-epic poems of the Restoration, the chief example of which is *The Last Instructions to a Painter,* a work that in many ways anticipates the mode that Dryden and Pope were to perfect.

As Yeats observed, "We make out of our quarrel with others, rhetoric, but the quarrel with ourselves, poetry." From the political crises of the Protectorate Marvell first contrived a poem that succeeds brilliantly in combining these opposed perspectives and styles, but the paradoxes so brilliantly explored in the *Horatian Ode* yielded inevitably to the simpler modes of public advocacy, as the complex hopes Marvell attached to the Lord Protector were defeated by his death and by the Restoration of the uninspiring and untrustworthy Charles II. Yet despite his advocacy of Cromwell, *The First Anniversary of the Government under His Highness the Lord Protector* (1655) maintains a judicious point of view in its metaphysical celebration of Cromwellian *virtu,* and it is only in the patriotic indignation of the major Restoration satires, both in verse and in prose, that commitment limits the full exercise of the imagination. When the degenerate regime of Charles II and his brother could no longer sustain the heroic, Marvell had no choice but to write in the partisan mock heroic.

In his career we can thus trace a major development in the poetry of the seventeenth century in which political circumstances made the ironic, contemplative mode of Marvell's greatest poems out of date. His later career demonstrates the "dissociation of sensibility" that Eliot deplored as a feature of the literary revolution in post-Restoration England. Marvell's lyric poems, which could organize varieties of conflicting experience, gave place to political poems with an analytical and partisan interest in public affairs. The transition reflected or exemplified other such major developments of the later seventeenth century as the shift from fancy to judgment as senior partner in the term *wit* and the growing concern with man as a more superficial political creature rather than as a being capable of infinite spiritual growth. The newly established priority of consensus over personal responses as the basis of value judgments (Marvell's "parti-color'd mind") and the prevalence of objective and denotative over connotative and subjective language also contributed to the declining power of Marvell's poetic imagination.

Whoever compiled the posthumous *Miscellaneous Poems* of 1681 decided to lead off the collection with the orthodox and unexceptionable *Dialogue between the Resolved Soul and Created Pleasure,* an utterly conventional dialogue celebrating a victorious spiritual combat. Without irony or real effort, the resolved soul parries and surmounts a series of temptations to sensuality or ambition that are expressed in the worn currency of dialectical psychomachia. The poem begins with a rousing exhortation to the soul to put on the full armor of God:

> Courage my Soul, now learn to wield
> The weight of thine immortal Shield.
> Close on thy head thy Helmet bright.
> Ballance thy Sword against the Fight.
> See where an Army, strong as fair,
> With silken Banners spreads the air.
> Now, if thou bee'st that thing Divine,
> In this day's Combat let it shine:
> And shew that Nature wants an Art
> To conquer one resolved Heart.   [1–10][1]

The strength and gusto of this injunction is reinforced by the succinct diction, strong rhyme-words, and especially the emphatic trochaic substitutions, in contrast to which the central couplet on the army of created pleasure seems unsubstantial. Like Satan in *Paradise Regained* Pleasure sets forth her delights at some length, while the Soul responds in a laconic style that suggests not so much resolution as indifference. Pleasure's mode is hyperbolic:

> Welcome the Creations Guest,
> Lord of Earth and Heavens Heir.
> Lay aside thy warlike crest,
> And of Nature's banquet share:
> Where the Souls of fruits and flow'rs
> Stand prepar'd to heighten yours.   [11–16]

Soul brushes aside the solicitations like a person trying to catch a train:

> I sup above, and cannot stay
> To bait so long upon the way.   [17–18]

The temptations offered to touch, smell, and sight are also briefly dismissed in a confident but almost pat manner, as though the Soul were responding by rote:

> A Soul that knowes not to presume
> Is Heaven's and its own perfume.   [29–30]

One may be tempted to ask whether Soul is not already presuming by affirming its lack of presumption. At any rate, its confidence that Heaven is its destination is untroubled:

> When the Creator's skill is priz'd,
> The rest is all but Earth disguiz'd.   [35–36]

Temptations to the ear require more than such rote replies, and Soul demonstrates real feeling for the first time:

> Had I but any time to lose,
> On this I would it all dispose.
> Cease Tempter. None can chain a mind
> Whom this sweet Chordage cannot bind.   [41–44]

The wit of "sweet Chordage" indicates potential for an *engaged* response, and this speech evokes enthusiastic praise from a chorus that concludes the first series of temptations. The more complex temptations Soul counters with rhetorical questions that turn back on Pleasure the problem of discriminating the truly good from the specious. To the final offer of unlimited knowledge, Soul returns to an easy gnomic paradox:

> None thither mounts by the degree
> Of Knowledge, but Humility.   [73–74]

And the examinee wins the unqualified plaudits of the chorus.

The dialogue is remarkable among Marvell's poems for its simplicity— one might even say for its facility. Little of the intellectual or imaginative vigor for which he is famous appears. The Soul learns nothing in its trials because its response to them is simply a series of conditioned reflexes. Although there is no evidence of irony to qualify the Soul's assurance, its character is as remote from those that figure in the other dialogues and lyrics as one could possibly imagine. What remains bothersome is why Marvell allowed himself to present the drama of salvation in such an undramatic and psychologically uninteresting way.

Usually Marvell explores the varieties of human experience through complex and sometimes bizarre hypotheses. Perhaps this dialogue is an experiment in hypothesizing the responses to temptation of a soul that has perfected the virtues of a Pauline Christian warrior. Yet the soul is unmoved by love and indifferent to the Redeemer and the gifts of grace without which, one would suppose, it cannot aspire to salvation. Against the narcissistic lures of Pleasure it offers what may be a narcissistic Stoicism: "A Soul that knowes not to presume / Is Heaven's and its own perfume." Those who find the Son in *Paradise Regained* priggish may have such a figure in mind.

In contrast, *A Dialogue between the Soul and the Body* explores in a way more typically Marvellian the dilemmas and contradictions in human nature so serenely dealt with in the first poem. The claims and counterclaims of the adversaries are fully dramatized, but they are not resolved. There is no chorus to award the palm to either of the dualities whose interinvolvement they equally deplore. Body's complaints are as intelligently and forcefully argued as those of Soul. Each raises a despairing cry for deliverance from the tyranny of the other. Soul opens its case with a brilliant indictment of Body's properties, which totally impede its own proper needs:

> O who shall, from this Dungeon, raise
> A Soul enslav'd so may wayes?
> With bolts of bone that fetter'd stands
> In feet; and manacled in Hands.
> Here blinded with an Eye; and there
> Deaf with the drumming of an Ear.
> A Soul hung up, as 'twere, in Chains
> Of Nerves, and Arteries, and Veins.
> Tortur'd, besides each other part,
> In a vain Head, and double Heart.   [1–10]

The brilliance of this lies in the punning, oxymoronic representation of sheer incompatibilities, especially in the notion of fettering feet, drumming ears, and manacling hands and in the vivid arraignment of the life-giving neural and circulatory systems of Body as chains that hang Soul as though it were the corpse of a convicted felon, the whole dilemma summed up in Soul's torture by "a vain Head and double Heart." Even in these terms ambiguity responds to the views of the contending parties: from Body's standpoint the vain head is empty; for Soul, the head's aspirations are unrealizable, while the auricle and ventricle of the heart reflect the irresolvable doubleness of the situation.

The capacity of Soul and Body to recognize, while deploring, the needs of its enemy is also apparent in Body's countercharge:

> O who shall me deliver whole
> From bonds of this Tyrannic Soul?
> Which, strecht upright, impales me so,
> That mine own Precipice I go;
> And warms and moves this needless Frame:
> (A Fever could but do the same.)
> And wanting where its spight to try,
> Has made me live to let me dye.

> A Body that could never rest,
> Since this ill Spirit it possest.   [11–20]

"Needless" incorporates Body's purely physical view of itself, with an intu-
ition of Soul's discomforting aspirations as a mere "fever." The indictment is
confirmed in the concluding complaint against Soul as an "ill Spirit" that
presents it as a sickness possessing Body. Traditional topoi about man's cloven
nature are intensified by the conviction that the fatal jointure of radically
incompatible parties is far worse than simple opposition. The enigma could
suggest Marvell's apprehensions about political and religious schismatics who,
in this period, were threatening the social order.[2]

The rest of the poem elaborates on the idea that Body's health is Soul's
illness and vice versa. Body is given four extra lines in its final statement,
which led one early reader to conclude that the poem was incomplete, but this
should not prevent us from seeing that Body has a slightly larger view of the
dilemma than does Soul:

> What but a Soul could have the wit
> To build me up for Sin so fit?
> So Architects do square and hew
> Green Trees that in the Forest grew.   [41–44]

Body sees Soul's aspirations as malignant, but its rhetorical question uninten-
tionally suggests Soul's redemptive aspect, just as the concluding couplet,
while urging the priority of nature over art, expresses a nostalgia for a vegeta-
tive dormancy that would preclude Soul's equally dazzling but fruitless self-
awareness.

The unresolved dialogue avoids the normal closure of a metaphysical
poem. Contradictions and incompatabilities are not solved through the language of paradox, nor does either of the parties apprehend a divine Architect
whose inscrutable purposes may be held responsible for them. Marvell is more
interested in fission than fusion, as we see in *A Definition of Love, The Coronet,
The Garden, Mourning,* and the Mower poems. The theme is expressed most
clearly in the conclusion of *The Definition of Love:*

> Therefore the Love which us doth bind,
> But Fate so enviously debarrs,
> Is the Conjunction of the Mind,
> And Opposition of the Stars.

On the *Dialogue between the Soul and the Body* I find John Klause persuasive:
"[Marvell] refuses to derive comfort from a paradoxical view of the human
composite or compound, allowing no synthesis to overcome the dreadful
antitheses that produce destructive ironies rather than healing paradoxes."[3]

In *To His Coy Mistress* the lover again postulates a Fate equally disbar-
ring, albeit indifferent rather than envious, and proposes a satisfaction of
desire so violent as to hasten, rather than retard, extinction. In withdrawing

from the *locus amoenus* of *The Garden,* Marvell wistfully looks back on a state of splendid isolation where he enjoyed for a while an unmediated relationship to nature:

> Such was the happy Garden-state,
> While Man there walk'd without a Mate:
> After a Place so pure, so sweet,
> What other Help could yet be meet!
> But 'twas beyond a Mortal's share
> To wander solitary there:
> Two Paradises 'twere in one
> To live in Paradise alone.   [41–48]

Disappointed hopes dominate Marvell's lyrics, whether the goal is the enjoyment of love or the enjoyment of solitude. The innocent pastoral setting of the Mower is destroyed by unrequited passion for Juliana or corrupted by man's hybridizing: "The Pink then grew as double as his Mind." Love and nature are at odds: "Like her fair Eyes the day was fair; / But scorching like his am'rous Care;" "For She my Mind hath so displac'd / That I shall never find my home."

Much richer than the naive pastoral views of the Mower and even the complex dialectic of the Soul and the Body is Marvell's exploration of internal contradictions in *The Coronet.* Confronting in a brief lyric Milton's problem in devoting a poem to God in *Paradise Lost,* Marvell's examination of motives leads him to a dilemma where an act of poetic creation requires its own destruction in sacrificial renunciation. Artistic creativity, requiring self-assertion, is hopelessly entangled with pride and thus demands not only its own abnegation but the willing annihilation of the self. Yet self-annihilation leaves no creative identity to express praise of the creator. Art is inevitably tainted by pride:

> When for the Thorns with which I long, too long,
>   With many a piercing Wound,
>   My Saviour's Head have crown'd,
> I seek with Garlands to redress that Wrong;
>   Through every Garden, every Mead,
> I gather flow'rs (my fruits are only flow'rs)
>   Dismantling all the fragrant Towers
> That once adorn'd my Shepherdesses head,
> And now when I have summ'd up all my store,
>   Thinking (so I my self deceive)
>   So rich a Chaplet thence to weave
> As never yet the king of Glory wore:
>   Alas I find the Serpent old
>   That, twining in his speckled breast,
>   About the flow'rs disguis'd does fold,
> With wreathes of Fame and Interest.   [1–16]

The serpent seems to be inseparable from the chaplet Marvell is weaving with such care. It even simulates the wreath he wishes to make, just as the highly implicated texture and movement of the verse, with its parenthetical suspensions, expresses the hopelessly tangled motives of the artist. The poem, to this point a false coronet woven of contradictory wishes, must then be destroyed:

> Ah, foolish Man, that would'st debase with them,
> And mortal Glory, Heavens Diadem!
> But thou who only could'st the Serpent tame,
> Either his slipp'ry knots at once untie,
> And disintangle all his winding snare:
> Or shatter too with him my curious frame:
> And let these wither, so that he may die,
> Though set with skill and chosen out with Care.
> That they, while Thou on both their Spoils dost tread,
> May crown thy Feet, that could not crown thy Head.[17–26]

The shift from the intricate verse patterns of the opening passage to the straightforward pentameter couplets of this conclusion reinforces the sense of a resolution achieved through dissolution of the dilemma posed by the coronet, the irreconcilable motives of the artist's praise and self-interest, the poem itself, and ultimately the poet.

An Horatian Ode upon Cromwell's Return from Ireland (1650) opens with a gesture dismissing the themes and styles of lyric retirement and contemplation to assess Cromwell's career at a critical moment. In this assessment it employs features of dialectic in the most complex and metaphysical lyrics. The alternating tetrameter and trimeter couplets tend to balance the claims of Cromwell's de facto power against the de jure rights of the executed king.

Retirement is associated with an ancient lyric tradition; emergence and action with a rejection of the tradition and involvement in the unprecedented phenomenon of Cromwell, who "through adventrous war / Urged his active star." "The forward youth who would appear" orients himself toward an indeterminate future of adventure, and the subtle chiaroscuro of pastoral with its "shadows" in which he sang "his Numbers languishing," together with "his Muses dear" must now be forsaken as irrelevant to the activism of the new man. In turning away from the retired mode of lyric meditation and "oyling th' unused Armours rust," the forward youth will emulate his chief,

> Who, from his private Gardens where
> He liv'd reserved and austere,
>   As if his highest plot
>   To plant the Bergamot,
> Could by industrious Valour climbe
> To ruine the great Work of Time.   [29–34]

Yet an important distinction lies between Cromwell's disciplined retirement in his garden and the suggestion of self-indulgence in the youth's "Numbers languishing." Cromwell's garden experience is implicitly a preparation for a public career in contrast to the youth's past indifference to public affairs. At the age of twenty-nine Marvell seems to project on the ephemeral figure of the forward youth a wry version of his own career as lyric poet. The dismissal is, however, conditional. It depends on the forward (foresighted, ambitious, precocious, perhaps immature) wish to appear. The youth's appearance might stem from an untimely commitment to a theme and style of appearances in celebrating the achievements of a hero who has nullified the legitimate role of the heir apparent: Prince Charles's hereditary right to the throne is never mentioned in the poem.

The dismissal is further qualified by Marvell's identification of the opportunistic youth with Cromwell's amoral grasping of power:

> So restless *Cromwell* could not cease
> In the inglorious Arts of Peace,
>   But through adventrous War
>   Urged his active star.   [9–12]

Restless and *inglorious* can be glossed from the poem *On a Drop of Dew*. On earth the soul rolls "restless and unsecure, / Trembling lest it grow impure," but "Congeal'd on Earth. . . . does, dissolving, run / Into the Glories of th' Almighty Sun." Marvell thus detaches himself from the youth's rejection of lyric poetry as an inglorious art and his adventurous (possibly reckless) submission to a restless pursuit of a glory that may be only a projection of his drive toward self-aggrandizement. For the "inglorious Arts of Peace" he may substitute the "wiser Art" of Cromwell, who "twining subtile fears with hope" wove a fatal net for King Charles. Such a Machiavellian art, contrived from opportunism and deceit, is implacably kinetic and incapable of achieving the stasis of great lyric art like Marvell's. The youth and Cromwell are alike committed to being driven by an interminable pursuit of a power and glory in which there can be no rest:

> But thou the Wars and Fortunes son
> March indefatigably on. . . .
>
> .   .   .   .
>
> The same *Arts* that did *gain*
> A *Pow'r* must it *maintain*.   [113–14, 119–20]

The insistent momentum of Marvell's Horatian mode, created by the diastole and systole of alternating iambic tetrameter and trimeter couplets, emulates Cromwell's indefatigable pursuit of power. But the forward drive of the verse is interrupted by the "memorable scene" to which the king is led by Cromwellian wiles. Machiavellian *virtù* contrives

That Charles himself might chase
To Caresbrooks narrow case.   [51–52]

The castle on the Isle of Wight in which Charles sought refuge proved a cul-de-sac. In attempting to escape through a narrow window, he was apprehended and taken to London for trial and execution:

> That thence the Royal Actor borne
> The *Tragick scaffold* might adorn,
>   While round the armed Bands
>   Did clap their bloody hands.   [53–56]

The tragic performance of the royal actor was interrupted as Cromwell's troopers were ordered to drown out his final speech by their mocking applause. In contrast

> *He* nothing common did, or mean,
> Upon the memorable scene:
>   But with his keener Eye
>   The Axes edge did try:
> Nor call'd the *Gods* with vulgar spight
> To vindicate his helpless Right,
>   But bow'd his comely Head
>   Down, as upon a Bed.   [57–64]

The memorable scene provides a static moment for contemplation. The inactive "acting" of the Royal Actor born is an implicit criticism of Cromwell, "urging his active star." The moment is isolated from the kinetic and future-directed thrust of Cromwell's career, just as Shakespeare's Richard II's "acting" is juxtaposed with Bolingbroke's ambitious pursuit of power as an end in itself; but Charles, in contrast to Richard, does not vainly invoke divine intervention. Yielding to the realities of secular power he ultimately enacts a Christlike passion.

The royal aesthetic thwarts Cromwellian arts. The memorable scene suggests the dynastic and ritualistic character of an action of which Cromwell is incapable. The usurper's opportunistic drive is ironically devalued by the grace with which his victim adorns the tragic scaffold, just as the relentless forward thrust of the verse that has led to this moment is thwarted by prominent trochaic substitutions: "*He* nothing common did, or mean"; "*But* with his keener Eye"; "*Nor* call'd the *Gods* with vulgar spight"; "*Down,* as upon a Bed."

Perhaps our unfamiliarity with minds as truly liberal and complex as Marvell's has made it hard to recognize the integrity, as well as the subtlety, of his vision in *An Horatian Ode,* a poem central to his poetic and political development alike. Following the example of J. B. Leishman, critics have begun to recognize the crucial Horatian element in the ode:[4] the capacity to feel at once two different ways toward each of two opposed figures and to greet a victory with feelings of relief and regret. It is now evident that Horace provides a clue to Marvell's sensibility and that such a poem as his ode on Cleopatra's defeat at Actium (*Carmina,* 1. 37) can illuminate the *Horatian Ode* as nothing else can:

Caesar, ab Italia volantem

remis adsurgens, accipiter velut
mollis columnas aut leporem citus
    venator in campis nivalis
    haemoniae, daret ut catenis

fatale monstrum. Quae generosior
perire quarens nec muliebriter
    expavit ensem nec latentis
    classe cita reparavit oras.

ausa et iacentem visere regiam
voltu sereno, fortis et asperas
    tractare serpentes, ut atrum
    corpore combiberet venenum,

deliberata morte ferocior,
saevis Liburnis scilicet invidens
    privata deduci superbo
    non humilis mulier triumpho.

[. . . and Caesar, when his galleys
Chased her from Italy, soon brought her, dreaming
    And drugged with native wine,
Back to the hard realities of fear.

As swiftly as the hawk follows the feeble
Dove, or in snowy Thessaly the hunter
    The hare, so he sailed forth
To bind this fatal prodigy in chains.

Yet she preferred a finer style of dying:
She did not, like a woman, shirk the dagger
    Or seek by speed at sea
To change her Egypt for obscurer shores,

But gazing on her desolated palace
With a calm smile, unflinchingly laid hands on
    The angry asps until
Her veins had drunk the deadly poison deep,

And, death-determined, fiercer than ever,
Perished. Was she to grace a haughty triumph?
    Dethroned, paraded by
Savage Liburnians? Not Cleopatra![5]]

As Steele Commager remarks,

in the Cleopatra Ode antithetical structure implies a double moral commitment. . . .
The images of hawk and tender dove, hunter and fleeing rabbit, are crucial in the
word's truest sense, for they mark the point at which poetic intentions cross. . . . The
lines act as a kind of pivot to divert our sympathies from Caesar to Cleopatra, and a

straightforward song of triumph slides into what has been justly termed a "panegyric of the vanquished queen."[6]

Poetic intentions cross in much the same fashion in the central passage from Marvell's ode, which begins in praise of Cromwell and "slides into" what might be termed "a panegyric of the vanquished king":

> What Field of all the Civil Wars
> Where his were not the deepest Scars?
>   And Hampton shows what part
>   He had of wiser Art:
> Where, twining subtile fears with hope,
> He wove a Net of such a scope,
>   That Charles himself might chase
>   To Caresbrooks narrow case:
> That thence the Royal Actor borne
> The *Tragick Scaffold* might adorn,
>   While round the armed Bands
>   Did clap their bloody hands.
> *He* nothing common did, or mean
> Upon that memorable Scene:
>   But with his keener Eye
>   The Axes edge did try:
> Nor call'd the *Gods* with vulgar spight
> To vindicate his helpless Right,
>   But bow'd his comely Head,
>   Down, as upon a Bed.   [II, 45–64]

Horace gives us the clue to this poem and to much that seems equivocal or contradictory in the poetry of Marvell. In the ode, according to John Coolidge, Marvell, under the pressure of events in midcentury England, "seems to have found in Horace the classical model of a poet maintaining a difficult kind of integrity in a period of great change."[7] Here we contemplate the late monarch with sympathy unclouded by sentimentality and his destroyer with admiration moderated by judgment, recognizing the gains and losses of a momentous revolution without taking refuge in equivocation or detachment.

An Horatian Ode is a key to Marvell's temper as man and poet. The ode's dialectic, in which opposing elements fuse into a comprehensive and complex point of view, comprises a kind of tragic realism: under the guise of eternity Charles is a tragic figure, but the ode is very time conscious—the pressure of time and Cromwell's thrusting activity is continually felt—and the tension between past, present, and future is very strong.

The ode also assimilates thematic and structural aspects of Eclogue I. Virgil anticipates Marvell in his handling of the issues raised by political upheaval, the Augustan settlement after the collapse of the Republic:

> Tityre, tu patulae recubans sub tegmine fagi
> silvestrem tenui musam meditaris avena:

> nos patriae finis et dulcia linquimus arva;
> nos patriam fugimus: tu, Tityre, lentus in umbra
> formosam resonare doces Amaryllida silvas.   [1–5]

> [You, Tityrus, lie under your spreading beech's
> covert, wooing the woodland Muse on slender
> reed, but we are leaving our country's bounds
> and sweet fields. We are outcasts from our country;
> you, Tityrus, at ease beneath the shade, teach the
> woods to re-echo "fair Amaryllis."[8]]

Meliboeus, evicted from his farm, "must now forsake his muses dear," while Tityrus meditates on them as he plays and sings his numbers languishing in the shade of the beech tree. Shadows are the privileged milieu of the fortunate old shepherd; Meliboeus must be transplanted to some alien land, perhaps to the cruel sun of Africa, "At nos hinc alii sitientis ibimus Afros" (64). Augustus, "the Wars and Fortunes son," has made Tityrus a "fortunatus senex":

> fortunate senex, hic inter flumina nota
> et fontis sacros frigus captabis opacum.   [51–52]

> [Fortunate old man! amidst familiar rivers
> and sacred fountains you will enjoy the cool shade.]

In Marvell's ode, Charles's illuminating grace has yielded to the thunder and lightning of the careerist that had roused the poet to wonder and amazement. As an Oedipus-like son of *tuché* (the Wars and Fortunes son), the palpable virtues of Cromwell to which Marvell pays tribute—justice, goodness, moderation, courage—cannot win for his forced power the sovereignty he needs. The arts with which he has contrived his conquests turn out to be as much his masters as his instruments, and he is condemned to maintain his power by an exhausting and indefatigable exercise of them, while the security of an established reign will forever elude him.

Marvell did not follow the example of his forward youth in the ode by leaving his books and taking down the corslet of the hall to follow Cromwell's fortunes. Instead, he joined the household of Lord General Fairfax, who had retired from command of the parliamentary forces because of a disagreement with Cromwell over Cromwell's plan to invade Scotland in 1650. Lady Fairfax had vehemently attacked the judges at the trial of Charles I, and the noble couple were making their dissatisfaction with Cromwell evident by withdrawing to Nunappleton House in Yorkshire. Marvell joined them as tutor in foreign languages to their only child, Mary, and it is reasonable to suppose that he wrote *The Garden* and his pastoral poems during this rural sojourn. He also wrote *Upon Appleton House,* a major work in his poetical career. Elusive of categories, this long poem has been seen as a country-house poem in the tradition of Ben Jonson, as a topographical poem like *Cooper's Hill,* as a universal history, as a long meditation, as a critique of the retired life, as a

praise of the retired life, as a poem marking a transition from the contemplative to the active life, as a brief epic, as a georgic, or as an extended panegyric
on the Fairfax family. It may be illuminated by most of these categories, but
their multiplicity suggests a poem that is protean both in its themes and in its
stylistic virtuosity.

   Upon Appleton House is notable for the various and shifting points of view
of its unreliable guide, views which challenge the reader to find in his fanciful
impressions a comprehensive vision of experience. Where *To Penshurst* is a
model of epideictic coherence and clarity, praising the organic economics of
hospitality in a great but unostentatious country house, Marvell goes out of
his way to bring down the edifice which is the ostensible object of his praise.
The expectations we bring to this country-house poem from Jonson, Herrick,
Carew, and Waller are more often thwarted than fulfilled. The house, its
gardens, fields, rivers, and forests seem to exist only as material for a surrealist
repertory of shifting impressions and projections. Hospitality and social interaction, major themes in the genre, are virtually ignored. The praise of the
Fairfaxes is perfunctory, and the customary priorities established from
Homer's tribute to the royal family in their Phaeacian palace and honored by
Virgil and Horace and Martial are largely ignored. The main focus of attention is the mind of the poet's ("Marvell's") playful persona.

   In thwarting our generic expectations Marvell seems bent on defamiliar-
izing the expected phenomenological conventions. He sees things unsteadily
and he does not see them whole. Shifts in perspective magnify the minute and
diminish the large. Shapes are unfixed and indeterminate. Identities are fluid
and metamorphosis runs riot. The traditional progress which surveys the
estate seems whimsical and arbitrary. The emphasis on traditional moral
values is spasmodic and unreliable.

   We are told, at the outset, that the house is a model of Jonsonian
restraint: "Within this sober Frame expect / Work of no forrain Architect."
Does this sober frame refer to the poem and to the house as well? The sobriety
of the house is defined negatively, as not the work of a foreign architect

> Who of his great design in pain
> Did for a model vault his Brain.   [5–6]

After extended comments on the pretensions of builders as opposed to the
modest needs of inhabitants, using as examples the dens of beasts, birds'
nests, and tortoise-shells, Marvell asks, "What need of all this marble crust /
T'impark the wanton mote of dust?" Assuming that the inhabitant unreasona-
bly demands of his dwelling "more room alive than dead," he then celebrates
Appleton House as a minimal tomblike dwelling as humble as that shown to
Aeneas by Evander and once visited by Hercules,

> In which we the dimensions find
> Of that more sober age and mind,

> When larger sized Men did stoop
> To enter at a narrow loop;
> As practising, in doors so strait
> To strain themselves through *Heavens Gate*.   [27–32]

This minimalist monument will be visited in future times by those fascinated by the discrepancy between its narrow confines and the greatness of the Fairfaxes, "And some will smile at this, as well / As Romulus his Bee-like cell" (39–40). The Jonsonian theme emerges briefly in the observation that "Humility alone designs / Those short but admirable lines." The sober frame thus appears to include the poem as well as the house, "lines" alluding both to the dimensions of the house and the terse octasyllabic octets. So much for the emphasis on humility and sobriety. As the master enters, the dwelling loses its "straitness:"

> Yet thus the laden House does sweat,
> And scarce indures the *Master* great:
> But where he comes the swelling Hall
> Stirs, and the *Square* grows *Spherical*.   [49–52]

Although Marvell had just derided those who "vainly strive t'immure / The *Circle* in the *Quadrature*," the entrance of Fairfax results in the greater three-dimensional anomaly of immuring the cube in the sphere, an impossibility aimed at praising the perfection of the master.[9] The extravagant conceit violates the "short but admirable lines" designed by humility. It owes something, obviously, to the *multum in parvo* motif so often used in inscriptions on tombs: the house is but an inn "to entertain / Its Lord a while, but not remain." If "these holy mathematicks / Can, in ev'ry figure equal man," the bizarre figure also owes something to Michelangelo's drawing of a man whose outstretched hands and feet touch simultaneously the corners of a square and the perimeter of a circle.

   Why does Marvell begin by emphasizing the sober frame of Appleton House with its "short but admirable lines," only to subject it to an impossible metamorphosis? One would not be disturbed if the metamorphosis preserved its figural function, but Marvell insists on making the impossible actual by treating radical contradictions literally. What happens here is quite different from the geometrically illustrated paradoxes of *The Definition of Love*, which conclude with a statement confirmed by logic and common sense:

> Therefore the Love which us doth bind,
> But Fate so enviously debarrs,
> Is the conjunction of the Mind,
> And opposition of the Stars.   [29–32]

   The effect of Marvell's bizarre affirmation of impossibilities, already condemned as vain in the opening of *Upon Appleton House*, puts the reader on notice that the poet is not to be trusted. Intoxicated by the limitless possibilities of a fancy that can blithely ignore material reality, he proceeds to lead us through a series of experiences bred of unbridled fancy, as he admits:

> Out of these scatter'd *Sibyls* leaves
> Strange *Prophecies* my Phancy weaves.   [577–78]

This corresponds to the kind of distortion of reality that he ascribes to the machinations of the "subtle nuns," whose persuasions to Isabella Thwaites typically devalue and reify religious symbols:

> Within this hold Leisure we
> Live innocently, as you see.
> These walls restrain the World without,
> But hedge our liberty about.   [97–100]

No sober frame, the nunnery cultivates an indulgent sensuality that mocks the piety it affects to preserve:

> Here we, in shining Armour white,
> Like *Virgin-Amazons* do fight.
> And our chaste *Lamps* we hourly trim,
> Lest the great *Bridegroom* find them dim
> Our *Orient* breaths perfumed are
> With incense of incessant pray'r.
> And Holy-water of our Tears
> Most strangely our Complexion clears.   [105–12]

In a burlesque skirmish the young Sir William Fairfax rescues his bride and demolishes the nunnery from which the stones of Appleton House will be quarried:

> Thenceforth (as when th'Inchantment ends
> The castle vanishes or rends).   [269–70]

The former cloister falls to Isabella Thwaites:

> Though many a *Nun* there made her vow,
> 'T was no *Religious House* till now.   [289–90]

The potentially sacrilegious destruction of a religious institution is countered by its reformation.

Against such corrupt figurations, Marvell turns to the symbolic specifications of the gardens laid out by Sir Thomas Fairfax:

> From that blest bed the *Heroe* came,
> Whom *France* and *Poland* yet does fame:
> Who, when retired here to Peace,
> His warlike studies could not cease:
> But laid these Gardens out in sport
> In the just figure of a Fort;

> And with five bastions it did fence,
> As aiming one at eve'ry Sense.   [281–88]

To the conceit of the garden as fort our guide attributes defensive power against the sensuality cultivated by the nuns. Like restless Cromwell in the ode, this Fairfax "could not cease" from his warlike studies, but, reversing Cromwell's career, he diverted his energies from war to the meditative combat. His successors, however, convert the spiritual garden into a miniature military camp, whose martial flowers "as on parade" gently mock the incumbent's retirement from public life. The memorable lament for the destruction of "that dear and happy Isle, / The Garden of the World erewhile" (321–22) in the Civil War seems to regret the withdrawal of a commander-in-chief

> Who had it pleased him and *God,*
> Might once have made our Gardens spring
> Fresh as his own and flourishing.   [346–48]

He did, to be sure, "with his utmost skill, / Ambition weed and Conscience till,"

> But he preferr'd to the *Cinque Ports*
> These five imaginary Forts:
> And, in those half-dry Trenches spann'd
> Pow'r which the Ocean might command.   [349–52]

From this moment, the lord general virtually disappears from the poem. The equivocal tribute over, Marvell's "progress" occupies the remaining half. His unstable perceptions are characterized by a series of shifting perspectives on the landscape of Nunappleton. In descending into the "Abbyss" of "that unfathomable Grass" (369–70), he escapes from the rigidly limited model of the garden. The dimensions of smaller and larger are reversed as "Men like Grashoppers appear, / But Grashoppers are Gyaunts there" (371–72).

> They, in their squeaking Laugh, contemn
> Us as we walk more low than them:
> And from the Precipices tall
> Of their green spires, to us do call.   [373–76]

The meadow, transfigured into a body of water, allegedly offers deep discoveries that would elude one contemplating half-dry trenches, yet all the divers come up with are flowers, to "prove they've at the Bottom been" (384).

In *The Garden* and the pastoral poems the details of the poet's milieu are fixed, though they form the subject of his shifting speculations. In the central speculative visions of *Upon Appleton House* both the landscape and perceptions of it are fluid. The reality of nature is subordinated to the metamorphoses of art and of the poet's fancy, and the scene is one "Where all things gaze themselves and doubt / If they be in it or without." The indeterminate interplay of subject and object and inside and outside raises radical doubts about the existence of any "reality":

> No Scene that turns with Engines strange
> Does oftner than these Meadowes change.
> For when the Sun the Grass hath vext,
> The tawny Mowers enter next;
> Who seem like *Israelites* to be,
> Walking on foot through a green Sea.   [385–90]

The "Engines strange" are largely the fanciful ingenuities of the observer. The Israelites "massacre" the grass, unwittingly slaying the rail, "Fearing the Flesh untimely mow'd / to [them] a Fate as black forebode" (399–400). But "bloody Thestylis" disputes this view, and "Greedy as Kites has trust it up, / And forthwith means on it to sup" (403–04). In an astonishing breach of narrative convention, she bursts out of the framework of art to assert a more cheerful interpretation:

> When on another quick She lights,
> And cryes, "He call'd us *Israelites*;
> But now, to make his saying true,
> Rails rain for Quails, for Manna Dew."   [405–08]

Thestylis blithely exposes as sentimental and false the mower's somber reflection on the meaning of the event. As gifts of God for the people of God, the quails, even "quick," are for consumption, not rumination. Her interruption of the narrative frame with a commonsense observation deflates the self-indulgent fantasies of the narrator. Although one critic has seen in this part of the poem "the universal history of mankind,"[10] it seems instead a parody of the particular meditation on the natural scene at which Marvell excelled.

    Thestylis' remark does not prevent Marvell from moralizing ponderously on the plight of the rails, after which he turns the scene from mock pathos to mock horror:

> Unhappy Birds! what does it boot
> To build below the Grasses root;
> When lowness is unsafe as height,
> And Chance o'ertakes what scapeth Spight?
> And now your Orphan Parents Call
> Sounds your untimely Funeral.
> Death Trumpets creak in such a Note,
> And 'tis the *Sourdine* in their Throat.
>
> .   .   .   .
>
> The Mower now commands the Field:
> In whose new Traverse seemeth wrought
> A Camp of Battail newly fought:
> Where, as the Meads with Hay, the Plain
> Lyes quilted ore with Bodies slain:
> The women that with forks it fling
> Do represent the Pillaging.   [409–16; 418–24]

The horror, unlike the pathos of the rails' untimely death, is distanced. "Seemeth" and "represent" combine with the simile to give the battlefield/ hayfield association a purely hypothetical status. As if weary of pursuing the emblematic mode further, Marvell concludes the mowing with a highly evocative scherzo:

> And now the careless Victors play,
> Dancing the Triumphs of the Hay;
> Where every Mowers wholesome Heat
> Smells like an *Alexander's sweat.*
> Their Females fragrant as the Mead
> Which they in *Fairy Circles* tread:
> When at their Dances End they kiss,
> Their new-made Hay not sweeter is.   [425–32]

The harvest ritual dance introduces for the only time an authentic pastoral vision, one which momentarily corrects Marvell's sentimental distortions. Here the celebration of georgic fulfillment comes close to Shakespeare and Herrick, a moment of rejoicing sanctioned even by Virgil, whose sons of Theseus at harvest time "gaily danced in the soft meadows" (Georgics, II, 383–84).

The ritual moment fades into a further series of speculative, masquelike views: the meadow with its haycocks is like a calm sea, showing its rocks, like an Egyptian desert with pyramids, or like Roman tombs rising "in hills for Soldiers Obsequies." This scene then withdraws, and the stubble field "brings a new and empty face of things," "as smooth and plain, / As Clothes for *Lilly* strecht to stain" (403–04). The tabula rasa poses no limits to the poetic fancy: it is the world at creation, a bullring before the bulls have entered, a pattern for the Levellers, a common on which villagers can graze their cattle, which reminds the poet of the sixth day of Creation in *Gondibert.* The cattle, "shrunk in the huge Pasture show / As Spots, so shap'd, on Faces do" (459–60) or as fleas seen in "Multiplying Glasses"; their slow motions are like those of constellations. As the meadow is flooded by the waters from Denton, Marvell ends this portion of his survey with a trite topsy-turvy Ovidian spectacle attributed to the flooding of the meadows.[11] The various scenes dissolve as the observer enters his most intense experience in the "fifth element" of the forest.

Marvell's deliquescent perceptions of shifting scenes up to this point have been random and essentially uncreative. To endow these random projections with the import of a survey of universal history is wide of the mark. Except for the harvest festival, the projections have led nowhere. The sober frame, which had promised a shaping vision of important possibilities, has surrendered to unframed and trifling fancies that fail to invest common phenomena with deep portents. The program has been abandoned.

Sequestered in the wood, the observer becomes the spectacle and, enamored of retirement, performs masquelike metamorphoses in a false version of meditation. Like the nunnery, the wood is a temple that excludes the outer world and generates egocentric and sensual fantasies. A surrealistic pathetic fallacy operates: to protect the nightingale, the thorn "draws within its shrunken claws," the stock-doves mourn despite "their equal love," herons drop their firstborn as a tribute to their Lord, the woodpecker efficiently tests the soundness of timber, and "Marvell" finds in this an allegory of the punishment for corruption. Despite acute renderings of his natural environment, he cannot resist the temptation to immerse his identity in this surrealist *paysage moralisé:*

> Thus I, *easie Philosopher,*
> Among the *Birds* and *Trees* confer:
> And little now to make me wants
> Or of the *Fowles* or of the *Plants.*
> Give me but Wings as they, and I
> Streight floating on the Air shall fly:
> Or turn me but, and you shall see
> I was but an inverted Tree.   [561–68]

Like the "traitor worm" in the oak, Marvell's fancy "taints" everything it touches. Vivid and minute observation of natural phenomena is relentlessly subjected to ungoverned fantasies that serve the demands of his ego. "Since from the beginning he knows what his conclusions will be, his tone is not desperate; yet the arch Clevelandism and the casual fantasizing do not hide the clash of principles that makes for inquietude in an '*easie Philosopher*' (561) whose unruffled manner . . . is not always a straightforward indicator of his feeling."[12] In concluding his reflections, the observer claims to have achieved a broad historical vision:

> Out of these scatter'd *Sibyls* leaves
> Strange Prophecies my Phancy weaves:
> And in one History consumes,
> Like *Mexique-Paintings,* all the plumes.
> What *Rome, Greece, Palestine,* ere said
> I in this light *Mosaick* read.   [577–82]

A big claim, but what revelation has he found? Even as an "*easie philosopher*" his reflections have been void of ideas or concepts. Instead of specifying his "*Mosaick*" revelations Marvell moves on to a series of histrionic poses that end in a wish for a mock crucifixion. If the survey is a kind of meditation, it lacks direction and climax. As a quest it has none of the disciplined intellectual and imaginative energy that characterizes a true psychomachia.

Marvell's flamboyant and self-indulgent impressionism as an "*easie philosopher*" is abruptly terminated by the advent of Maria as the genius loci. The *libertin* mode, culminating in a passage of piscatory eclogue, is dismissed hurriedly:

> But now away my Hooks, my Quills,
> And Angles, idle Utensils.
> The young *Maria* walks to night:
> Hide trifling Youth thy Pleasures slight.
> "Twere shame that such judicious Eyes
> Should with such Toyes a Man surprize;
> She that already is the *Law*
> Of all her *Sex,* her *Ages Aw.*   [649–56]

By her advent "*Nature* is wholly *vitrifi'd.*" Maria,

> like a sprig of *Mistleto,*
> On the *Fairfacian Oak* does grow;
> Whence, for some universal good,
> The *Priest* shall cut the sacred Bud;
> While her glad *Parents* most rejoice,
> And make their *Destiny* their *Choice.*   [739–44]

The poem at last admits a purpose and divulges a future, however indeterminate now, that will lead out of the poet's labyrinthine preoccupations and Lord and Lady Fairfax's constraining retirement. Marvell appears to be abandoning, under Maria's influence, the *libertin* play and the languishing "numbers" of metaphysical decadence, but not without a final coup de main:

> But now the *Salmon-Fishers* moist
> Their *Leathern Boats* begin to hoist;
> And, like *Antipodes* in Shoes,
> Have shod theyr *Heads* in their *Canoos.*   [769–72]

The simile links for the last time actuality with a casual and unrewarding bit of fancy. The concluding injunction, "Let's in: for the dark *Hemisphere* / Does now like one of them appear" (775–76) may signalize "Marvell's" return to actuality. It may also hint at a personal recognition that his sojourn at Nunappleton, "an *Inn* to entertain / Its *Lord* a while, but not remain," is about to end. If this interpretation holds, "Let's in" corresponds to the lines with which Virgil takes leave of the *Eclogues:*

> surgamus: solet esse gravis cantantibus umbra,
> iuniperi gravis umbra, nocent et frugibus umbrae.
> ite domum saturae, venit Hesperus, ite capellae.   [X, 75–77]

[Let us rise; the shade often brings peril to singers. The juniper's shade brings peril; hurtful to the corn, too, is the shade. Get ye home, my full-fed goats—the evening star comes—get ye home!]

Although the word *liberal* has now lost its meaning on both sides of the Atlantic and was not a significant term in Marvell's time, I am inclined to attribute some of his great strength and abiding influence to a liberal imagination and a liberal conscience. His ode on Cromwell always reminds me of E. M. Forster's *Two Cheers for Democracy*. His career as poet and public servant was marked by independent judgment and a talent for making responsible discriminations. Early in 1655 Marvell published *The First Anniversary of the Government under His Highness the Lord Protector,* outstanding among poems on affairs of state for its special blend of political realism and piety. It explores the proposition that Cromwell may be a Heaven-sent ruler and that the power maintained so indefatigably at the end of the *Horatian Ode* might now, God willing, be settled on Cromwell as Lord Protector. In any event, Marvell's wisdom in the ways of innocence and experience appears brilliantly in his figurative representation of the ways in which the political opposition may help to sustain the Protectorate. He sees in Cromwell another Amphion, using his instrument (the Instrument of Government, 1653, which established the Protectorate) to produce political harmony out of discord.

> Such was that wondrous Order and Consent,
> When *Cromwell* tun'd the ruling Instrument.   [67–68]

Hostile monarchs look with mingled awe and dread on Cromwell and his mighty ships of war:

> Yet if through these our Fears could find a pass;
> Through double Oak, and lin'd with treble Brass;
> That one Man still, although but nam'd, alarms
> More than all Men, all Navies, and all Arms.
> Him all the Day, Him, in late nights I dread,
> And still his Sword seems hanging ore my head.   [373–78]

Cromwell is endowed with a teleological drive that sets him apart from monarchs and ordinary people, who are trapped in the circles of a malignant eternal return:

> Like the vain curlings of the watry Maze,
> Which in smooth Streams a sinking Weight dos raise;
> So Man, declining always, disappears
> In the weak Circles of increasing Years;
> And his short Tumults of themselves Compose,
> While flowing Time above his Head does close.   [1–6]

Marvell thus challenges conservative historiography, so persistently to be embodied in Dryden's poetry, with its emphasis on the present repetition of past events. Against the Virgilian emphasis on return (Iam redit et Virgo) and re-creation (magnus ab integro saeclorum nascitur ordo) central to Dryden's view, Marvell affirms a more orthodox Christian vision of a unique divine intervention in human affairs. Kings "with vain Scepter strike the hourly Bell,"

> While indefatigable *Cromwell* hyes,
> And cuts his way still nearer to the Skyes,
>
> .   .   .   .
>
> Learning a Musique in the Region clear,
> To tune this lower to that higher Sphere.   [41–42, 47–48)

The Cromwell who was enjoined at the end of the *Horatian Ode* to march indefatigably on has now achieved the destiny and destination he formerly lacked. He does not make his destiny his choice, but, Marvell hesitantly suggests, he might be *chosen:*

> Hence oft I think, if in some happy hour
> High Grace should meet in one with highest Pow'r,
> And then a seasonable People still
> Should bend to his, as he to Heavens will,
> What we might hope, what wonderfull Effect
> From such a wish'd Conjuncture might reflect.
> Sure, the mysterious Work, where none withstand,
> Would forthwith finish under such a Hand:
> Fore-shortned Time its useless Course would stay,
> And soon precipitate the latest Day.   [131–40]

This is a step toward the fulfillment of the millennial hopes Marvell wistfully entertained for Fairfax:

> And yet there walks one on the Sod
> Who, had it pleased him and *God,*
> Might once have made our Gardens spring
> Fresh as his own and flourishing.   [345–48]

Marvell's engagement with Cromwell in *The First Anniversary* is something new in his poetical career. The hypothetical, contradictory, dégagé pose that characterizes *Upon Appleton House* gives way to a new heroic mode in which actuality and hope fuse. Nowhere is this seen more clearly than in the brilliant metaphors, musical and architectural, that resolve conflicting forces:

> Then our *Amphion* issues out and sings,
> And once he struck, and twice the pow'rful Strings.
>   The Commonwealth then first together came,
> And each one enter'd in the willing Frame;
> All other Matter yields, and may be rul'd;
> But who the Minds of stubborn Men can build?
> No Quarry bears a Stone so hardly wrought,
> Nor with such labour from its center brought;
> None to be sunk in the Foundation bends,
> Each in the House the highest Place contends,
> And each the Hand that lays him will direct,
> And some fall back upon the Architect;
> Yet all compos'd by his attractive Song,
> Into the Animated City throng.

> The Common-wealth does through their Centers all
> Draw the Circumference of the publique Wall;
> The crossest Spirits here do take their part,
> Fast'ning the Contignation which they thwart;
> And they, whose Nature leads them to divide,
> Uphold, this one, and that the other Side;
> But the most equal still sustein the Height,
> And they as Pillars keep the Work upright;
> While the resistance of opposed Minds,
> The Fabrique as with Arches stronger binds,
> Which on the basis of a Senate free,
> Knit by the Roofs Protecting weight agree.   [73–98]

The harmonious architecture of the Protector employs the recalcitrant gravity of "crossest Spirits" to sustain the dome of the Commonwealth's City. Metaphorical precision, as in *The Definition of Love,* constitutes an authoritative proof of Cromwell's brilliant achievement in reconciling the recalcitrant individualism of various sectarians with the grand harmonic design, a design anticipated in *Musicks Empire:*

> *Jubal* first made the wilder Notes agree;
> And *Jubal* tun'd Musick's first *Jubilee:*
> He call'd the *Ecchoes* from their sullen Cell,
> And built the Organs City where they dwell.   [5–8]

The firmness of Cromwell's political structure is reflected in the thick cacophony of that remarkable line, "Fast'ning that Contignation which they thwart." In constructing this sober frame, Cromwell halts the erosion of the temporal process, "And still new Stopps to various Time appl[ies]." The complex association of architecture and music and politics is extended through Cromwell's lute, which is the Instrument of Government that created the Protectorate.

Annabel Patterson has convincingly argued that, in evaluating the unique figure of Cromwell in *The First Anniversary,* Marvell explored the ways in which he differed from biblical types like Gideon, Elijah, and Noah as much as he traced resemblances.[13] Despite his commitment to Cromwell, and his conditional position that "If these the Times, then this must be the Man," Cromwell, as elusive of categories, must be an unrepeatable figure as the possible instrument of apocalypse. His death obviously canceled teleological expectations, and in *On the Death of the Lord Protector* the poet returns "to a concept of time and history essentially repetitive,"[14] and the late Protector, now no longer unique, takes his place in the perspective of chronicle. Despite the rather feeble observation on son Richard "That a Cromwell in an Houre a Prince will grow," the window of opportunity has been decisively closed. Unique among panegyrics, *The First Anniversary* scrutinizes political realities, finding in Cromwell the possible architect of a stable mixed state. Providence, in its infinite wisdom, declined to fulfill such a hope. It is not the poet's role, Marvell felt, to challenge that decision.

CHAPTER FIVE

Satire and Sedition

The Restoration, as we have often been told, was a great period of satire. Dryden, whose name provided a synonym for the age, has received more acclaim for *Absalom and Achitophel* than for any of his other works in verse or prose. The greatest English poem of its kind, *Absalom* unites two dominant interests of the Restoration period: politics and satire.

Absalom and two or three other poems by Dryden have virtually monopolized critical and historical accounts of Restoration satire. Literary historians, in attempting to show how Dryden the satirist typified his age, give passing notice to a few of his contemporaries. Usually they pay brief tribute to *Hudibras*, to the *Satire against Mankind*, to the *Satires against the Jesuits* (largely, one suspects, because Dryden praised Oldham), and to Marvell's mock-heroic and political lampoons (often dismissed as "crude"). There the typical account of Restoration satire ends. This customary emphasis on Dryden's preeminence, coupled to a corresponding neglect of his contemporaries, confronts us with a strange situation, for Dryden towers over a void. The other satirists by virtue of whom he is affirmed to be typical and preeminent remain almost unknown.

Those who derive their impressions of the period from such sources may wonder at the fact that in quantity and popularity satire stood first among the various kinds of nondramatic verse written between 1660 and 1714. More than 3,000 satirical pieces from this period survive in print. Of these approximately 1,200 were published in various collections between 1689 and 1716, the best known of which were entitled *Poems on Affairs of State* (*POAS*). *POAS* (also commonly called *State Poems*) was a leading poetical miscellany for thirty years, and about thirty volumes were printed. In addition, some 2,500 poems on state affairs survive only in manuscript.

This mass of satirical verse is directed at every aspect of public affairs, from national issues of the greatest consequence to the most trivial incidents of life at court. The early editors who named these "Poems on Affairs of State" had more in mind than we would ordinarily infer from the title. The affairs of state that the poems celebrate are as likely to be love affairs of kings and courtiers as they are the matters of public policy that we normally associate with the term. While political or ecclesiastical matters are their chief concern, many of the poems are devoted in whole or in part to literary battles and court gossip. Their focus is almost invariably personal and particular. Even where great historical events and issues form the basis of these poems—battles, treaties, plots, acts of Parliament—their ultimate emphasis is upon the men and women involved. Those who held power or aspired to it in this period of British history formed a compact and well-known group compared with the amorphous bureaucracies of our own day. Figures with no official position in the government also influenced public policy deeply. Aside from those of recognized importance in high offices of Church and State—kings, chief ministers, members of Parliament, judges, bishops, and courtiers—power was often centered in royal mistresses and favorites, in political careerists and adventurers. Some, like Louise de Kéroualle or John Ayloffe, were agents of other powers and exerted a pro-French or pro-Dutch influence on king or Parliament. Others, like Father Patrick or Titus Oates, sought to bring corresponding influences to bear on political and ecclesiastical affairs. There were, in addition, those shadowy figures of the back stairs who ministered variously to the royal or ducal pleasures—the Chiffinches, Bab Mays, Killigrews, and Brounckers, whose minor positions at court were by no means always commensurate with their true importance.

Influence radiated outward from the acknowledged and unacknowledged centers of power in Church and state, in Parliament and the diplomatic and military services, to lend ephemeral importance to various actors, spies, ladies-in-waiting, and adventurers. Beyond these, in terms of influence, came some of the writers on public affairs. A few, like the Court Wits, had a certain standing at Whitehall. Two or three were professional men of letters, like Dryden. Some were dedicated amateurs, like Marvell. Many were denizens of Grub Street or propagandists for outlawed political or religious sects who shrouded themselves in anonymity. At the furthest range we encounter figures of the most marginal importance as far as state affairs are concerned—bullies, fops, bawds, *beaux-garçons* and their misses, green and gullible heirs of country squires. At this point political satire merges with social satire.

This varied world centered on Whitehall and Westminister is vividly reflected in the *State Poems* by a corresponding variety in tone and technique. The poems range from the gravity and patriotic fervor sometimes evident in Marvell, Dryden, or Oldham, through the irreverent raillery of *The History of Insipids,* to ribald catalogues of court vices devised by anonymous hacks. In form they range from sophisticated and complex mock-heroic poems to doggerel sung in the streets by peddlers.

However crude or sophisticated, however trivial or grave its subject, Augustan satirical verse is remarkable for the freedom with which it attacks public figures and institutions that would in other ages have been immune from such attacks. Until the quarrel between Charles I and Parliament reached its crisis in civil war, there was very little topical satire on affairs of Church and state. What little there is usually shrouded itself in allegories and ambiguities like Spenser's *Mother Hubbard's Tale* or Skelton's *Why Come Ye Not to*

Court? Until the 1630s most English satire was typical rather than topical. This is as true of Chaucer's arraignment of worldly ecclesiastics as it is of Langland's, and it is also true of the Elizabethan satirists of the 1590s, Donne, Martston, and Hall, the imitators of Juvenal, Persius, Horace, and Martial, whose works attracted ecclesiastical censure in spite of their concern with types rather than individuals.

Verse satire directed explicitly at public figures and institutions first appeared in England as the Civil War broke out.

The ferment of political activity, the quarrels over methods of government and religious dogma, the animosities which separated and the shifting alliances which united the peoples, their fears, hopes, ideals and misunderstandings were reflected in the varied literature of an immensely productive epoch. . . . Writers of popular ballads were unceasingly prolific; in response to a new demand the press was born—a noisy, precocious infant; political satire developed from clumsy adolescence to ferocious maturity.[1]

The inauguration of this new literary epoch may be marked by the invocation to his caustic muse of the Royalist poet, John Cleveland:

> Come, keen iambics with your badgers' feet,
> And badger-like bite till your teeth do meet![2]

For the next eighty years the political warfare of Cavalier and Roundhead, of Court Party and Country Party, of Whig and Tory found increasingly uninhibited expression in satirical verse.

From 1640 to about 1740, then, one finds leading poets as well as poetasters and ballad-makers increasingly concerned with political and religious issues or with the underlying ideological and metaphysical questions reflected in these issues. Public affairs become, accordingly, a leading subject for such writers as Cleveland, Wither, Brome, Denham, Butler, Wild, Marvell, Rochester, Ayloffe, Oldham, Dryden, Garth, Mainwaring, Defoe, Pope, and Swift.

The Civil War and the Interregnum stand as a watershed between the old order and the new. The old order, with its mystique of monarchy and its divinely sanctioned hierarchies in Church, state, and society so richly exemplified under Elizabeth, was shaken under James and shattered under Charles. The deathblow was struck on the scaffold outside Whitehall Palace on January 30, 1649, and Marvell, the poet who later so diligently undermined the authority of Charles II's government, commemorated this occasion, as we have seen, with extraordinary percipience and judgment in *An Horatian Ode*. The "helpless Right" of the reign of Charles I exemplifies the Stuart dilemma from right up to the last vain Jacobite rising. For the remainder of the century the underlying issue between Cavalier and Roundhead or Tory and Whig was really the contest between a view of monarchy as divinely ordained and sanctioned and an opposing view of monarchical power as limited by certain inalienable rights of the subject. The issue is reflected specifically in the period between the Restoration and the Glorious Revolution as a conflict between royal prerogative and parliamentary privilege.

The execution of Charles I demonstrated, as Marvell's ode shows, that the theoretically unlimited divine right was in fact limited by the power opposed to it. When the English found that they could pull down kings and set them up again, divine right became a polite fiction. Opposition writers during the Restoration were not slow to discover flaws in the ancient rights affirmed by royalists and Anglicans, and they went back to Henry VIII to suggest that these had their real origin in purely human urgencies. As one satirist wrote of Charles II,

> The virtues in thee, Charles, inherent
> (Although thy count'nance be an odd piece)
> Prove thee as true a God's vicegerent
> As e'er was Harry with the codpiece.[3]

Once the divinity that doth hedge a king had been stripped away by events, political writers anxious to defend the liberties of the subject against the encroachments of royal power turned with alacrity to the task of exposing the human weaknesses of their monarchs. From Rochester's attacks on Charles II to Pope's on George II one finds a flood of trenchant, bitter, sometimes obscene, and sometimes witty verse purporting to expose every imaginable weakness and folly in the reigning monarch. Satirical Roundheads had confined themselves to attacks on Charles I's ministers and officers, but from about 1670 on, often under the influence of the counter-myth of the Classical Republicans, kings themselves were attacked as freely as Old Nol or the Rump had been.

As dissatisfaction with the administration of Charles II grew, opposition satirists exercised their utmost ingenuity to discredit their rulers. For a while—in the 1660s especially—the pretense was maintained that Charles was a great king with misguided counselors. But at about the time of the secret entente with France and the Third Dutch War, unmitigated personal abuse was directed at him and at the whole Stuart dynasty. As long-suffering Britannia puts it in John Ayloffe's *Britannia and Raleigh* (1674),[4]

> Raleigh, no more: too long in vain I've tri'd
> The Stuart from the tyrant to divide.
> As easily learn'd virtuosos may
> With the dog's blood his gentle king convey
> Into the wolf and make him guardian turn
> To the bleating flock by him so lately torn.
> If this imperial oil once taint the blood,
> It's by no potent antidote withstood.
> Tyrants like lep'rous kings for public weal
> Must be immur'd, lest their contagion steal
> Over the whole: th' elect Jessean line
> To this firm law their scepter did resign;
> And shall this stinking Scottish brood evade
> Eternal laws by God for mankind made?   [141–54]

The republican satirist here entirely subverts the traditional sanctions of monarchy, transforming the sanctifying chrism from a symbol of divine ordination into a mark of tyrannical power and affirming God-given rights in the subject while denying them in the sovereign.

At a less abstruse and philosophical level this iconoclastic attitude toward royalty appears in the casual and familiar treatment of the king even in poems written by his friends. To the Court Wits Charles was merely the first gentleman of England, with all that the term implied, and his well-known gentlemanly vices did nothing to maintain the myth that he was God's viceregent and Defender of the Faith. A revealing anecdote touches on this last point. In the course of a theological debate concerning matters of faith Charles is reported to have observed to a court lady that all wise men were of one religion (the skepticism of the king was well known). When she asked him what religion that was, he answered that wise men never tell. Political and ecclesiastical upheavals, sectarianism, the breakdown of even the appearance of conventional moral standards in the court, the efflorescence of empirical thinking about political institutions exemplified in the works of Hobbes and Locke, and the growth in experimental science sponsored by the Royal Society paralleled the widespread skepticism and libertinism in the seats of power and influence.

Apologists for Charles II and his brother could only help to delay—they could not arrest—the progressive disintegration of traditional attitudes toward monarchy. The greatest satirist of the period, who had represented Charles in *Annus Mirabilis* (1667) as a heroic figure like Aeneas, was obliged, fifteen years later, in *Absalom's* opening lines, to make concessions to the well-established satirical image of the king. Dryden could only counter the ad hominem attacks of the Marvells and Rochesters by simultaneously conceding and belittling the king's human weaknesses while affirming the divine authority of his office. Dryden's conservative political poetry marks the end of the era of divine right. Parliamentary prerogative and the concept of the subject's inalienable rights won a decisive victory seven years later.

The intense and widespread interest in politics and satire which dominated the half-century following Charles II's Restoration is reflected in the large number of known literary men who produced these poems—Dryden, Marvell, Butler, Rochester, Oldham, Swift, Pope, and others. There were, in addition, many nobleman and gentlemen who wrote mainly on affairs at court and formed a clique of cognoscenti: the duke of Buckingham, the earl of Mulgrave, Henry Savile, Sir Fleetwood Sheppard, Sir George Etherege, Sir Charles Sedley, Lord Buckhurst, and others. The largest group, most of them unidentified, includes both the little-known patriots who wrote out of a deep concern and the minor hacks who wrote for bread. Among the former John Ayloffe, secret agent, propagandist, and associate of Marvell, is an outstanding representative, and there is also the irrepressible Stephen College, who was executed for his lampoons on Charles II. The commercial hacks are the hardest to identify, possibly because there is little stylistic distinction or ideological consistency in their works, or because their social insignificance prevented the gossip that surrounded the literary activities of the others.

In other respects as well circumstances conspired to make the *State Poems* inaccessible to modern readers. Not only are they unrepresented in modern anthologies and editions and their authors largely unknown, but their concentration on the topical requires much elucidation. The particularity which made them popular in their own day makes them teasing and inscrutable in ours. The great majority of these poems issued anonymously from the author's hands, were copied by nameless scribes in "scriptoria," and were distributed surreptitiously.

The chief reason for the traffic in manuscripts during the Restoration period was the government's strenuous effort to prevent the publication of anything that could be construed as critical of its policies or personnel. Satires which in any way reflected on Charles or James, their ministers or mistresses, were produced and circulated at the risk of severe penalties. A Treason Act was the first statute passed by the Cavalier Parliament. It included in the category of overt offenses "all printing, writing, preaching, or malicious and advised speaking calculated to compass or devise the death, destruction, injury, or restraint of the sovereign, or to deprive him of his style, honor, or kingly name." In 1683 Algernon Sidney was convicted and executed when the act was interpreted to extend to unpublished and uncirculated writings. Thus circulation in manuscript, though it often mitigated the risks, could not always avoid penalties for treason.

The Licensing Act of 1662 extended the statutory basis for suppressing dissident literature. This Act prohibited "the printing or importing of any books or pamphlets containing doctrines contrary to the principles of the Christian faith or to the doctrine of government or of governors in Church or State." This Act lapsed with the dissolution of the Cavalier Parliament in 1679 and was followed by a royal proclamation ordering the seizure of libels and the arrest of their authors and printers, with a reward of £40 payable to informers.

The Licensing Act was rarely resorted to in practice, but it provided judges with justifications to proceed more rigorously under the common law. Its importance was principally due to the powers of search and seizure vested in the crown, delegated to the secretaries of state, and exercised by that watchdog of the press, Sir Roger L'Estrange. Armed with these powers, L'Estrange ferreted out the authors and publishers of seditious literature. A perennial culprit was Francis "Elephant" Smith, who was imprisoned from 1661 to 1663 for printing *Annus Mirabilis, the Year of Prodigies,* the first of those radical pamphlets to which Dryden's *Annus Mirabilis* was a rejoinder. L'Estrange was highly successful in discovering other inflammatory literature, such as the last speeches of the regicides executed in October 1660; or *Prelatic Preachers* (1663), an attack on episop-acy; or *A Treatise of the Execution of Justice* (1663), which advocated the assassination of King Charles.

At first sight it may seem strange, in view of the spate of radical prose pamphlets produced in the early 1660s, that there should have survived almost no verse satires attacking the government. Up to 1666 the number of such pieces is negligible. The earliest antigovernment verse satires of any substance written in this period are the second and third *Advice to a Painter*, which deal with the Dutch War in the years 1665 and 1666. The explanation for the production in the early 1660s of so much opposition prose and so little verse may be that prose pamphleteers were violently radical and seditious and would have been at any time irreconcilable to the restored Stuart monarchy, while most verse satirists seem to have been more moderate and to have conceived of themselves as members of a loyal opposition. It is only in the disenchantment of the 1670s that attacks on monarchy begin. Before that time nearly all the verse satirists seem to have accepted, or to have made a pretense of accepting, the institution of monarchy.

From 1660 to 1666 both Charles and his ministers seem to have received nothing but panegyrics from the poets. Dryden set the pace with *Astraea Redux* and *To My Lord Chancellor*. Waller's eulogistic *Instructions to a Painter*, which celebrates the Duke of York's victory over the Dutch at Lowestoft in June 1665, brought the honeymoon to an end by providing the model for Marvell's parodic *Second Advice to a Painter*, the first substantial satiric attack in verse and the first of a series of important poems in the genre. This and *Third Advice*, which followed *Second Advice* a year later, are highly circumstan-tial narrative poems exposing the fiascos of the war against the Dutch in the summers of 1665 and 1666 and assigning blame with considerable satiric skill to York, various ministers of Charles, courtiers and court ladies, naval of-ficers, and servile members of Parliament.

Although the two advices specifically excluded the king from criticism and affirmed a deep loyalty to him, the government evidently regarded them with concern. Not only were they among the few opposition satires printed in the reign, but the large number of unlicensed editions (some with a false Breda imprint) testify to their popularity. They seem, furthermore, to have enjoyed an unusually wide circulation in manuscript before they were printed. Finally, copies reached the innermost recesses of the government at Whitehall and Westminster.

The government's efforts to suppress the advices and ferret out the pub-lisher, "Elephant" Smith, are a further indication of the concern with which they regarded them: "Questions to be put to the Master and Wardens [of the Stationer's Company] relative to their late searches for unlicensed books; their seizure of other printers and presses, as well as Milburn's and Darby's; sale of a tract on the firing of the city, and of Second and Third Advice to a Painter,

offered by Fras. Smith."[5] A few months later, in July 1667, we find another
record of attempts to censor these satires:

Declaration of William Burden. Fras. Smith of the Elephant and Castle, Strand,
asked him to let Johnson, a printer living in his house, print two or three sheets of
verse, called "The Second and Third Advice to a Painter." Asked if they reflected on
the Lord Chancellor, Duchess of Albemarle, and others of the Court; refused either to
allow it to be printed at his house or to help him to a printer. Told Royston, a
warden of the Stationers' Company, of this business, and advised him to look after it.[6]

According to a second entry of the same date, Smith was summoned before
Lord Arlington, the secretary of state. It must have been a stormy interview,
since Arlington was the object of a devastating attack in *Third Advice* and was
not a man known for his sense of humor. Despite the penalties which Smith
presumably suffered on this occasion, he evidently continued to defy the law
during the next two decades. On 16 September 1670 he was "ordered to enter
into a recognizance of £100 to appear at the next Quarter Sessions of Middle-
sex" for having sold scandalous pamphlets.[7] On 11 June 1684 he was tried
before Judge Jeffreys for "printing and publishing a scandalous libel called
The Raree Show," the lampoon on Charles II which had been a contributory
factor in the execution of its author, Stephen College, on a charge of high
treason three years earlier. This time Smith was convicted and sentenced "to
pay a fine of £500, to stand in the pillory at the Palace yard at Westminister,
at the Temple, and at the Royal Exchange, and the libel to be burnt by the
common hangman, and to have a paper set on him signifying his crime, to
find sureties for his good behavior for life, and to be committed till all was
done."[8]

"Elephant" Smith was merely the best-known and most persistent of the
booksellers and publishers who attempted to defy censorship and circulate
satirical verse in print. On the same day that Smith received his sentence from
Jeffreys one Jane Curtis was tried and convicted for publishing *Justice in
Masquerade,* a lampoon on Jeffreys's friend and associate, Lord Chief Justice
Scroggs. Sometimes attempts were made by the victims of censorship to evade
penalities by subornation. On 18 October 1683 a bookseller named John How
admitted that he had bribed a member of the Stationers' Company to drop
proceedings against him for publishing a poem attacking Scroggs, the Duke
of York, and the Duchess of Portsmouth as Papists ("His Holiness has three
grand friends").[9] The authors of these pieces were, of course, much harder to
find than publishers and booksellers, unless, like the foolhardy College, they
openly defied the authorities. Yet the government's agents seem to have
conducted their search for satirical poets with some vigor if not with much
success. When Queen Mary's pregnancy in 1687 seemed to jeopardize hopes
of a Protestant successor to the throne, one of the lampoons produced upon
the occasion provoked an intense search for the culprit. The incident is reported in the blasé tones of a young scholar named Richard Lapthorne: "It

seems there is some idle brain hath made a lampoon relating to the late thanksgiving and a strict inquiry is made after the author who, if he be discovered, will according to deserts be severely punished."[10]

The Licensing Act of 1662 applied only to printed libels, but in 1677, L'Estrange recommended to the Libels Committee of the House of Lords that the legal definition be extended to include manuscript material, "because it is notorious that not one in forty libels ever comes to the press, though by the help of manuscripts they are well-nigh as public." Pepys, as we shall see, received the second, third, fourth, and fifth advices one by one in manuscript form before they were printed together in 1667.

The government's attempt to extend censorship to unpublished material led to extremes of injustice and brutality in the case of Algernon Sidney, one of the most dedicated of the Classical Republicans. Judge Jeffreys sent Sidney to the scaffold for merely possessing an allegedly subversive manuscript. Thus neither publication nor circulation needed to be proven. This travesty of the legal process became in its turn the subject of a telling satirical attack:

> Algernon Sidney,
> Of Commonwealth kidney,
> Compos'd a damn'd libel (ay, marry, was it!)
> Writ to occasion
> Ill blood in the nation,
> And therefore dispers'd it all over his closet.[11]

This spirited rejoinder to the tyrant Jeffreys shows, as does the great volume of other satires written in the cause of freedom, that neither fine, prison, pillory, nor scaffold was adequate to deter the satirists.

The assumption that many such poems enjoyed a wide distribution in manuscript is further supported by the large number surviving in this form. In the Osborn collection at Yale, for example, there are many satires copied out on single sheets or folios, folded as though for the pocket, and occasionally bearing an addressee's name on the outside.

While many manuscript lampoons were passed around among friends or tacked to the doors of enemies, there was a well-organized business in their commerical reproduction and sale. Robert Julian, facetiously known as the "secretary of the Muses," kept himself supplied with brandy for years through the proceeds from such a clandestine clearinghouse. Julian was himself the subject of numerous lampoons, one of which describes his function in clear, if unflattering terms:

> Thou common shore of this poetic town,
> Where all our excrements of wit are thrown—
> For sonnet, satire, bawdry, blasphemy
> Are empti'd and disburden'd all on thee.[12]

On 12 November 1684 Julian was convicted of "making and publishing that scandalous libel, Old Rowley the King." For this and other items he was sentenced to pay a fine of 100 marks and stand in the pillory.[13] Julian had a successor in the business, one Capt. Warcup, addressed in the "Letter to C———W———" as "thou second scandal-carrier of the town."

Coffeehouses must have been among Julian's best customers. Roger North in the *Examen* notes that during the 1670s these establishments "began to be direct seminaries of sedition and offices for the dispatch of lying."[14] An order for their suppression was issued in 1675 but not enforced. In 1677 King Charles was reported to be highly incensed by those proprietors who, "to gain a little money had the impudence and folly to prostitute affairs of state indifferently to the views of those that frequent such houses, some of them of lewd principles, and some of mean birth and education."[15] Affairs of state were a mystery about which ordinary subjects should be kept ignorant. In 1616 Charles's grandfather had expressed more emphatically this traditional attitude toward the *arcana imperii:*

That which concerns the mystery of the king's power is not lawful to be disputed; for that is to wade into the weakness of princes, and to take away the mystical reverence that belongs unto them that sit in the throne of God. . . . As for the absolute prerogative of the Crown, that is no subject for the tongue of a lawyer, nor is lawful to be disputed. It is atheism and blasphemy to dispute what God can do; good Christians content themselves with his Will revealed in his Word: so it is presumption and high contempt in a subject to dispute what a king cannot do, or say that a king cannot do this or that, but rest with that which is the king's revealed will in his law.[16]

James I's statement enunciates a belief in divine right that was, as we have seen, increasingly discredited as the century wore on, but the quasi-religious instinct that affairs of state were not the concern of the subject lingered, especially in the writings of Dryden. The various ways in which the governments of Charles II and James II tried to embody this principle through censorship and suppression of all real news helped actually to induce the writing and circulation of satire. The outpouring of verse on public affairs during the Restoration showed a strong and widespread desire to penetrate the barrier of silence which the government and its monopoly *Gazettes* and *Intelligencers* maintained around national issues. Undoubtedly the "seditious" literature disseminated through the coffeehouses did much to educate, arouse, and—sometimes—to mislead the English in this crucial period.

These political satires, whether printed or not, found their way also into the hands of the great and powerful. They circulated in the very citadels of government, in Whitehall and Westminster. There is, for instance, the well-known anecdote of Rochester's banishment from court for accidentally showing Charles II a lampoon on the king himself.[17] A large manuscript volume in the Osborn collection containing many satires on James II and bearing his arms testifies to the royal interest in keeping track of opposition writing. The story of the circulation of the second and third *Advices* provides us with an unusually interesting and well-documented case. Here we have abundant evidence of the impact on a high government official of this kind of political verse, and, in addition, a strong presumption that the same pieces were employed in an attempt to influence the House of Commons.

The *Second Advice to a Painter* and its sequels, as we have seen, deal circumstantially with British naval fiascos in the Dutch War of 1665–67. Samuel Pepys, who was probably the most experienced and knowledgeable official in the Restoration navy, noted down in his diary his impressions of each of these satires as it came into his hands. Of *Second Advice,* which he received from his old friend, Sir H. Chumley, he wrote: "I am sorry for my Lord Sandwich's having so great a part in it."[18] Edward Montagu, earl of Sandwich, had succeeded the duke of York as commander-in-chief of the navy in the late summer of 1665. *Second Advice* attacks Sandwich, who was a close friend and patron of Pepys, for incompetence in general and especially for a flagrant breach of naval regulations and procedures in sharing a rich Dutch prize with his officers before the vessels had been through the prize court. In view both of his intimate knowledge of naval affairs and of his close relation to Sandwich, Pepy's comment on *Second Advice* seems like an implicit acknowledgment of the poem's veracity.

Another friend of Pepys, Mr. Brisband ("a good scholar and a sober man") gave him at Whitehall a manuscript of *Third Advice to a Painter,* "a bitter satire upon the service of the duke of Albemarle the last year." Again the future secretary of the admiralty seems to acknowledge the effectiveness and fidelity of the satire: "I took it home with me and will copy it, having the former, being also mightily pleased with it."[19]

The crowning disaster of the war occurred in the summer of 1667, when the Dutch fleet sailed almost unopposed up the Thames and Medway and destroyed or captured many English men-of-war. During an inspection of defensive installations in this third summer of the war, Pepys and some colleagues met with "the several Advices to a Painter, which made us good sport, and indeed are very witty" in exposing "the folly of our masters in the management of things at this day."[20] These may, of course, have been in one of the early printed editions, but there is no way of knowing. At the end of that summer Pepys found a manuscript of *Fourth Advice* at a friend's house and noted that it "made my heart ache, it being too sharp, and so true."[21]

Several significant conclusions may be drawn from all this. First, that Pepys saw at least three of four important satires in manuscript is an indication of the effectiveness of this mode of circulation. Second, the future "savior of the navy's" having received these pieces from close friends in the government indicates that Restoration political satire was by no means circulated only among the politically disaffected. In the third place, the fact that Pepys, who knew as much about naval affairs as anyone in England, should affirm the sharpness and truth of these satires is an impressive testimonial to their importance.

The circulation of political lampoons in the centers of government was not limited, however, to such methods as we find in the case of Pepys. There is on record an attempt to influence the entire House of Commons by distributing copies of a verse lampoon to each member. The incident occurred in February 1668 during a debate on the naval miscarriages of the war just ended. On the twelfth, "several small printed papers in rhythm [rhyme] were by a porter conveyed to the doorkeeper of the House of Commons under several coverts directed to the respective members of the House.[22] Our authority goes on to say that "the matter of them is libellous and the whole thing shows the author to be more fraught with malice than poetry." Henry Verney supplies additional details of the incident: "Yesterday a fellow brought a bag of about 400 letters for Parliament to the door and slunk away; they were printed books of verses, a downright libel, quite like Wither's *Abuses Whipped and Stripped*."[23] Two days later, we are told, "a libel was conveyed to the Speaker of the House of Commons of such a nature that it was not thought to fit to be published even in that great Council."[24]

At this time the House was investigating the disastrous division of the fleet in 1666, when a large force under Prince Rupert was detached to attack a French force wrongly reported to be in the Channel. The main fleet under the duke of Albemarle encountered the Dutch shortly after and was saved from annihilation after a bloody three days' battle by Rupert's last-minute reappearance. The House was interested chiefly in two questions: who was responsible for the false report that the French were in the Channel, and who was responsible for the decision to divide the fleet before the imminent appearance of the Dutch? It is possible that the "printed books of verses" which Verney mentions bore upon these and other questions of naval mismanagement. At any rate Marvell, whose *Third Advice* arraigns Arlington for the intelligence failures, is quoted in Grey two days after the satires were delivered to the doorkeeper to the same effect:

Mr. Marvell, reflecting on Lord Arlington somewhat transportedly said: "We have had Bristols and Cecils Secretaries and by them knew the king of Spain's Junto and letters of the Pope's cabinet; and now such a strange account of things. They money allowed for intelligence so small, the intelligence was accordingly—a libidinous desire in men for them—the place of Secretary ill gotten, when bought with £10,000 and a barony." He was called to explain himself, but said the thing was so plain it needed it not.[25]

Political satire is related to historical events in two ways. It is a record of events, a history, however distorted by partial views and private motives. It also can exert some influence upon the events themselves. The political verse of the Restoration played a considerable part in the determination of large issues in England: the question of a Protestant or a Catholic succession, for one, and the relative power of royal prerogative and Parliament for another. Viewed either as history or as an instrument of party warfare, Restoration political satire is marked by a circumstantial and highly personal approach to events. As history and as propaganda, it purports to tell the real story, to set the record straight, and its prime method is to present the reader with a plausible body of purported fact. For us who are studying these events three hundred years after they happened, two questions arise. How accurately do the *State Poems* reflect events? To what extent did they influence them?

From 1665 on, every aspect of public affairs in England was subjected to the satirist's increasingly minute and bitter scrutiny. Charles's personal faults, which might have been tolerated in a monarch whose political and religious inclinations were more congenial to his subjects, were magnified until he was depicted as another Sardanapalus. The mistresses, whose greed supposedly drained off vast sums appropriated for the national welfare and whose alien creeds threatened the liberties of Charles's subjects, were exposed to appalling but sometimes justified invective. No drunken frolic, brawl at court, bribe in Parliament, not an instance of cowardice or chicanery in the navy, nor of hypocrisy or bigotry in the Church escaped satirical notice. The Restoration is a period unusually rich in detailed records: the diaries of Pepys, Evelyn, Dering, Luttrell, and Milward, the letters of Rochester and Savile, of Etherege, Marvell, and Henry Verney; the memoirs of Grammont, Barillon, North, Burnet, and Clarendon; the state papers and newsletters—all contribute to the rich documentation. Nearly every item of even the slightest public interest in such sources is mentioned in the thousands of poems on public affairs which have survived. The most important of these, set in chronological order with their occasions and persons identified, comprise a priceless record. Their particularity and involvement and gossipy interest in everything that happened give them something of the appeal that we find in Pepys's diary. The pictures they paint are always, to some extent, distorted. The mirror they hold up to flawed human nature is often flawed itself, but thanks to rebuttals and apologias and to the abundance of other dependable records, the modern student of Restoration history and manners can still get at kinds of truth through this medium.

What, then, can be said of these poems as history? The writer of commendatory verse selects his details, softens his focus, and heightens his colors to produce an image heroic or benign of king, queen, or chancellor. The satirist, on the other hand, despite the pretense of delivering unvarnished truth, distorts and colors realities for his own political and aesthetic purposes. *Second Advice* reveals, for example, the many unheroic realities that Waller omitted or glossed over in *Instructions to a Painter,* but Waller's panegyrical treatment of the war of 1665 reminds us that Marvell underrated the courage of James and the magnanimity of Clarendon in his parody.

In the preface to *Annus Mirabilis* Dryden implied just such a discrepancy between the heroic or the satirical image and reality. In defending his adaptation of Virgilian tropes and phrases, he writes:

Such descriptions or images, well wrought, which I promise not for mine, are, as I have said, the adequate delight of heroic poesy; for they beget laughter; for the one shows nature beautified, as in the picture of a fair woman, which we admire; the other shows her deformed, as in that of a lazar or of a fool with distorted face and antic gestures, at which we cannot forbear to laugh, because it is a deviation from nature.

It is a step beyond Dryden's statement to say that the fair woman and the lazar are two images of one person, but a comparison of Dryden's massive apologia for the regime of Charles II with, say, *Third Advice* suggests that this is true. In *Annus Mirabilis* Dryden bent his energies on painting anew, with a palette of heroic colors, such figures as the king, the duke of York, and the duke of Albemarle, whom the satirists depicted in livid colors and grotesque postures.

The juxtaposition of a heroic poem like Waller's *Instructions to a Painter* or *Annus Mirabilis* with satiric poems dealing with the same figures and events sheds new light not only upon the events themselves but on the techniques of the heroic and satiric modes in topical poetry. The poems of Waller and Dryden, of Marvell and Rochester, are mutually illuminating. In the first place the underlying aesthetic assumptions of both modes are thrown into relief by comparison. The heroic, as Dryden's important comment suggests, is designed to "beget admiration" or wonder; the satiric (or burlesque) to "beget laughter." The heroic mode aims at an imaginative identification of contemporary persons and events with the heroic tradition in epic or biblical accounts. The technique necessarily entails a careful selection from the available mass of fact, an idealizing or heightening of the details selected, and a cunning association of these details with mythic precedents. The satiric artist also selects from the available mass of fact, but pays particular regard to details which may appear as grotesque and incongruous. His technique depends upon a vivid and realistic treatment of detail, and, if he employs heroic associations, he does so in order to denigrate the present reality by contrast with a nobler past. Thus Dryden, in *Annus Mirabilis*, projects upon Charles II Aeneas's pious care for his people and his country's destiny, while Marvell draws grotesque analogues between Ovid's fabulous artificer and the cunning political architect he sees in Clarendon. An example of the difference between the two modes is found in the accounts of the wounding of the British admiral Monck in the Three Days' Battle. Monck's breeches were shot away, and he suffered a minor wound in the buttocks. Dryden permits himself a moment of grave levity before reasserting the epic mood:

> Our dreaded Admiral from far they threat,
>> Whose batter'd rigging their whole war receives.
> All bare, like some old oak which tempests beat,
>> He stands, and sees below his scatter'd leaves.

> Heroes of old, when wounded, shelter sought,
>   But he, who meets all danger with disdain,
> Ev'n in their face his ship to anchor brought,
>   And steeple high stood propp'd upon the main.
>
> At this excess of courage all amaz'd,
>   The foremost of his foes a while withdraw:
> With such respect in enter'd Rome they gaz'd,
>   Who on high chairs the god-like fathers saw.   [241–52]

As Hooker judiciously remarks, "Dryden's raillery is admirable by the best standards of his age: it is a gentle thrust, serving to reveal or heighten certain admirable qualities in the object of raillery—in this instance, the duke's unshaken courage." In treating the same incident Marvell employs mock modesty and a Ciceronian disclaimer in advising his painter:

> But most with story of his hand or thumb,
> Conceal (as Honor would) his Grace's bum,
> When that rude bullet a large collop tore
> Out of that buttock never turn'd before.
> Fortune, it seem'd, would give him by that lash
> Gentle correction for his fight so rash,
> But should the Rump perceiv't, they'd say that Mars
> Had now reveng'd them upon Aumarle's arse.   [123–30][26]

Here something like heroic dignity is momentarily assumed to emphasize by contrast the prevailing effect of broad humor. Heroic personifications of Honor and Fortune wage a vain struggle with low words like *bum* and *arse*. In the lines which follow this passage Marvell, like Dryden, brings in further analogues from the heroic tradition, but with an effect that is directly opposite to Dryden's:

> The long disaster better o'er to veil,
> Paint only Jonah three days in the whale,
> Then draw the youthful Perseus all in haste
> From a sea-beast to free the virgin chaste,
> (But neither riding Pegasus for speed,
> Nor with the Gorgon shielded at his need);
> For no less time did conqu'ring Ruyter chaw
> Our flying gen'ral in his spongy jaw.
> So Rupert the sea dragon did invade,
> But to save George himself and not the maid,
> And so arriving late, he quickly miss'd
> E'en sails to fly, unable to resist.   [131–42]

In this account of Prince Rupert's attempt to rescue the beleaguered Monck the mythical allusions to Jonah, Perseus and Andromeda, and St. George have a discordant effect. They underscore by contrast the irrelevance of heroic attitudes to the present "long disaster." The effect of the passage runs counter to that which Dryden gains by his sonorous lines on Rome's "god-like fathers." It awakens the reader's skepticism where Dryden's weighty lines excite awe. The conflicting techniques and strategies of the heroic and mock-heroic genres tend to illustrate the basic ideological oppositions of the century: on the one hand the appeal to faith in traditional values, rituals, and myths, on the other the appeal to empirical, skeptical, and critical attitudes toward experience.

As I have already suggested, circumstances in this period aroused skeptical and critical attitudes toward authority. The actual characters and conduct of great Restoration figures often seem like those found in satires in other ages. The truth could be stranger than fiction, and the Restoration satirist of court life was rarely called upon to strain his powers of invention. As Rochester wrote of his enemy, Sir Carr Scroope,

> in thy person we more clearly see
> That satire's of divine authority,
> For God made one on man when he made thee,
> To show there were some men as there are apes,
> Fram'd for mere sport, who differ but in shapes.   [4–8][27]

In his famous portrait of Zimri, Dryden took few liberties with the historical duke of Buckingham. The wits and bravoes of this period, like Charles himself, were a self-conscious lot, and one suspects them at times of trying to imitate the hyperboles that imagination drew of them. Sir Robert Howard sometimes seems to have modeled his haughty demeanor on the heroes of his own dramas. One is driven to wonder if Restoration life imitated art more than in other periods.

In matters of politics the same rule often applies. Marvell's satirical account of England's defeat by the Dutch in 1667 and the parliamentary and diplomatic maneuvers which accompanied it is a primary source for historians. In her scholarly edition of the parliamentary diary of John Milward, Caroline Robbins draws upon *Last Instructions* continually for illustration and confirmation of her author. When Charles II, with the aid of Clifford, "the mad Cethegus of the age," and Arlington, evolved in secret the Grand Design of making England a dependency of Louis XIV and the Catholic Church, the worst suspicions of the satirist fell short of the truth.

If Charles, the ironist, "never said a foolish thing, nor ever did a wise one," at least he managed to preserve the crown for his humorless brother James, who wore it with a difference and only for a short time. Charles embodied the Restoration spirit of compromise, whereas James was intractable and wrongheaded. The best that could be said of Charles has been said by the exponent of compromise, the Earl of Halifax:

That yieldingness, whatever foundations it might lay to the disadvantage of posterity, was a specific to preserve us in peace for his own time. If he loved too much to lie upon his own down-bed of ease, his subjects had the pleasure, during his reign, of lolling and stretching upon theirs. As a sword is sooner broken upon a feather-bed than upon a table, so his pliantness broke the blow of a present mischief much better than a more immediate resistance would perhaps have done.

Ruin saw this, and therefore removed him first to make way for futher overturnings.[28]

We come now to the second relationship between political satire and history. To what extent did the enormous output of the Restoration satirists influence the course of history? Some of the answers to this question have already been implied. Circulation of these pieces in defiance of severe legal penalties and a vigilant censorship raises a strong presumption in favor of their effectiveness. Obviously we are not likely to find well-documented instances of political conversion. Yet the testimony of such a distinguished public servant as Pepys in favor of the force and authenticity of some of these pieces is an indication of their impact. And the sheer volume of Restoration satire, with its evidently wide circulation even in government circles, shows its significance as a political instrument.

The implicit question with which this part of our discussion opened was what effect, if any, political verse had in contributing to the downfall of James II. The issues which led to the Revolution of 1688 had been alive in the 1660s. The Protestant, liberty-loving subjects of Charles had been alerted to the dangers of "Popery and arbitrary government" for many years, partly through the agency of surreptitiously distributed satires. What made them revolt against James was not so much a change in royal policy on the questions of religion and prerogative as it was the crystallization in James of tendencies long associated with both the brothers.

For twenty-five years before the Revolution the satirists had driven home again and again the dangers inherent in the authoritarian and Catholic proclivities of Charles and his brother. In 1688, then, the public had only to learn of a long-feared plot for their forced conversion to rise against James. Feeling against their Catholic ruler and his mercenary Irish soldiers found its most popular expression in Lord Wharton's famous ballad, *Lilliburlero,* which was directed, oddly enough, not against James, as almost everyone supposed, but against Lord Talbot.

The influence of *Lilliburlero* cannot, of course, be measured, but it seems to have provided James's outraged subjects with an intoxicating distillate of the rebellious feelings which had found expression in thousands of satirical songs and poems over the years. Its popularity must have been largely due to the catchy tune Purcell composed for it. Bishop Percy went so far as to say that *Lilliburlero* "had once a more powerful effect than either the Philippics of Demosthenes or Cicero, and contributed not a little towards the great revolution of 1688."[29] Macaulay, on the other hand, regarded it as "the effect and not the cause of that excited state of public feeling which produced the

Revolution."[30] David Hume was probably nearer the truth in saying that it "both discovered and served to increase the general discontent of the kingdom."[31] Here is Wharton's devastating trifle:

> Ho, brother Teague, dost hear de decree,
>   Lilli burlero, bullen a-la;
> Dat we shall have a new debittie,
>   Lilli burelero, bullen a-la;
>   Lero lero, lero lero, lilli burlero, bullen a-la.
>
> Ho, by my shoul, it is a Talbot,
> And he will cut de Englishman's troat.
>
> Though, by my shoul, de English do prat,
> De law's on dare side, and Chreist knows what.
>
> But if dispense do come from de pope,
> Weel hang Magno Cart and demselves on a rope.
>
> And the good Talbot is made a lord,
> And he with brave lads is coming aboard.
>
> Who'll all in France have taken a swear,
> Dat day will have no Protestant heir.
>
> Oh, but why does he stay behind?
> Ho, by my shoul, 'tis a Protestant wind.
>
> Now Tyrconnel is come a-shore,
> And we shall have commissions gillore.
>
> And he dat will not go to mass
> Shall turn out and look like an ass.
>
> Now, now, de heretics all go down,
> By Chreist and St. Patrick, the nation's our own![32]

As we have seen, *Poems on Affairs of State* are concerned in detail with the issues of the period. Judged as literature, topical satire so deeply embedded in historical fact seems to suffer from a double disability. In the first place, satire has often been granted only a grudging and precarious status as a literary genre. In the second, satire directed at ephemeral issues and persons seems above all to lack the autonomy or universality of true poetry.

If satire has suffered as a literary genre, the satirist has often been to blame for this neglect. For the satirist often disavows the art and pretends to give only a factual account of things as they are. In taking satire literally, we all too often accept this pretense and confine ourselves to the historical circumstances of the work. Thus, as one writer has put it, "Satire is denied the independence of artistic status and made a biographical and historical document, while the criticism of satire degenerates into discussion of an author's moral character and the economic and social conditions of his time."[33] Lytton

Strachey's view of Pope's satires as boiling oil ladled out by an ape is typical of this approach.[34]

In our own time satire has begun to receive serious critical attention as literature. Northrop Frye has considered it as one of four basic literary "myths."[35] Mary Claire Randolph and Maynard Mack have explored in different ways the arts which the satirist pretends not to use.[36] Alvin Kernan and Robert C. Elliott have greatly advanced our understanding of satires as literary artifacts,[37] and several excellent critical studies have helped to rescue the Augustan satirists from an exclusively historical, biographical, or cultural approach.

As a consequence we are less inclined than former ages to treat satire only as a social document. This is especially true of the more obviously fictional satires in which the relation of the author to his characters or subject is remote, oblique, or impersonal. Menippean satire, which emphasizes the scene rather than the satirist, is perhaps more readily accepted as literature than is formal satire in which the satirist plays a prominent part. Maynard Mack has shown, however, that even in those satires where Pope seems to speak in propria persona he in fact employs a variety of satiric masks. We should be alert, therefore, to the differences between the real author and the identities he assumes.

The richest satire, as the example of the Augustans reminds us, is that which transmutes concrete historical realities into universals. Its fictions include but transcend historical fact. It employs freely any of the means by which poetry is made from the passing shows of our experience, but it has recourse most frequently to a series of techniques which, though not necessarily peculiar to it, the great satirists have made their own. For convenience these may be categorized as the satirical persona, the satirical butt, the audience for whom the satire is written, the scene, and the action. The satirical persona includes such popular types as "the scourge of villainy," the naïf, the honest man, the cynic, and the patriot. He may be identified by the author's name, or by a pseudonym, or he may be nameless. The butt has a corresponding range of identities: the various types of folly, greed, and vice under the names of living persons, or in the guise of historical or legendary figures. The audience addressed is usually more shadowy than the two principals. Sometimes, of course, as in the simpler kinds of lampoon, it is the butt himself. Sometimes it is the sober, hardheaded adversarius, like Pope's Arbuthnot. Usually, it is not identified specifically, but its character is implied by the assumed identity of the satirist and the nature of the appeals and arguments used. In some cases the satirist addresses a figure representing the virtues and values he finds lacking around him: Queen Elizabeth, Sir Walter Raleigh, Shakespeare, Horace, and so forth. Wherever a specific auditor is addressed, we also find ourselves, of course, as members of an audience who are overhearing it all. Scene and action, especially in topical satires like those collected in *Poems on Affairs of State,* are usually contemporary places and events: a debate in the Commons, a council of war aboard the *Royal Charles,* dalliance at Whitehall. Frequently, however, a contemporary event is associated with some historical, biblical, or mythological incident or place: the court of Nero, the trials of David, the loves of Pasiphaë in Cretan legend.

There is corresponding variety in the structural forms employed. The ballad is generically used to produce an effect of ironic naiveté. The satirical song often jars ironically with the associations of the familiar tune to which it is set. Even the mock litany, the crudest and least successful of forms, shows an attempt to be indirect, oblique, and wry. Among the more sophisticated devices are the naive confession, the dialogue, the dream, the vision, the beast fable, and the sessions of the poets. Among the more ambitious and technically complex we find the advice to the painter and the mock epic.

In painter poems the satirist adopts the mask of the patriotic ironist who in turn engages a painter to depict the satirical scene. This strategy serves to heighten the sense of realism, to justify the emphasis on quasi-visual detail, and to make us accept more readily a satiric revelation which does not seem to depend on the satirist's personal attitude toward the material. There are many other ways, of course, for the satirist to feign objectivity, but this is one of the most effective because of the apparent disengagement and because of the authority with which we tend to endow what we seem to be seeing. The arrangement of narrative "instruction" with large tableaux interspersed with sketches or full-length portraits of the principal figures permits a great deal of structural and tonal variety. Occasionally, too, the figures themselves speak, heightening our sense of authenticity. Perhaps the peak of satirical indirection is in Marvell's *Third Advice* where the poet describes the duchess of Albemarle to the painter, who draws such a speaking likeness of her that she begins in fact to speak and delivers a satirical exposé of the administration, at the same time unconsciously revealing her own earthy vulgarity. The rich irony of this is crowned in the solemn envoy to the king by the framing of the Duchess' splenetic diatribe as "Cassandra's song" and by the concluding identification of this erstwhile seamstress with Philomela:

> So Philomel her sad embroid'ry strung,
> And vocal silks tuned with her needle's tongue.
> The picture dumb in colors loud revealed
> The tragedies of court so long concealed
> But when restored to voice, increased with wings,
> To woods and groves, what once she painted, sings.   [451–56]

The tragic vision and the satiric vision are thus potently combined. Such vivid, quasi-pictorial effects are of course not confined to this genre of satire. *Annus Mirabilis* employs such visual details without the painter machinery. As Jean Hagstrum observes, "in order to make us understand, Dryden wanted first to make us see," and, like the painter-poet, gives us "visual images that do not come directly from nature but from the canvases of baroque artists and emblematists."[38] In *Mac Flecknoe* and, above all, in *Absalom and Achitophel,* he brought the pictorial technique to its perfection in satiric modes by bringing together "images that beget admiration" and "images that beget laughter."

In relating Dryden's poetry on public affairs to that of his contemporaries we find, accordingly, new and unexplored areas of significance, both thematic and aesthetic. If we read *Annus Mirabilis* with the painter poems of the 1660s, or *Mac Flecknoe* with the literary satires of the next decade, or *Absalom and Achitophel* with the long series of lampoons on Charles II and Buckingham and Shaftesbury, the phrase "the Age of Dryden" takes on new life and meaning. An aspect of this is suggested by Hagstrum's remark "that in drawing the analogy between painting and satire, Dryden followed the example of Marvell and other seventeenth-century satirists, who had used this parallel frequently enough to make it a convention."[39]

The poetic images of great satire, as I have said, grow out of and supersede historical truth. The duke of Buckingham, fixed for all time as Zimri, sadly acknowledged this principle in his unpublished poem, "To Dryden:"

> As witches images of man invent
> To torture those they're bid to represent,
> And as that true live substance does decay
> Whilst that slight idol melts in flames away,
> Such and no lesser witchcraft wounds my name,
> So thy ill-made resemblance wastes my fame.[40]

In this complaint the duke unwittingly hit upon the primitive origins of satire in witchcraft, which Elliott has described. The satirist's images may bear as little resemblance to the living original as the magician's wax figures, but they can be equally destructive.

Dryden's Zimri is one of those satiric portraits that, like Pope's Sporus, overwhelms by its vividness and life the historical person who served as its model. If we compare Dryden's creation with another sketch of Buckingham from an anonymous Restoration satire, we can see how closely Dryden's technique is related to that practiced by his contemporaries.

On the Prorogation attacks Buckingham for advising Charles to prorogue Parliament in 1671. The satirist adopts the character of a loyal member of Parliament who has faithfully represented the king's interests without reward and, usually, against the dictates of conscience:

> And must we, after all our service done
> In field for father and in House for son,
> Be thus cashier'd to please a pocky peer
> That neither Roundhead is nor Cavalier,
> But of some medley cut, some ill-shap'd brat,
> Would fain be something if he knew but what?
> A commonwealth's man he owns himself to be,

And, by-and-by, for absolute monarchy,
Then neither likes, but, some new knicknacks found,
Nor fish nor flesh, nor square is nor yet round.
Venetian model pleaseth him at night;
Tomorrow, France is only in the right.
Thus, like light butterflies, much flutter makes,
Sleeps of one judgment, of another wakes.
Zealous in morn, he doth a bishop make,
Yet before night all bishops down he'd take.
He all things is, but unto nothing true,
All old things hates, but can abide no new.   [72–89][41]

This passage marks a great advance over the crude personal invectives of the
Commonwealth period. First, it employs the occasion of the prorogation as an
effective dramatic context for the outburst. Second, the satirist's mask as a
Royalist appealing to the king against the king's evil advisor disarms any
suspicion we might have that personal animus motivates the attack. Finally, the
details of the portrait are all integrated with the central animating principle of
the character: his constant inconstancy. The portrait moves through an accumu-
lation of significant incidentals to final enunciation of a general truth in the last
couplet. The apparently random character of the images—Buckingham is a
shapeless piece of cloth, neither fish nor flesh, square nor round, a fluttering
butterfly—is exactly appropriate to the erratic impulses of the character. Even
the rhetorical movement and rhythm are responsive to the tone and meaning,
most obviously in the lines,

Thus, like butterflies, much flutter makes,
Sleeps of one judgment, of another wakes.   [84–85]

This portrait of Buckingham has the autonomous poetic life of true satire.

I think it very likely that Dryden had seen this passage, because his
portrait shares with it central conceptions and techniques. But regardless of
this possibility, the important point is that the anonymous passage exemplifies the formal and stylistic features by which satire can transmute history
into poetry. Dryden's lines are more concentrated and fluent, but they are of
the same creative kind:

A man so various that he seemed to be
Not one, but all mankind's epitome.
Stiff in opinions, always in the wrong;
Was everything by starts and nothing long:
But, in the course of one revolving moon,
Was chemist, fiddler, statesman, and buffoon:
Then all for women, painting, rhyming, drinking;
Besides ten thousand freaks that died in thinking.
Blest madman, who could every hour employ
With something new to wish, or to enjoy!   [545–54]

There is no need to multiply examples from the almost unknown works of minor Augustan satirists. Many such pieces fail to transmute history into poetry. On the other hand, here and there a passage, or sometimes a whole poem, will be touched by the true satiric art into poetry. In episode, description, or characterization, the critical question remains the same: has the satirist succeeded, by masks, indirections, ironies, and myths, in freeing the poem from the trammels of historical circumstance and in bestowing upon it the poetic autonomy of true satire? In a thousand unknown examples, in a bewildering array of formal and satirical devices, we can find topical verse struggling toward the condition of an art which the great Augustans, profiting by these examples, brought to perfection.

Indiscriminate hyperbole in the grand style defeats itself and gives birth to mock-heroic. So Waller's *Instructions to a Painter,* with its blithe disregard for the naval miscarriages in the Battle of Solebay and the administrative failures that contributed to it, was an irresistible target for a mock-heroic revisioning of the events that led up to the duke of York's failure to seize a victory over the retreating Dutch. Waller's soft focus, otiose similes, and heroic clichés almost inevitably invited a factual and detailed account of what really happened. Marvell, in the *Second Advice to a Painter,* shattered Waller's servile panegyric, which was intended to restore the time-serving poet of the Commonwealth to the graces of Charles II and his brother. Marvell opens with a reexamination of the painter genre which Waller had borrowed from Francesco Busenello's poem celebrating a Venetian naval victory over the Turks near Crete:

> Nay, Painter, if thou dar'st design that fight
> Which Waller only courage had to write,
> If thy bold hand can, without shaking, draw
> What e'en the actors trembled when they saw
> (Enough to make thy colors change like theirs
> And all thy pencils bristle like their hairs)
> First, in fit distance of the prospect main,
> Paint Allin tilting at the coast of Spain:
> Heroic act, and never heard till now,
> Stemming of Herc'les' Pillars with his prow!
> And how two ships he left the hills to waft,
> And with new sea-marks Dover and Calais graft.   [1–12][42]

A squadron led by Sir Thomas Allin had attacked Dutch merchantmen before war was declared, and two of its ships had run aground. Needless to say, Waller had not mentioned this embarrassing and unheroic prelude to the Second Dutch War. Marvell goes on to survey instances of corruption in the naval administration (which doubtless contributed to Pepys's heartache when he read the poem) and of ineptitude and cowardice, especially among the gentlemen volunteers, one of whom was implicated in giving orders to quit the pursuit of the retreating Dutch.

Waller had depicted the duchess of York's visit to the fleet at Harwich in romantic terms:

> Spreading our sails, to Harwich we resort,
> And meet the beauties of the English court.
> Th'illustrious duchess and her glorious train
> (Like Thetis with her nymphs) adorn the main.
> The gazing sea-gods, since the Paphian queen
> Sprung from among them, no such sight had seen.   [79–84][43]

Marvell responded with burlesque:

> See where the duchess with triumphant tail
> Of num'rous coaches, Harwich does assail!
> So the land crabs, at Nature's kindly call,
> Down to engender at the sea do crawl.
>
> . . . .
>
> One thrifty ferry-boat of mother-pearl
> Sufficed of old the Cytherean girl;
> Yet navies are but properties, when here
> (A small sea-masque and built to court you, dear)
>
> . . . .
>
> O duchess! If thy nuptial pomp were mean,
> 'Tis paid with int'rest in this naval scene.
> Never did Roman Mark within the Nile
> So feast the fair Egyptian Crocodile,
> Nor the Venetian duke, with such a state,
> The Adriatic marry at that rate.   [55–58; 63–66; 69–74]

The inferences suggested by that lingering "triumphant tail" are wittily developed in the allusion to the duchess's wedding, which was performed in secret because of her advanced pregnancy. As the ambitious daughter of the ambitious Chancellor Clarendon, Anne Hyde was one of Marvell's favorite satiric targets.

Three court friends of the duke had been killed standing near him, and Waller had seized the opportunity for outrageous hyperbole:

> Happy! to whom this glorious death arrives,
> More to be valued than a thousand lives!
> On such a theatre as this to die,
> For such a cause, and such a witness by!
> Who would not thus a sacrifice be made
> To have his blood on such an altar laid?   [149–54]

Marvell countered this tasteless nonsense with a biting, if equally tasteless, account of the death of the earl of Falmouth:

> Falmouth was there (I know not what to act—
> Some say 'twas to grow duke, too, by contact);
> An untaught bullet in its wanton scope
> Quashes him all to pieces and his hope.
> Such as his rise such was his fall, unpraised:
> A chance shot sooner took than chance him raised.
> His shattered head the fearless duke distains
> And gave the last-first proof that he had brains.   [181–88]

Against this unfortunate courtier Marvell commemorates two distinguished professional captains who also died in the battle: "Lawson, whose valor beyond fate did go / And still fights Opdam in the lakes below," and Marlborough ("None more prepared was or less fit to die"). Nor does Marvell succumb to Waller's treatment of the battle as a baroque spectacle when he directs his painter to "draw the battle terribler to show / Than the Last Judgment was of Angelo" (111–12). Marvell's attention, unlike Waller's soft focus, fixes on "the noise, the smoke, the sweat, the fire, the blood." In contrast to this horror he exposes the greed which led Sandwich, commander-in-chief, to expropriate booty that should have been distributed through the court of prizes, an offense whose consequences he escaped by his abrupt appointment as ambassador to Spain.

After a survey of the futility of the war, Marvell ends his poem, as Waller does, with an address to the king. Picking up Waller's facile allusion to England as a new Crete where a new Zeus is born, Marvell turns the reference into an attack on Clarendon, "If thou art Minos, be a judge severe / And in's own maze confine the engineer" (355–56). Thus Waller is reversed.

The *Third Advice to a Painter* addresses itself to naval maneuvers in the Four Days' Fight of 1666. With Sandwich safe in Spain, the command of the fleet had been invested jointly in Prince Rupert, an aging Cavalier hero, and the redoubtable Albemarle. Marvell opens this poem with a search for an appropriate painter. Lely's a Dutchman and "may intelligence impart," so he turns to the miniaturist Gibson, whose tiny paintings might be appropriate to "drawing in little, how we do yet less." The division of command, hailed derisively in "United Gen'rals! sure the only spell / Wherewith United Provinces to quell," establishes a motif of bifurcation which Marvell exploits in the decision to divide the fleet and send Rupert off in pursuit of French forces wrongly reported to be in the Channel. He speculates that the intelligence may have been contrived by Albemarle's foes in the government. Albemarle, unaware of this duplicity, attacks the superior Dutch force but is beset by "chained dilemmas through our sinewy shrouds." Finding " 'twas now in vain to fight," he "imps his plumes the best he may for flight." Rupert shows up in time to avert disaster, and with the lucky help of fog, the British manage to escape: "Old Homer yet did never introduce, / To save his heroes, mist of better use." The rescue of the beleaguered Aeneas in the *Iliad* provides

Marvell with the perfect context for an indecisive engagement falsely represented as a victory:

> Now joyful fires and the exalted bell
> And court gazettes our empty triumph tell.
> Alas, the time draws near when overturned
> The lying bells shall through the tongue be burned;
> Paper shall want to print that lie of state,
> And our false fires true fires shall expiate.   [163–68]

In place of these congratulatory media, Marvell finds a spokesman and artist who can tell the truth. In employing as his artist Albemarle's duchess, a plain-spoken seamstress, Marvell instructs his painter, "Paint thou but her, and she will paint the rest." Thus freed from the constraints of the advice-to-a-painter mode, Marvell, through the duchess, indicts the government for malfeasance and nonfeasance. "Arraigning past, and present, and *futuri*," this "Presbyterian sibyl," after a detailed account of corruption and oversight, urges her husband to attend to the practical needs of the navy:

> 'Tis true, I want so long the nuptial gift,
> But (as I oft have done) I'll make a shift,
> Nor with vain pomp will I accost the shore,
> To try thy valor at the Buoy of th' Nore.
> Fall to thy work there, George, as I do here:
> Cherish the valiant up, cowards cashier,
> See that the men have pay and beef and beer.
>
> . . . .
>
> See that thou hast new sails thyself and spoil
> All their sea market and their cable-coil.
> Tell the king all, how him they countermine;
> Trust not, till done, him with thy own design.
> Look that good chaplains on each ship do wait,
> Nor the sea diocese be impropriate.
> Look to thy pris'ners, sick, and wounded: all
> Is prize; they rob even the hospital.
> Recover back the prizes, too: in vain
> We fight, if all be taken that is ta'en.   [321–28; 337–46]

Such practical advice about coping with the real needs of the navy can be certified from Pepys, who, as a commissioner, was constantly frustrated by difficulties in paying and properly victualing his seamen and especially incensed by the misdeeds of his patron, Sandwich: "The great evil of this year and the only one ended is the fall of My Lord of Sandwich whose mistake about the Prizes hath undone him, I believe, as to his interest at Court" (6 December 1665). When her beleaguered husband is recalled to help cope with the disastrous Fire of London, the duchess sums up the ruinous year 1666:

> "Woe's me! what see I next? Alas, the fate
> I see of England and its utmost date!
> Those flames of theirs at which we fondly smile,
> Kindled like torches our sepulchral pile.
> War, fire and plague against us all conspire;
> We the war, God the plague, who raised the fire?
> See how men all like ghosts, while London burns,
> Wander and each over his ashes mourns!
> Dear George, sad fate, vain mind, that me didst please
> To meet thine with far other flames than these!
> Cursed be the man that first begat this war,
> In an ill hour, under a blazing star.
> For others' sport two nations fight a prize;
> Between them both religion wounded lies.
> So of first Troy the angry gods unpaid
> Razed the foundations which themselves had laid.   [413–28]

In lines to the king she urges him to hear her "Cassandra's song ere Fate destroy, / By thy own navy's wooden horse, thy *Troy*" (447–48).

Marvell ends the *Third Advice,* as we have seen, with lines that match in their intricacy and lyric power anything that he wrote:

> So Philomel her sad embroid'ry strung,
> And vocal silks tuned with her needle's tongue.
> The picture dumb in colors loud revealed
> The tragedies of court so long concealed
> But when restored to voice, increased with wings,
> To woods and groves, what once she painted, sings.   [451–56]

Through her passionate commitment to the truth the "monkey duchess" has been apotheosized into an eloquent figure who is the authentic voice of tragedy and truth. The advice-to-the-painter convention was never used with more sublimity and force than in this haunting metamorphosis.

Dryden could not have failed to see this poem while he was composing a heroic vindication of Charles II and his regime. In *Annus Mirabilis, the Year of Wonders, 1666,* he treated plague and fire as heavenly visitations brought on the nation by the guilt of Dissenters and presented the king and the duke of York as heroic princes in the tradition of Aeneas. The poem is dedicated to the duchess in a fulsome Walleresque panegyric. In its masterful adaptation of Davenant's *Gondibert* stanza it achieves a gravely poignant mood, especially in describing the situation where both Rupert and the Dutch are disabled:

> The warlike Prince had severed from the rest
>   Two giant ships, the pride of all the main;
> Which, with his one, so vigorously he pressed
>   And flew so home they could not rise again.

Already battered, by his lee they lay,
    In vain upon the passing winds they call;
The passing winds through their torn canvas play,
    And flagging sails on heartless sailors fall.

Their opened sides receive a gloomy light,
    Dreadful as day let in on shades below;
Without, grim death rides bare-faced in their sight,
    And urges ent'ring billows as they flow.

When one dire shot, the last they could supply,
    Close by the board the Prince's main-mast bore.
All three, now helpless, by each other lie,
    And this offends not, and those fear no more.

So have I seen some fearful hare maintain
    A course till tired before the dog she lay;
Who, stretched behind her, pants upon the plain,
    Past pow'r to kill as she to get away.

With his lolled tongue he faintly licks his prey,
    His warm breath blows her flix up as she lies;
She, trembling, creeps upon the ground away,
    And looks back on him with beseeching eyes.

The prince unjustly does his stars accuse,
    Which hinder'd him to push his fortune on;
For what they to his courage did refuse,
    By mortal valour never must be done.

This lucky hour the wise Batavian takes,
    And warns his tattered fleet to follow home;
Proud to have so got off with equal stakes,
    Where 'twas a triumph not to be o'ercome.   [505–36]

Though often guilty of an idealizing bias, Dryden here presents fairly—and with a Horatian breadth of view that transcends the partisan—the tragically inconclusive nature of the Four Days' Fight. The closely observed simile is utterly different from the inflationary and unreflective allusions to the natural world with which Waller sprinkles his *Instructions to Painter*.

Annus Mirabilis is nonetheless propaganda. Like most of Dryden's political poems, it draws over real characters and events a network of Virgilian and biblical analogies designed to win our consent to his idealized view of Charles II and his regime. What is left out of *Annus Mirabilis,* faulty intelligence, criminal negligence in communicating with Rupert, lack of supplies, and widespread corruption in the naval administration (from which even Pepys benefited), must be suppressed because subversive of Dryden's heroic intent.

Marvell's *Last Instructions to a Painter* outdoes its predecessors in comprehensiveness and in modulating between instances of the heroic and the anti-heroic. Its opening search for a painterly technique appropriate to its subject is partly determined by an anonymous "Reply to Mr. Waller's Many Advisers" composed after the *Third Advice*. The "Reply" takes particular offense at the low burlesque mode: "I'll tell you where a painter you may find. / Look out some canvas stainer, whose cheap skill / With rhythms and stories alehouse walls doth fill" (94–96). Marvell takes up the suggestion at the beginning of his poem:

> After two sittings, now, our Lady State
> To end her picture, does the third time wait.
> But, ere thou fall'st to work, first, Painter, see
> It ben't too slight grown or too hard for thee.
> Canst thou paint without colours? Then 'tis right:
> For so we too without a fleet can fight.
> Or canst thou daub a sign-post, and that ill?
> 'Twill suit our great debauch and little skill.
> Or hast thou marked how antic masters limn
> The aly-roof with smoke of candle dim,
> Sketching in shady smoke prodigious tools?
> 'Twill serve this race of drunkards, pimps, and fools.   [1–12]

The recalcitrance of the subject to artistic representation leads to the desperate conclusion that frustration and anger can find expression only in action painting, in which chance may finish what art could only begin. The poise achieved at the end of *Third Advice* can no longer be maintained in the face of outrageous evil and folly.

The new technique produces three single-mindedly contemptuous portraits. The earl of St. Albans is depicted as a gross, self-indulgent, credulous oaf. Then Marvell paints the duchess as a sexual virtuoso.

> Paint then again Her Highness to the life,
> Philosopher beyond Newcastle's wife.
> She naked can Arch'mede's self put down,
> For an experiment upon the crown.
> She perfected that engine, oft assayed,
> How, after childbirth to renew a maid,
> And found that royal heirs might be matured
> In fewer months than mothers once endured.
> Hence Crowther made the rare inventress free
> Of's Highness's Royal Society.   [49–58]

Considerable information about the duchess is crammed into this knotty passage. Through an Archimedean experiment in hydrostatics she can prove that she is not a light woman but true gold. No virgin when Crowther performed her marriage to the duke, she can outdo her bluestocking friend, the duchess of Newcastle, by restoring virginity. The gestation period of her royal infants is shorter than normal, which explains why she gave birth to the first so soon after her wedding. Her "experiment upon the crown" reiterates Marvell's reflections on the ambitions of her and her father, Clarendon. A few lines later she is accused of plotting to poison York's mistress, Lady Denham, a claim for which there is no evidence.

The utmost in character assassination is reserved for the king's unfaithful mistress, Barbara Palmer, countess of Castlemaine:

> Paint Castlemaine in colors that will hold
> (Her, not her picture, for she now grows old):
> She through her lackey's drawers, as he ran,
> Discerned love's cause and a new flame began.
> Her wonted joys thenceforth and court she shuns,
> And still within her mind the footman runs:
> His brazen calves, his brawny thighs (the face
> She slights), his feet shaped for a smoother race.
> Poring within her glass she readjusts
> Her looks and oft-tried beauty now distrusts;
> Fears lest he scorn a woman once assayed,
> And now first wished she e'er had been a maid.   [79–90]

The last line in this passage employs the same device used in *Second Advice* where Falmouth's shattered head gives "the last-first proof that he had brains."

Last Instructions is grounded on the aesthetics of the ugly, but the ugly is defined, implicitly and explicitly, by the beautiful. Castlemaine's sordid passion can even transcend itself in the lovely line, "And still within her mind the footman runs." Her lust aspires, briefly, to the ideal. The complex effect of Marvell's description eludes Dryden's categories of heroic images that show nature beautified and burlesque images that show nature diminished. Grace and ugliness, for Marvell, are inherent in the characters and their actions, as in Michelangelo's painting of the Last Judgment.

In contrast to these examples of what Annabel Patterson calls "the impropriety topos" Marvell supplies in his descriptions of loyal but independent members of Parliament a combination of idealism and hardheaded practicality:

> A gross of English gentry, nobly born,
> Of clear estates, and to no faction sworn;
> Dear lovers of their king, and death to meet,
> For country's cause, that glorious think and sweet;
> To speak not forward, but in action brave,
> In giving gen'rous, but in counsel grave;
> Candidly credulous for once, nay twice,
> But sure the devil cannot cheat them thrice.   [287–94]

The allusion to Horace's famous ode—*dulce et decorum est pro patria mori*—reinforces the heroic claims Marvell is making for these noble individuals. The rhetorical and prosodic balance of the couplets emphasizes the discriminating judgment of these patriots in contrast to the headlong and enjambed movement of the lines dealing with the reflexes that govern the vicious humors of self-indulgent and corrupt politicians, as in this character of Clarendon:

> Blither than hare that hath escaped the hounds,
> The House prorogued, the chancellor rebounds.
> Not so decrepit Aeson, hashed and stewed,
> With bitter herbs, rose from the pot renewed,
> And with fresh age felt his glad limbs unite;
> His gout (yet still be cursed) had left him quite.
> What frosts to fruit, what ars'nic to the rat,
> What to fair Denham mortal chocolate,
> What an account to Cart'ret, that, and more,
> A Parliament is to the chancellor. [355–44]

The equipoise in Dryden's poignant simile of the hound and hare immobilized by exhaustion is quite opposite to the exhilaration of the chancellor at the prorogation of Parliament.

In recounting the death of the heroic Douglas, Marvell modulates his style in the direction of baroque panegyric:

> That precious life he yet disdains to save
> Or with known art to try the gentle wave.
> Much him the honors of his ancient race
> Inspire, nor would he his own deeds deface,
> And secret joy in his calm soul does rise
> That Monck looks on to see how Douglas dies.
> Like a glad lover the fierce flames he meets
> And tries his first embraces in their sheets.
> His shape exact, which the bright flames enfold,
> Like the sun's statue stands of burnished gold.
> Round the transparent fire about him glows,
> As the clear amber on the bee does close,
> And, as on angels' heads their glories shine,
> His burning locks adorn his face divine. [671–84]

Douglas's more than human self-sacrifice is heightened by the sensuous and erotic images that, heedless of the realities of such a death, make the scene an emblematic apotheosis in the mode of Virgil's treatment of the death of Euryalus. Like Virgil, Marvell concludes his panegyric with promises of literary immortality:

> Fortunate boy! If either pencil's fame,
> Or if my verse can propagate thy name,
> When Oeta and Alcides are forgot,
> Our English youth shall sing the valiant Scot. [693–96]

In keeping with the decorum of the genre, Marvell asserts the possibility of pictorial immortality.

The stylistic versatility of the *Last Instructions to a Painter* continues the technical variety of the preceding poems, in marked contrast to the unreflecting hyperbole of Waller's original poem. It is also quite different from the irresponsible, fanciful virtuosity of *Upon Appleton House,* and it may be a reason for the frequent critical claim that the *Last Instructions* lacks unity.

THE CASE OF JOHN AYLOFFE

Perhaps no period in England's history has produced so much secret and violent political activity as the two decades which preceded the Revolution of 1688. When Charles II's leanings toward Catholicism and arbitrary power began to emerge through his devious negotiations with France in the 1670s, the champions and pretended champions of the Protestant cause and English liberties began to supplement parliamentary opposition with various clandestine activities which emerged as the Popish Plot, the Rye-House Plot, Monmouth's Rebellion, and the Revolution itself. As one might expect, the cause engaged both high-minded republicans like Sidney and treacherous self-seekers like Lord Howard of Escrick in schemes ranging from the brutal and shortsighted to the heroic and visionary.

The ambivalent character of the Whig cause is well represented by the elusive figure of John Ayloffe, whose deep involvement in the political events of the period contrasts strongly with the obscurity in which historians have allowed him to remain. Aside from a brief entry in the *Dictionary of National Biography* (supplemented by important additions and corrections),[44] the only generally available account of Ayloffe's career is a page or so in Macaulay: "Though political sympathy had drawn him toward the Puritans, he had no religious sympathy with them, and was indeed regarded by them as little better than an atheist. He belonged to that section of the Whigs which sought for models rather among the patriots of Greece and Rome than among the prophets and judges of Israel."[45] No doubt Macaulay was correct in regarding Ayloffe as a classical republican, for, like Harrington or Russell or Sidney, he looked to Venice or to ancient Rome rather than to Israel for his inspiration. A close examination of Ayloffe's astonishingly diverse career makes one wonder, however, whether he is faithfully represented as such a lofty and idealistic Whig champion. In the service of noble ends Ayloffe often resorted to devious and violent means of which a Harrington or a Sidney would not have approved, while distinguishing himself from other violent and devious, but unreliable, partisans by his unremitting devotion to the cause.

In spite of Ayloffe's high connections and his flamboyant career, obscurity continues to surround his personality, even after a full examination of what turns out to be a quite well-documented life. Occasionally one catches a glimpse, in some witty, impudent, or defiant word or act, of a passionate nature which Ayloffe must have labored to conceal. The terse comments of Ayloffe's connections such as Christopher Hatton or the Hydes that he was "distracted" (mad) makes the riddle of his character all the more teasing, especially if one reflects that his political career from beginning to end was thoroughly representative of the radical segment among the Whigs and that he was a trusted associate of both Shaftesbury and Marvell.

Ayloffe, the son of John Ayloffe, was born in Foxley, Wiltshire, about 1645. His aunt, Anne Ayliffe or Ayloffe (the name appears in a variety of forms), had become in 1629 the first wife of Edward Hyde, the future earl of Clarendon, who long afterward spoke of the poet's father as one "whom he dearly loved."[46] Ayloffe matriculated at St. Edmund Hall, Oxford, in July 1662 and entered the Inner Temple, before the gates of which he was finally executed, in 1664. Of his subsequent legal career we know nothing for certain, although he may be the Ayloffe who represented Skinner in the famous case against the East India Company in 1667.

The next we hear of John Ayloffe is the wooden shoe episode which created such a stir. The following is Charles Hatton's account:

October 28, 1673

Monday last the Parliament met, and, as soon as the door of the House of Commons was open, a kinsman of ours, John Ayliff (as is reported), rushed in and went up to the Speaker's chair; and the woman which kept the door seeing him fling something under it, imagining it had been a fireball, cried out, "Treason! treason!" whereupon the doorkeepers came and apprehended him with a sabot the king of England's arms blazoned and "utrum" writ under, and on the right side the king of France's arms and "horum" under written. They kept our kinsman prisoner, till some of the members came who knew him; and they told the doorkeepers he was distracted, and bid them let him go. You cannot imagine how much this sabot is talked on, and what infinite number of people go to see it.[47]

Seven years later Henry Hyde, second earl of Clarendon, son of the first earl by his second wife, writes about "Mr. Jo. Ayloffe, who about seven years since put a wooden shoe and a chaplet in the Speaker's chair and had been roughly handled for it, but that Sir Jo. Morton at my request excused him as a person distracted." Here history seems to repeat itself, for twenty years earlier we find the first earl supporting "the petition of Mr. Ayliff, in behalf of his mother, for mediation with her creditors" and testifying "that the lady is a person of quality, and one to whom he is much indebted, and that the debts were incurred chiefly during her lunacy; therefore he desires to get her out of prison, and put her into the hands of her son." It is noteworthy that both John Ayloffe and a woman who was possibly his mother (at any rate a relative) should have been regarded as lunatics by the Hydes.

Despite the friendly intervention of Hatton and Clarendon, Ayloffe eventually suffered exile as a partial consequence of the wooden shoe incident. Among the papers of the marquis of Bath is an item described as follows: "Original petition to the king by John Ayloffe who stands charged with placing The Appeal and The Votes of Parliament in the Speaker's chair for which he has suffered two years' exile.—Asks pardon" (HMCR, IV: 235). The Votes of Parliament has not survived, but The Appeal is unquestionably the enormously effective pamphlet attacking English foreign policy composed in Holland and first circulated in London in March 1673, the full title being England's Appeal from the Private Cabal at Whitehall to the Great Council of the Nation, the Lords and Commons in Parliament Assembled. In identifying the French alliance with widespread fears of popery at home, the Appeal succeeded in arousing in Parliament an opposition so powerful as to force Charles to make peace with Holland. This was the masterstroke of the propaganda "fifth column" directed by Peter Du Moulin, William of Orange's secretary, in which Ayloffe and Marvell played vital parts. No doubt his work in helping to print the *Appeal* was far more influential than the emblem of the wooden shoe, but they both carried the same message.

Although Ayloffe petitioned for pardon, exile had not made him penitent. In June 1674, according to the code deciphered by K. H. D. Haley,[48] he was active in the Du Moulin underground, presumably taking advantage of his exile in Holland to work at its headquarters. While helping to smuggle propaganda into England, he was also producing verse satires attacking the government, the king, the Stuart dynasty, and monarchy in general. Evidence now makes it possible to assign to him one of the most significant verse satires of the period—*Britannia and Raleigh,* sometimes attributed to Marvell,[49] and this attribution facilitates his identification by internal evidence as author of a number of other important pieces. It now appears that this obscure and shadowy figure deserves a place among leading Restoration political satirists.

Ayloffe finally paid with his life for his involvement in the disastrous rebellion of Monmouth and Argyle, although it seemed that he might be saved once more by friends in power: "Col. Ailiffe is civilly used upon my Lord Dumbarton's acquaintance and is thought may be saved upon his Lordship's intercession. Rombolt the malster, his head and quarters are boxed up for England by order from Court after they were set up here. Argyle's head is upon the west end of the Tolbooth, and all his arms and ammunition put in the castle" (*HMCR,* VII: 379). After grievously wounding himself in an attempt at suicide, Ayloffe was sent to London to be examined. Fox speculates that "his relationship to the King's first wife might perhaps be one inducement to this measure, or it might be thought more expedient that he should be executed for the Rye-House Plot . . . than for his recent acts of rebellion in Scotland."[50] Several sources describe an interview in which King James, in offering a pardon in return for information, is supposed to have remarked, "You had better be frank with me, Mr. Ayloffe. You know that it is in my power to pardon you." To this Ayloffe supposedly replied, "It may be in your power, but it is not in your nature." As Fox remarks, it is "one of those anecdotes which is believed rather on account of the air of nature that belongs to them, than upon any very good traditional authority" (p. 227). It is hardly conceivable that Ayloffe could have expected any clemency from the monarch he had so long and so persistently labored to destroy.

In any event, he did not escape again, but met his death under the old sentence of outlawry on October 30, 1685, upon a scaffold erected before the Temple gate. Richard Nelthorpe, a close friend and fellow rebel and a relation of Marvell's, died the same day.[51]

The chief document in an attempt to establish a canon of Ayloffe's verse satires is the copy of Marvell's *Miscellaneous Poems* to which a large manuscript section has been added. This item is Bodleian MS. Eng. poet. d.49, a description of which is given in Margoliouth's second edition of *Marvell's Poems and Letters* (1951). This text supplies Marvell's three poems on Oliver Cromwell, which were cancelled in all but one known copy of the *Miscellaneous Poems* (1681), and a large number of verse satires attacking the government of Charles II between 1666 and about 1676. As Margoliouth explains, the manuscript additions to the printed text were probably prepared after Marvell's death under the direction of his nephew, William Popple, with a view to publishing a complete collection of his lyric and satirical poetry.

This collection fell into the hands of Edward Thompson (a descendant, no doubt, of Marvell's correspondent and relative of that name) as he was completing his three-volume edition of Marvell in 1775. Thompson mentions it in his preface, and there are some important marginalia in his hand in the manuscript portion of the Marvell collection. For our purposes the most significant of these are the attribution of two satires sometimes regarded as Marvell's to "Mr. Ayloffe": *Advice to a Painter to Draw the Duke By* and *Britannia and Raleigh*. There is no way of knowing why Thompson ascribed these poems to Ayloffe, although internal evidence, as we shall see, suggests very strongly that they are not Marvell's.

The *Advice to a Painter to Draw the Duke By* (1673) employs the convention of the poet's instructing a painter to depict various individuals and scenes, which Marvell employed so skillfully in *Last Instructions to a Painter*, but, unlike its predecessor, its use of the convention is entirely perfunctory and unimaginative. In 1679, when the poem reappeared as a broadside, Henry Savile wrote a letter to Halifax encouraging him not to worry that the broadside "will have any effect to the prejudice of those you are concerned for." The piece is clearly not by Marvell, but there seems little reason to share Margoliouth's conjectural attribution to Savile.

The *Advice* is a saturnine personal attack on the duke of York as a bloody and besotted tyrant surrounded by counselors who are popish cutthroats. The characterization is wooden. York is made to say,

> Shall these men dare to contradict my will
> And think a prince o'th' blood can e'er do ill?
> It is our birthright to have power to kill.[52]   [25–27]

Everything is described with melodramatic exaggeration. York and Clifford, "the mad Cethegus of the age,"

>   had each too great a mind
> To be by justice or by law confin'd.
> Their boiling heads can hear no other sounds
> Than fleets and armies, battles, blood, and wounds.   [61–64]

There is no trace of Marvell's characteristic wit.

Britannia and Raleigh strikes exactly the same strident, humorless note in describing James:

> When she had spoke a confus'd murmur rose
> Of French, Scotch, Irish, all my mortal foes;
> Some English, too, disguis'd (oh shame!) I spi'd,
> Led up by the wise son-in-law of Hyde.
> With fury drunk, like Bacchanals, they roar,
> "Down with that common Magna Charta whore!"   [105–10]

A personification of French tyranny is described as recommending to Charles the same kind of brutal violence attributed to James in the other poem:

> Bribe hungry priests to deify your might,
> To teach your will's the only rule of right,
> And sound damnation to those dare deny't.   [85–87]

Britannia finally abandons her attempts to defend Charles and concedes that the Stuart dynasty is innately corrupted by tyrannical ambition:

> Raleigh, no more; too long in vain I've tri'd
> The Stuart from the tryant to divide.
>
> . . . .
>
> If this imperial oil once taint the blood,
> It's by no potent antidote withstood.
> Tyrants, like lep'rous kings, for public weal
> Must be immur'd, lest their contagion steal
> Over the whole. Th'elect of Jessean line
> To this firm law their scepter did resign.
> And shall this stinking Scottish brood evade
> Eternal laws, by God for mankind made?   [141–42; 147–54]

In abandoning the Stuarts she abandons monarchy also, turning to the republicanism represented by "the serene Venetian state." Z. S. Fink emphasizes *Britannia and Raleigh's* "truly Harringtonian vision" and observes that the poem's "mere existence is striking evidence of the revival of classical republicanism, at least as an ideal, in the 1670's."[53] An attempt is also made to give the satire a historical perspective by introducing various Roman tyrants and heroes (Tarquin and Publicola), just as Ayloffe's *Advice* compares Lord Clifford to Cethegus, and *Marvell's Ghost*[54] compares the Stuarts to Nero and Tarquin.

The *Advice* was written in 1673 or thereabouts and *Britannia and Raleigh* about a year later. If we turn to other satires of this period which can be attributed with some confidence to Marvell, such as *Upon His Majesty's Being Made Free of the City, On the Statue Erected by Sir Robert Viner,* and *The Statue at Charing Cross,* we find a wholly different satirical tone and technique. Their treatment of Charles and James is humorous and rueful, but not bitter, and they are neither anti-Stuart, antimonarchical, nor republican. They are marked by irony and ridicule but not by hatred. Charles is "the mimic so legally seiz'd of Whitehall" and we are told that if James becomes king "The whole nation may chance to repent it." A witty balance is maintained quite unlike the vehemence which informs the other poems, with their portentous allusions to Roman history.

In *Marvell's Ghost,* which was printed as Ayloffe's after his death (an ascription there is no reason to question), we find the same earmarks of style and content that appear in the *Advice* and *Britannia and Raleigh.* The tone is undeviatingly somber. The ghost of the patriot Marvell accuses Charles and James of villainies that "would make the son of Claudius smile," and the Stuarts are described as a "spurious race . . . design'd for Britain's over-throw." Britain is doomed unless

> she to those resentments come
> That drove the Tarquins out of Rome,
> Or such as did in fury turn
> Th'Assyrian's palace to his urn.   [43–47]

These characteristics are also found in Ayloffe's little-known tribute to a fellow conspirator, Sir Thomas Armstrong, who was hanged in 1684 for his part in the Rye-House Plot. Armstrong, said to be related by marriage to Clarendon, was perhaps a kinsman by marriage to Ayloffe.[55] The poem appears in B.M. Add. MS. 1094, and its circumstantial ascription is convincing: "By Mr. Ayliff who was hang'd at Temple Bar Octbr 30 1685." Again Ayloffe attributes to the Stuarts insatiable and Neronian malignancy:

> His carcass [Armstrong's] stands a monument to all,
> Till the whole progeny a victim fall,
> And like their father tread the stage (which some
> In a blasphemous strain call martyrdom).
> For they in guilt transcendently excell
> All that e'er poets or historians tell.
> To act fresh murders and with flames devour
> Is but the recreation of their power,
> And they alone are for destruction chose
> That either Rome or tyranny oppose.
> Tarquin and Nero were but types of these,
> In whom all crimes are in their last degrees,
> Swelling like Nile in a prodigious flood
> Of execrable villainy and blood.

The recollection of Marvell's description of Charles I's death in this context ("He nothing common did or mean / Upon that memorable scene") points to one fundamental difference in outlook and sensibility between him and Ayloffe.

Another piece that has been attributed to Marvell on the basis of unreliable printed texts shows the same signs of Ayloffe's attitude and manner. *Nostradamus' Prophecy* (1672), like most of the other pieces under discussion, employs a visionary framework to expose the corruption and degeneracy of king and court. Charles is again described as a tyrant assiduously modeling himself on foreign patterns:

> When the English Prince shall Englishmen despise
> And think French only loyal, Irish wise;
> Then wooden shoes shall be the English wear,
> And Magna Charta shall no more appear;
> Then th' English shall a greater tyrant know
> Than either Greek or Gallic stories show.   [37–42]

The passage foreshadows Ayloffe's placing the wooden shoe under the Speaker's chair, an event which occurred shortly after the poem was written. From the tyranny thus symbolized the satirist turns to "wish in vain Venetian liberty," thus striking the note on which *Britannia and Raleigh* concludes.

Oceana and Britannia is a sequel to *Britannia and Raleigh.* In the first poem Britannia relates her efforts to reform Charles II and to maintain her loyalty to the Stuart line, then describes the monstrous actions of Charles and his brother which had driven her reluctantly to espouse a republic on the Venetian model. In the second poem she heralds the imminent establishment of such a republic, which Oceana describes in specifically Harringtonian terms ("Propose, resolve, agrarian, Forty-One"), after the Stuarts have been indicted as worse than Roman tyrants.

Perhaps the chief conclusion to be drawn from John Ayloffe's life and works is the striking mixture of republican idealism and political extremism one finds in both, a mixture which made possible his intimate association with the most reckless and violent members of the Whig opposition and with the most thoughtful and high-principled as well. Probably no other figure of that turbulent era reveals such a close connection between abstract political theory and ruthless political action. He was, by his own lights, a dedicated patriot, but one who could resort to chicanery in the defense of his cause; a doctrinaire republican whom probably no actual political settlement could ever have satisfied. Although he died for his pursuit of liberty under a real tyrant, the gallows before Temple Bar seems to have been an inevitable conclusion to such a career in any period. As a satirist he must be distinguished sharply from those like Marvell and Dryden (both moderates in their own ways) whose viewpoints were based on some kind of reasonable consensus of ideas and aims. Ayloffe's satirical viewpoint was uncomprisingly individualistic.

 CHAPTER SIX

Dryden, the New Virgil

Despite the serious personal risks entailed by Marvell's political activity in the 1670s, he published witty and incisive prose attacks on political and ecclesiastical tyranny. *The Rehearsal Transprosed* (1672), a defense of freedom of conscience, won the admiration of Charles II himself. In it Marvell attacks ecclesiastical tyranny in the form of Samuel Parker, a former Puritan and friend of Milton, but now the Archdeacon of Canterbury and an eager proponent of religious persecution to compel uniformity. To write against such a man in support of religious toleration in 1672 was a dangerous matter, and the risk was greatly increased when Marvell, accused of hiding himself in anonymity, boldly printed his name to the "Second Part" with the following legend on the title page:

Occasioned by Two Letters: The first Printed, by a nameless Author, Intituled, A Reproof, &c.
    The Second Letter left for me at a Friends House, Dated Nov. 3, 1673. Subscribed J.G. and concluding with these words; If thou darest to print or Publish any Lie or Libel against Doctor Parker, by the Eternal God I will cut thy Throat![1]

Marvell's witty strategies, which exemplify the workings of a highly intelligent and independent mind, were to win from Jonathan Swift outspoken admiration as well as the flattery of imitation in *A Tale of a Tub*.
    Marvell's title was a slap at Dryden, who had been attacked earlier as the eccentric dramatist Bayes in the Duke of Buckingham's enormously successful farce *The Rehearsal*. In his commendatory poem for the second edition of *Paradise Lost* (1674) praising the freedom of Milton's blank verse as against the trivializing rhymes of Dryden's operatic version, Marvell gave another twist to the knife:

> Well mightst thou scorn thy Readers to allure
> With tinkling Rhime, of thy own Sense secure;
> While the Town-Bayes writes all the while and spells,
> And like a Pack-Horse tires without his Bells.   [45–48]

In the preface to *Religio Laici* (1682) Dryden replied by calling Marvell "the first Presbyterian scribbler who sanctified libels and scurrility to the use of the good old cause."
    These brief encounters between two leading poets of the age indicate

profound and far-ranging differences in almost every area. Marvell and Dryden were opposites in religion, politics, literary style, and sensibility, and many of the crucial issues of the age are found in what we know or what we can intuit of these oppositions. Since it was an age where religious and political issues were inseparable and exercised a profound influence on the content and even the style of letters, the differences can be seen most succinctly by comparing Marvell's *Last Instructions to a Painter* with Dryden's *Annus Mirabilis* (written in 1667 and 1666, respectively; see Chapter 5), or *The Rehearsal Transprosed* (1672; *Part II,* 1673) with *Religio Laici* (1682). Although Dryden, like Marvell, had served Cromwell and written an elegy upon him, he also, unlike Marvell, had composed a panegyric for Charles II on his Restoration, for which he was often, though unfairly, chided. Dryden's career resembles Marvell's in his adherence to a succession of different political and religious positions, but his underlying motives differed radically from Marvell's. Against Marvell's independence and passionate commitment to individual freedom, Dryden's inherent and cautious conservatism stands out. Yet Dryden's conservatism is not like the conservative elements in Marvell's makeup—a deep attachment to rights more ancient than those asserted by Charles and James—but rather an instinct to preserve the status quo, whatever it might be. For Dryden "innovation {was} the blow of fate," and he constantly sought, through all the shifts and turns of his religious and political career, for institutional authority in church and state and for a conservative consensus to uphold the status quo. Dryden led the reaction against individualistic literature, political liberalism, and personal religion exemplified at its best in Marvell and Milton and at its worst in the rabid political and religious sects and metaphysical eccentricities which plagued English life and letters from the time of the Civil War. In letters, at least, Dryden won the battle by establishing a conservative, tradition-oriented consensus as the norm of the new poetry. Social man became the hero of Restoration poetry and drama. Marvell's solitary contemplative gave way to Dryden's honored kinsman surrounded by political suitors at his country house, and later to Pope in his grot thronged with "chiefs, out of war, and statesmen, out of place." Nothing approaching the scrupulous inwardness of Marvell's lyrics appeared again until the Romantic Revival, although Pope and Collins succeeded in molding a social idiom into the illusion of inwardness, seeking to give relief to a nation which had suffered profoundly from war, plague, fire, and civil dissension. Dryden prescribed balms and lenitives for the health of the troubled nation; Marvell, corrosives and abstersives. When, fifteen years later, the nation's peace was threatened by the Popish Plot and the ambitions of Shaftesbury and Buckingham and Monmouth, Dryden showed that he had achieved the subtlest and wittiest satirical style yet seen in England. The introductory lines in *Absalom and Achitophel* on the polyphiloprogenitive David act as an effective rejoinder to satirical images of the king (like Marvell's) by combining a loyal regard for him with a witty and tactful acknowledgment of his faults.

When we compare two examples of polemical prose, Dryden's preface to *Religio Laici* and Marvell's *Rehearsal Transprosed,* we find corresponding distinctions. Dryden's prose is that of a spokesman; Marvell's that of an independent-minded individual. Dryden speaks for a consensus of like-minded, levelheaded, witty gentlemen. Marvell, in exercising his own judgment and feelings freely, exemplifies the sturdy individual sticking up for personal rights. Dryden, like many conservatives before and since, fears and despises the individualistic tendencies of religious nonconformity:

While we were Papists, our Holy Father rid us, by pretending authority out of the Scriptures to depose princes; when we shook off his authority, the Sectaries furnish'd themselves with the same weapons; and out of the same magazine, the Bible: so that the Scriptures, which are in themselves the greatest security of governors, as commanding express obedience to them, are now turn'd to their destruction; and never since the Reformation has there wanted a text of their interpreting to authorize a rebel. And 'tis to be noted by the way that the doctrines of king-killing and deposing, which have been taken up only by the worst party of the Papists, the most frontless flatterers of the Pope's authority, have been espous'd, defended, and are still maintain'd by the whole body of Nonconformists and Republicans.[2]

An extraordinary indictment (by implication, of course) of all those who were apprehensive about a Catholic successor to the throne and the arbitrary tendencies of Charles II and his brother! As Marvell had written of another Mr. Bayes, "The Church of England is much oblig'd to Mr. Bayes for having proved that Nonconformity is the sin against the Holy Ghost."

Marvell held a higher opinion of what M. C. Bradbrook and M. G. Lloyd Thomas call "the English capacity to evolve a suitable form of government as if by an instinctive process of self-adjustment":[3]

In all things that are insensible there is nevertheless a natural force always operating to expel and reject whatsoever is contrary to their subsistence. . . . The common People in all places partake so much of Sense and Nature, that, could they be imagined and contrived to be irrational, yet they would ferment and tumultuate at last for their own preservation. Yet neither do they want the use of Reason, and perhaps their aggregated Judgment discerns most truly the Errours of Government, forasmuch as they are the first, to be sure, that smart under them. In this only they come to be short sighted; that though they know the Diseases, they understand not the Remedies; and though good Patients, they are ill Physicians. The Magistrate onely is authorized, qualified and capable to make a just and effectual Reformation, and especially among the Ecclesiasticks.[4]

Marvell did not share Dryden's aristocratic contempt for the average citizen, nor did he share Dryden's perhaps exaggerated respect for authority in political and religious matters. There was no question, however, as to his stand on the rightful authority of the secular power: "Power of the Magistrate does most certainly issue from the Divine Authority. The Obedience due to that Power is by Divine Command; and Subjects are bound both as Men and as

Christians to obey the Magistrate Actively in all things where their Duty to God intercedes not."[5] While Marvell and Dryden in their writings on public issues (and even a layman's faith was a public issue then) shared a deep concern for the welfare of Church and state, while both took positions near the center on these issues, and while both usually tried to advance moderate positions through conciliatory strategies, they were temperamental, philosophical, and spiritual opposites. Stylistically, the distinction between them can be elusive. Dryden's social tone has the voice of a cultivated, witty man of the world advancing arguments which we, who ipso facto are also cultivated, well-bred, and witty, must inevitably accept. Against this wonderfully insinuating style Marvell tends to sound more like an individual speaking to another individual, an effect unquestionably due in part to the independent emphasis of the puritan tradition as against the Anglican emphasis on the catholic and the communal. Dryden's style is normative, Marvell's more idiosyncratic; Dryden's humor is directed at aberrations from what society or certain institutions regard as good, Marvell's at the crushing weight of institutions misemployed to oppress the individuals they are meant to serve. Marvell's style is a witty demonstration of the operations of the free mind: "In the flexibility of his attack, Marvell produced what might roughly be taken as the prose version of the 'metaphysical' style. There is the same synchronization of the important with the trivial, the same free combination of colloquialism and learning, the same variety in the points of view."[6] The free combination of colloquialism and learning is certainly present in Dryden, but it is usually in the service of established authority.

When freedom was jeopardized by a more formidable enemy than Mr. Bayes in Charles II's suspension of parliamentary sessions between 1675 and 1677, Marvell's style became less variable and more somber, as in his last known work, An Account of the Growth of Popery and Arbitrary Government in England (1677). He died the following year, having rejected, according to unauthenticated rumor, an opulent offer from the king. His sudden death brought dark hints of political murder, but he seems to have been a victim only of medical incompetence.

Throughout his career as a political writer Dryden repeatedly used the theme of restoration as his central myth. Beginning with Astraea Redux (1660) we can trace through his writings on public affairs, whether they deal with the Stuart Restoration (the central political event of the age in Dryden's imagination), or the reestablishment of the Church, or the return of justice, or the reformation of poetry, or the rediscovery of historical truths, a remarkable preoccupation with a cosmogonic myth of restoration, recovery, or renewal after exile, defeat, or destruction. Although it assumes a variety of forms, such as Aeneas's flight from Troy and founding of Rome, or the establishment of the Augustan settlement following the Roman civil wars, or David's exile and subsequent victory over the plots of Saul or Absalom, or Christ's triumph over the temptations of Satan, the essential myth is the restoration of royal authority after a period of rebellious disorder.

It follows that no contemporary occasion or event is presented in itself, as a unique historical fact, without some counterpart drawn from the past, from Greek and Roman myth, or from the Bible. In the events of his own times Dryden always saw a recurrence of past events or the repetition of some archetypal pattern. His view of history is inescapably retrospective and cyclical. It dreads anarchy above all things, and, next to anarchy, innovation. The statement of one of our leading contemporary theologians defines perfectly the essence of Dryden's conservative political cosmos:

If . . . we examine the historical movements of political and social renewal, we will find that the "myth of the eternal return" was operative here as well. Ironically enough, all known movements for a new future were initiated under the banner of the category "re." We speak of renaissance, reformation, revolution, of revival, renewal, and restoration, etc. In all these movements men sought not the new of the future but "paradise lost" or the "golden age," the primitive natural condition of man or the original order of things. They sought their future in the past. They connected the renewal of the present with a "dream turned backward."[7]

Of all Dryden's poems, *Absalom and Achitophel* represents most completely and pervasively his lifelong affinity for seeing the present in terms of the past, while his preface to a translation of the *Life of Plutarch* (1685) shows his approach to history as a model for the future. History, he says,

helps us to judge of what will happen, by showing us the like revolutions of former times. For mankind being the same in all ages, agitated by the same passions, and moved to action by the same interests, nothing can come to pass but some precedent of the like nature has already been produced, so that having the causes before our eyes, we cannot easily be deceived in the effects, if we have the judgement enough but to draw the parallel.

In employing the myth of restoration to defend the status quo in Church and state Dryden was combating radical eschatological views derived from the apocalyptic books of the Old and New Testaments—Daniel, Revelation, and the prophecies of Isaiah—as well as from the epistles of St. Paul, which proclaimed the establishment of Christ's kingdom on earth by a unique divine intervention in human history, concluding with the destruction and redemption of the world. This vision is at the center of Christian eschatology. In Dryden's time it found one of its most powerful renderings in book XI of *Paradise Lost*. It also inspired, or was used to justify, many revolutionary political schemes in seventeenth-century England. In the breathing spell which followed the Restoration, Dryden found abundant evidence that political dissidents, by a reckless application of apocalyptic prophecy to contemporary affairs, were a threat to a precariously reestablished order. As a leading defender of and spokesman for this order from 1660 to his death in 1700, he devoted his energies and talents to discrediting political innovation by advanc-

ing the conservative myth of restoration against the radical myth of apocalypse. In 1660 he established the story of the exiled and restored David as a
model for Charles II:

> Thus banish'd David spent abroad his time,
> When to be God's Anointed was his Crime.
>
> [*Astraea Redux,* 79–80]

The identification and Dryden's practice of scanning history for "the like revolution of former times" were uncannily validated in 1681 when the Monmouth-
Shaftesbury conspiracy against Charles provided an obvious counterpart to the
conspiracy of Absalom and Achitophel against David. In what must have
seemed for Dryden a most compelling way, political circumstance provided him
with the fable for his greatest poem.

A more secular restoration motif, the Virgilian theme of the establishment of the peace of Augustus after the Roman civil wars, was interwoven in
the body of Dryden's political verse with the Davidic myth. In adapting this
pattern from history, Dryden cast himself as a new Virgil proclaiming a new
Augustan age of peace and prosperity. The role allowed him to dramatize
himself not only as a spokesman for the restored order and its laureate but as
the presiding genius of a new literary age, which was also a conservative age
bent on imitating the classics.

In all ways the Davidic myth and the Augustan myth, as Dryden employed them, served to dampen political ardor and instill obedience, a lesson
further reinforced in *Absalom and Achitophel* by telling allusions to the temptation and fall of man in *Paradise Lost.* In contrast to the excitements of apocalyptic myth with its prospect of imminent divine intervention, the conservative
myth as Dryden uses it was deliberately quiescent and cool. Apocalyptic riveted
its vision on the immediate future and emphasized the need to act; conservatism
saw the present in the past and urged passive acceptance.

The conservative does not ordinarily entertain large hopes (sometimes,
perhaps, because of having already much of what other people hope for). The
cyclical view of history is threatened by radical change, even if the innovator is
God. When considered alongside the myth of apocalypse, the conservative
myth seems secular in every sense of the word, especially if the religious
element is tempered, as in Dryden, by Augustan motifs. In such a cosmos God
becomes something of an abstraction, a dim coadjutor to the vicegerent king.
This low-keyed, secular quality in *Absalom and Achitophel* and Dryden's other
political poems can be more fully understood if in due course we compare it
with Marvell's vivid eschatological vision in the poems on Cromwell, with their
sense of the imminent pressure of the divine on human affairs.

In Dryden's political poems from *Astraea Redux* (1660) to *Absalom and Achitophel* (1681) we find a central motif of renewal and restoration following a crisis
of civil war, defeat, destruction, or exile. The contemporary event is always

presented sub specie aeternitatis by means of analogues usually drawn from
classical mythology, Roman history, or the Old Testament. No contemporary
event or issue is seen as unique, and the participants in these national dramas
are generally reduced to types. Dryden's good characters in the political poems
are especially lacking in individuality. The public-spirited and self-effacing
qualities of virtue as Dryden here conceives of it—in striking contrast to the
egotism of his dramatic heroes—helps to define the admired monarchs, statesmen, and warriors in terms of functions and relationships rather than in terms
of extraordinary gifts or *virtu*. This is plainly seen in the cases of Barzillai's
heroic son (in real life the earl of Ossory) and of the handful of faithful
followers David relies on in the crisis of *Absalom and Achitophel:*

> Now more than half a Father's Name is lost.
> His Eldest Hope, with every Grace adorn'd,
> By me (so Heav'n will have it) always mourn'd,
> And always honour'd, snatcht in Manhoods prime
> By unequal Fates, and Providences crime:
> Yet not before the Goal of Honour won,
> All parts fulfill'd of Subject and of Son;
> Swift was the Race, but short the Time to run.
> Oh Narrow Circle, but of Pow'r Divine,
> Scanted in Space, but perfect in thy Line!   [831 40]

Individuality enters the picture with Dryden's villains. The catalogue of rebels, dreamers, informers, and plotters includes more eccentric characters than
any other English poem except, perhaps, *The Canterbury Tales.* Wickedness is
conceived of as eccentric and egocentric. Each villain is wicked in a special
way, while the good are all good in the same way. Because they are incapable
of the reciprocal loyalties that link king and subject, master and servant, god
and man, or father and son, these villains are very much cut off from others.
Their eccentricity is further emphasized by idiosyncrasies of appearance and
manner. It is significant that none of the good characters in *Absalom and
Achitophel* is given a physical description, while all the evil ones are marked by
unforgettable physical features.

It follows that with Dryden's aversion to the idiosyncratic there should
be a corresponding aversion to novelty. The central conspirators of the Exclusion crisis are the slaves of the New. Achitophel is "Restless, unfixed in
principles and place, / In power unpleased, impatient of disgrace," and Zimri
is hailed as "Blest madman, who could every hour employ, / With something new to wish or to enjoy." Dazzled by ambition or bemused by mad
schemes for innovation, the rebel leaders are seen as prisoners of the moment.
The essence of Dryden's profound mistrust of political alteration is conveyed
in one of the most powerful couplets in *Absalom and Achitophel:*

> All other Errors but disturb a State;
> But Innovation is the Blow of Fate.   [799–800]

With his aversion to innovation Dryden also seems to feel a certain anti-intellectualism. Among David's supporters the only one to whom intellectual brilliance is attributed is "Jotham of piercing wit and pregnant thought," and even here the emphasis on perspicuousness rather than originality is significant. All the other virtuous characters, including the king, are recognized for their sense of duty and loyalty, not for their brilliance. Dryden's implicit anti-intellectualism is expressed in the much-quoted couplet:

> Great Wits are sure to Madness near ally'd;
> And thin Partitions do their Bounds divide.   [163–64]

Intellectual brilliance is as dangerous in its own way as the inner light of the spirit, that fallible guide of the sects:

> Plain Truths enough for needfull use they found;
> But men wou'd still be itching to expound:
> Each was ambitious of th' obscurest place,
> No measure ta'en from knowledge, all from GRACE.
> Study and Pains were now no more their Care;
> Texts were explain'd by Fasting, and by Prayer:
> This was the Fruit the private Spirit brought;
> Occasion'd by great Zeal, and little Thought.
>
> [*Religio Laici*, 409–16]

Devotees of novelty, whether in religion or politics, are doomed to an ephemeral existence:

> A Thousand daily Sects rise up, and dye;
> A Thousand more the perish'd Race supply.   [421–22]

Thus *Religio Laici* indicts the Dissenters whose shifting political allegiances *Absalom and Achitophel* had arraigned in these lines:

> For, govern'd by the Moon, the giddy Jews
> Tread the same track when she the Prime renews:
> And once in twenty Years, their Scribes Record,
> By natural Instinct they change their Lord.   [216–19]

Dryden's innovative Jews seem to illustrate Santayana's remark that "those who do not remember the past are condemned to repeat it." Perhaps the most striking aspect of Dryden's conservatism is that it permeates every part of his political verse. It is explicitly stated and argued; it is illustrated by a wide variety of examples; and it is represented in the very structure and style of the poems. All these aspects of Dryden's conservatism have been extensively treated by others, and so I would like to concentrate on the infrequently discussed subject of Dryden's concept of history in the political poems. This, I think, points to a radical issue which divided Conformist and Dissenter, Whig and Tory, Puritan and Anglican throughout the great religious and political crises of the seventeenth century.

In *Absalom and Achitophel,* his most important political poem, Dryden showed very clearly his central concern with the relationship of the present to the past. Because the story of David had already been widely used by various pamphleteers to figure forth the story of Charles II, it has often been assumed that Dryden's contribution to the use of myth was mainly a question of greater dexterity and wit. There is no doubt about the technical superiority of his poem over its models and predecessors, but this should not blind us to Dryden's real innovation in the use of Old Testament myth—the amalgamation of present and past. We do not see the present through an allegory from or an analogy with the past; we see past and present simultaneously. David neither simply stands for Charles II nor merely resembles him: David is Charles. Dryden is not saying that we can learn lessons from the past. He is everywhere affirming that we can only understand the present when it is amalgamated with the past.

At the heart of Dryden's conservatism is the feeling that past, present, and future coexist. We can see in Dryden those aspects of the Anglican temper defined by James Sutherland: "To some extent it is possible to see the division between Anglicans and Nonconformists as another aspect of the battle between the Ancients and the Moderns. The Anglican priest naturally felt himself to be the trustee of a venerable ecclesiastical tradition, performing the unvarying offices of the Church and celebrating its time hallowed ritual."[8] While Dryden's anticlericalism would have rejected such an assumption of an ecclesiastical role, he undoubtedly regarded himself as the trustee of venerable political and religious traditions and the celebrator of time-hallowed rituals. At the center of his thought throughout his career was something like what Eliade has called "the myth of the eternal return," in which the chief feature is a recurrent restoration and resanctification of the community after losses and violations. This "primitive" ontological conception Eliade describes thus:

An object or an act becomes real only insofar as it imitates or repeats an archetype. Thus, reality is acquired solely through repetition of participation; everything which lacks an exemplary model is "meaningless," i.e., it lacks reality. Men would thus have a tendency to become archetypal and paradigmatic. This tendency may well appear paradoxical, in the sense that the man of a traditional culture sees himself as real only to the extent that he ceases to be himself (for a modern observer) and is satisfied with imitating and repeating the gestures of another. In other words, he sees himself as real, i.e., as "truly himself," and precisely insofar as he ceases to be so.[9]

A brief survey of the recurrent rituals of restoration in Dryden's political verse will demonstrate this point. *Astraea Redux,* which proclaims the theme in its title, carries as its epigraph the first line from the most famous of Virgil's *Eclogues* (the fourth), in which the restoration of Justice is hailed: "Iam Redit & Virgo, Redeunt Saturnia Regna" (The Virgin now returns and the Saturnian reign). The restoration of Charles II after a long exile is thus identified with the restored Saturnian Age in which the departed Astraea (Divine Justice) returns to earth. Since Virgil was celebrating the birth of a prophesied redeemer in the fourth *Eclogue,* and since this poem was often regarded as an anticipation of the birth of Christ, the cosmogonic implications inherent in identifying Charles with the newborn son of the Consul Pollio could scarcely be more powerful. But Dryden extends them even further by including an identification with an Old Testament type as well:

> Thus banish'd David spent abroad his time,
> When to be God's Anointed was his Crime.   [79–80]

Toward its close the poem hails the inception of the new age under this new Augustus (yet another powerful identification):

> And now times whiter Series is begun
> Which in soft Centuries shall smoothly run.   [292–93]

In the next forty years Dryden's poetry is imbued with this theme of restoration, renewal, and return, finally dismissed in the haunting chorus of the *Secular Masque:*

> All, all, of a piece throughout;
> Thy Chase had a Beast in View;
> Thy Wars brought nothing about;
> Thy Lovers were all untrue.
> 'Tis well an Old Age is out,
> And time to begin a New.   [92–97]

The restoration of Charles II, with its archetypes of David's return from exile and the investiture of Augustus as emperor, becomes Dryden's central pattern for a long series of restorations. *To His Sacred Majesty, a Panegyrick on His Coronation* celebrates that crown "Preserv'd from ruine and restor'd by you." The motif of restoration is combined with Aeneas's escape from Troy and founding of Rome in a passage from *To My Lord Chancellor Presented on New-Years-Day, 1662:*

> When our great Monarch into Exile went
> Wit and Religion suffer'd banishment:
> Thus once when Troy was wrapt in fire and smoak
> The helpless Gods their burning shrines forsook;
> They with the vanquish'd Prince and Party go
> And leave their Temples empty to the fo:
> At length the Muses stand restor'd again
> To that great charge which Nature did ordain;
> And their lov'd Druyds seem reviv'd by Fate
> While you dispence the laws and guide the State.   [17–26]

Of course the conclusion of *Absalom and Achitophel* is the most prominent instance of the restoration theme—in fact Dryden is here emphasizing a re-restoration:

> Henceforth a Series of new time began;
> The mighty Years in long Procession ran:
> Once more the Godlike David was Restor'd,
> And willing Nations knew their lawful Lord.   [1027–30]

As Godfrey Davies remarked, the Godlike David is more Godlike than God, whose only function in this poem is to nod affirmatively in response to David's reassertion of his power.[10] These lines combine in an exemplary fashion all the main ingredients of Dryden's restoration myth: divine sanction, inauguration of a new age, the identification of the king as David with undertones of Aeneas, and the reestablishment of the nation's obedience to its lawful lord. In fact, Dryden's attachment to these themes verges on the tedious, and it becomes easy to anticipate the exact point in a poem at which these plangent heroic notes will come in. One foresees the climax of *Threnodia Augustalis:* Dryden's strategy is already dictated by past practice, and so the death of Charles is inevitably subordinated in the conclusion of the poem to the succession of his brother:

> with a distant view I see
> Th' amended Vows of English Loyalty.
> And all beyond that Object, there appears
> The long Retinue of a Prosperous Reign.
>
> . . . .
>
>   . . . While starting from his Oozy Bed
> Th' asserted Ocean rears his reverend Head;
> To View and Recognize his ancient Lord again:
>   And with a willing hand, restores
>   The Fasces of the Main.   [504–07; 513–17]

Although the myth is most centrally expressed in those numerous poems that deal with the restoration and succession of the Stuart line, Dryden extends it to include a variety of subjects, from Charleton's discoveries at Stonehenge to the duchess of York's return from a trip to Scotland. Sometimes its use seems perfunctory, as it does in the flattering condescension to the duchess, but it is more discriminating in the Charleton poem. Dryden wittily combines Dr. Walter Charleton's theory that Stonehenge was built by the Danes as a temple for the coronation of their kings with an allusion to Charles's alleged asylum there after the battle of Worcester and an implied reference to the founding of Rome:

> These Ruines sheltred once His Sacred Head
> Then when from Wor'sters fatal Field He fled;
> Watch'd by the Genius of this Royal place,
> And mighty Visions of the Danish Race.
> His Refuge then was for a Temple shown:
> But, He Restor'd, 'tis now become a Throne.   [53–58]

Stonehenge is implicitly identified with the temple of Apollo at Cumae where Aeneas descended into the underworld and saw mighty visions of the Roman race. Thus Dryden juxtaposes recent or contemporary events with mythic or historical counterparts in a distinctively Virgilian way. In an equally Virgilian way he establishes a relation between losses and gains in the fate of the royal line and the nation: defeat and flight, exile and wandering, become the swelling prologue to the imperial theme. *Il faut reculer pour mieux sauter.*

Dryden employs the same principle in treating the devastation of London by the Great Fire of 1666. Since the remarkable rebuilding of the city had scarcely begun, there was as yet little tangible reason for hailing London's renewal as he does in *Annus Mirabilis* (1667). Here is no actual equivalent to the Restoration of Charles, and so Dryden's implicit argument seems to be that, because the city was burned, it will be renewed like the Phoenix:

> 294
> Already, Labouring with a might fate,
>   She shakes the rubbish from her mounting brow,
> And seems to have renew'd her Charters date,
>   Which Heav'n will to the death of time allow.

> 295
> More great then humane, now, and more August,
>   New deifi'd she from her fires does rise:
> Her widening streets on new foundations trust,
>   And, opening, into larger parts she flies.   [1173–80]

At the height of the Exclusion crisis Dryden again used the legend of Noah and the Flood (another version of the basic theme) which he had first alluded to in the opening lines of *To His Sacred Majesty:*

> In that wild Deluge where the World was drownd,
> When life and sin one common tombe had found,
> The first small prospect of a rising hill
> With various notes of Joy the Ark did fill.   [1–4]

The *Epilogue to the King . . . at Oxford . . . 19 March 1680* treats the turbulence of the times and the desperate hope for a peaceful solution to the crisis in terms of the same myth:

> Our Ark that has in Tempests long been tost,
> Cou'd never land on so secure a Coast.
> From hence you may look back on Civil Rage,
> And view the ruines of the former Age.
> Here a New World its glories may unfold,
> And here be sav'd the remnants of the Old.   [17–22]

In this passage Dryden employs one of their favorite weapons against the predominantly Dissenting and Whiggish champions of Exclusion by appropriating to the king's side their customary designation of themselves as the saving remnant.

In an interesting anticipation of Pope's treatment of the *translatio studii* in the *Essay on Criticism* and *The Dunciad,* Dryden in 1684 hails the restoration to England of Greek and Roman learning in *To the Earl of Roscommon on His Excellent Essay of Translated Verse:*

> The Wit of Greece, the Gravity of Rome
> Appear exalted in the Brittish Loome;
> The Muses Empire is restor'd agen,
> In Charles his Reign and by Roscommon's Pen.   [26–29]

One concluding example will show how pervasive the theme of restoration is in Dryden's poetry. In a poem of pure compliment welcoming the duchess of York after one of her sojourns abroad Dryden turns the following dainty conceit:

> The Muse resumes her long-forgotten Lays,
> And Love, restor'd, his Ancient Realm surveys;
> Recalls our Beauties, and revives our Plays.
> [*Prologue to the Dutchess on Her Return from Scotland, 1682,* 30–32]

Whenever Dryden celebrates a public event, then, he combines it with some classical or mythic prototype and thus endows it with a kind of cosmic regularity and inevitability. A natural correlative to this is in his rejection of the search for novelty and innovation, already glanced at. It is given general force in the *Prologue to The Unhappy Favorite* (1682):

> Tell me you Powers, why should vain Man pursue,
> With endless Toyl, each object that is new,
> And for the seeming substance leave the True . . . ?   [12–14]

The erratic and perverted character of the crowd is emphatically expressed in these lines from *The Medal* (1682):

> Almighty Crowd, thou shorten'st all dispute;
> Pow'r is thy Essence; Wit thy Attribute!
> Nor Faith nor Reason make Thee at a stay;
> Thou leapst o'r all eternal truths, in thy Pindarique way!   [91–94]

In such a mob doctrines and tenets can only be ephemeral:

> The common Cry is ev'n Religion's Test . . .
>
> . . . .
>
> And our own Worship only true at home.
> And true, but for the time, 'tis hard to know,
> How long we please it shall continue so.
> This side to day, and that to morrow burns;
> So all are God-a' mighties in their turns.   [103; 106–10]

Dryden's most telling indictment of the sects is of course in *Religio Laici* (1682):

> The Common Rule was made the common Prey;
> And at the mercy of the Rabble lay.
> The tender Page with horney Fists was gaul'd;
> And he was gifted most that loudest baul'd:
> The Spirit gave the Doctoral Degree:
> And every member of a Company
> Was of his Trade, and of the Bible free.
>
> . . . .
>
> While Crouds unlearn'd, with rude Devotion warm,
> About the Sacred Viands buz and swarm,
> The Fly-blown Text creates a crawling Brood;
> And turns to Maggots what was meant for Food.
> A Thousand daily Sects rise up, and dye;
> A thousand more the perish'd Race supply.   [402–08; 417–22]

Dryden's attack on the sects here resembles that of Marvell in *The First Anniversary:*

> You who the Scriptures and the Laws deface
> With the same liberty as Points and Lace;
> Oh Race most hypocritically strict!
> Bent to reduce us to the ancient Pict;
> Well may you act the *Adam* and the *Eve;*
> Ay, and the Serpent too that did deceive.   [315–20]

Bernard Schilling, among others, has shown how, to Dryden, extravagances of style were as much to be avoided as moral or spiritual extravagances:

A form that lacks discipline is then appropriate for expressing rebellious sentiments, and suggests how the desire for political and social order led to so much control of literary expression. Behind all the vast structure of rule and law there is a fear lest individual energy, if given any chance at all, will assert itself dangerously. Hence the attack on such displays of energy as eloquence, vigorous figurative language, powerful original thought or speculation, and, worst of all, the force of human imagination, which might lead into a whole complex of dangers suggested by the term "enthusiasm."[11]

The conservative myth is celebrated in a style that avoids these pitfalls, a style which by its regularity and sobriety, its balance and rationality, and its irony and good humor enacts the meaning it expresses. In this neoclassical style wit is, in Dryden's phrase "a propriety of thoughts and words; or, in other terms, thoughts and words elegantly adapted to the subject."[12] Dryden's idea of invention, like Hobbes's, carried little emphasis on creating something new, but was a matter of seeking and recovering something that was lost, a "calling to mind."[13] In the preface to *Annus Mirabilis* Dryden describes the function of wit as searching "over all the memory for the Species or Ideas of those things which it designs to represent." Thus style was undergirded by a neoclassical psychology of literary creation, and, like both the style and the conservative myth, focused on the past, seeking what had been lost. Ancient truths, the same *hic et ubique,* were to be expressed under the aegis of Homer, Virgil, Aristotle, Horace, and the Bible.

The weight of this formidable neoclassical machinery was employed by Dryden to persuade moderates to accept the Stuart settlement. For Dryden the chief enemies of peace in Church and state were those who, with the battle cry of "Popery and Tyranny," were seeking to disturb the succession in the Exclusion crisis of 1681. It is appropriate that *Absalom and Achitophel,* a poem dealing with threats to the Stuart dynasty and to the principle of succession, should embody in every way the principles that underlie succession. In this view, the exclusive legitimacy of James as heir to the throne is an absolute right, not a relative one, and it is not negotiable. To tamper with it would be to tamper with divinely ordained law, to "touch the ark." Although Dryden goes to some lengths to present James as a worthy heir, his right to the throne is constitutionally independent of personal merit, and I suspect that a corresponding function of the raillery with which Charles's various love affairs are treated in the opening of *Absalom* is to undercut the notion of personal merit. Dryden enunciates (at least by implication) the doctrine of the king's two bodies—the natural and the politic—dealt with by Ernest Kantorowicz.[14] His basic assumption is that Charles, whatever his imperfections as a man, is the legitimate monarch, endowed with certain inalienable rights and corresponding responsibilities, chief among them in this crisis being the safeguarding of the succession.

Just as the Exclusionists would have threatened to destroy the succession and thereby the orderly continuity on which Church and state are founded, so, in an earlier national crisis of war, plague, and fire, the radical element threatened the continued existence of England by its apocalyptic interpretation of events. In *Annus Mirabilis* Dryden strategically deflects the linear, eschatological view of events with which the sects hailed the end of the world in 1666—and sought, in Marvell's memorable phrase, "to precipitate the latest day"—into the familiar cyclical cosmos of loss and renewal. War, plague, and fire had, as dissenting prophets declared, been a judgment of God for sin, but the sin, in Dryden's view, was that of the rebellious citizens of London and not of the allegedly profligate king and his court. So Dryden deftly turned the apocalyptic interpretation of events back upon the Dissenters and implicitly identified the origins of London's devastating fire with the career of the regicide dictator he had once celebrated in *Heroique Stanzas:*

213

As when some dire Usurper Heav'n provides,
    To scourge his Country with a lawless sway:
His birth, perhaps, some petty Village hides,
    And sets his Cradle out of Fortune's way:

214

Till fully ripe his swelling fire breaks out,
    And hurries him to mighty mischiefs on:
His Prince surpriz'd at first, no ill could doubt,
    And wants the pow'r to meet it when 'tis known:

215

Such was the rise of this prodigious fire,
    Which in mean buildings first obscurely bred,
From thence did soon to open streets aspire,
    And straight to Palaces and Temples spread.   [849–60]

It is hard for me to avoid the idea that Dryden was alluding here to the
Cromwell of Marvell's *Horatian Ode,* who

> . . . like the three-fork'd Lightning, first
> Breaking the Clouds where it was nurst,
>   Did thorough his own Side
>   His fiery way divide.
>
> .   .   .   .
> Then burning through the Air he went,
> And Pallaces and Temples rent:
>   And Caesars head at last
>   Did through his Laurels blast.
> 'Tis Madness to resist or blame
> The force of angry Heavens flame;
>   And, if we would speak true,
>   Much to the Man is due:
> Who, from his private Gardens, where
> He liv'd reserved and austere,
>   As if his highest plot
>   To plant the Bergamot,
> Could by industrious Valour climbe
> To ruine the great Work of Time.   [13–16; 21–34]

Nearly all Marvell's details appear in Dryden's stanzas: the obscurity of Cromwell's birth, his portentous role as a heaven-sent scourge, his sudden attain-
ment of power and his impetuous career, his "mighty mischiefs," the unpre-
paredness of his prince, and his rending of "Palaces and Temples." On stanza
213, quoted above, the California edition of Dryden notes: "Perhaps a reference to Cromwell, who came from the country and who was an obscure figure
until the 1640's. The passage was probably in Gray's mind when he wrote ll.
57ff. of the *Elegy.*"[15] If the three stanzas are taken together, however, we seem

also to get a subtle allusion to the hero of Marvell's ode and a rather surprising agreement between these two poets in their way of looking at the "dire Usurper" as an agent of apocalypse. Essential differences begin to appear only as the two poets develop in separate ways their estimate of the mighty mischiefs threatening "the great Work of Time." The differences are partly due to the circumstances under which the poems were written: in *An Horatian Ode* Marvell has to deal with the king's death as a fait accompli; in *Annus Mirabilis* Dryden is trying to ward off a repetition of the dire event predicted by the radical Dissenters. E. N. Hooker describes the polemical purpose of the poem thus:

Annus Mirabilis is, in one sense, a piece of inspired journalism, written to sway public opinion in favor of the royal government, which dreaded a revolution—a revolution which, according to republican propaganda, was to be ushered in by omens and portents, by "wonders" signifying the wrath of God against the king and his party. Because of the mystic properties of the figure "666," expectation of revolution had centered around the year 1666; years before, William Lilly had prophesied that "in 1666, there will be no King here, or pretending to the Crowne of England." Fear was widespread. Pepys, recording a conversation with Lord Sandwich on 25 February 1666, reported: "He dreads the issue of this year, and fears there will be some very great revolutions before his coming back again."[16]

Hooker goes on to enumerate some of the pamphlets which attempted to exploit these fears: *Mirabilis Annus, the Year of Prodigies; Mirabilis Annus Secundus: or the Second Year of Wonders;* and so on.

Not only did Dryden turn the enemy's guns back upon them, but he adopted and modified the prophecies of the sectarians about the impending end of the world and made them serve his view of restoration and renewal. Stanza 212 includes one of Dryden's few eschatological references in the political poems:

212
Yet London Empress of the Northern Clime,
   By an high fate thou greatly didst expire;
Great as the worlds, which at the death of time
   Must fall, and rise a nobler frame by fire.   [845–48]

But once again the eschatological catastrophe has been deflected into the cosmogonic cycle of renewal.

Schilling defines the conservative myth as used by Dryden in these words:

Dryden works from an inherited set of symbols and responses to them that make up a general interpretation of life. This might be called a mythology of order, a set of connected myths, drawing on the literary tradition from Rome through the Renaissance, on the Bible as read in the 17th century, on the political and religious experiences of the mid-century civil war, and on the assumptions of rule and control that dominate neoclassical literary theory.[17]

In this otherwise excellent summary, "the Bible as read in the 17th century"
calls for more definition. To a large extent one of the major issues of the
seventeenth century was how to read the Bible. The Brownists, Anabaptists,
Familists, Muggletonians, and Independents, as well as the Presbyterians
(among others) all had their own ways of reading the Bible, and these often
differed as much from each other as they did from the Anglican views of
Dryden. With good reason Dryden was alarmed by the divisive effects the
"private spirit" brought in its various interpretations of the holy text. He was
deeply concerned lest such independence of interpretation should lead to
further upheavals in Church and state. As Schilling observes. "If conservatism, like classicism, in Oliver Elton's phrase, is the triumph of obedience,
Dryden seems to have obeyed naturally. He seems free, with no sense of
straining toward what was required by neoclassical authority in art, by the
demands of political and religious order."[18] It was virtually inevitable, then,
that after writing *Absalom and Achitophel* and *The Medal* he would next direct
his attention to what might be regarded as the issue behind the issue of
Exclusion and the Popish Plot—the private spirit in religion which had
produced that "Headstrong, Moody, Murmuring race" whom "No King
could govern, nor no God could please." Thus in *Religio Laici* (1682) Dryden
fortified his conservative myth with pragmatic Anglican underpinnings. The
poem is not really about a layman's faith as much as it is about obedience to
the established church:

> In doubtfull questions 'tis the safest way
> To learn what unsuspected Ancients say:
> For 'tis not likely we shou'd higher Soar
> In search of Heav'n than all the Church before:
> Nor can we be deceiv'd, unless we see
> The Scripture, and the Fathers disagree.
> If after all, they stand suspected still,
> (For no man's Faith depends upon his Will;)
> 'Tis some Relief, that points not clearly known,
> Without much hazard may be let alone:
> And, after hearing what our Church can say,
> If still our Reason runs another way,
> That private Reason 'tis more Just to curb,
> Than by Disputes the publick Peace disturb.
> For points obscure are of small use to learn:
> But Common quiet is Mankind's concern.   [435–50]

With such gestures toward tolerance, Dryden is bent on enforcing the authority of the established church instead of making a confession of a layman's
faith. If we compare *Religio Laici* with the *O Altitudo*'s of its predecessor,
Religio Medici, the lack of content in Dryden's poem is as remarkable as its
commonsense tone. Here the medium, a style "Plain and Natural, and yet
Majestick," is indeed the message. Part of Dryden's conservative strategy is to

ascribe to certain public institutions like the Church, the monarchy, and the law the authenticity they claim without looking very deeply into the foundations for the claim. He is adept at begging the question while inducing a mood of agreement.

At the heart of the great political and religious conflicts of the English Revolution, then, we find a profound disagreement about the nature of history. At the height of the crisis, in his poems on Cromwell, Marvell turned to the apocalyptic visions of John, Revelation, and Daniel. He found there the sanctions for a revolutionary Christian orthodoxy, at the same time rejecting the democratic views of the Anabaptists, Levellers, and other separatists as anarchical, and the conservative, cyclical view of history as heretical, secular, and futile—"the vain curlings of the wat'ry maze." Against the forward eschatological thrust of such revolutionary doctrines Dryden deployed a view of history that was retrospective in every sense of the word.

A central myth in which both Dryden and Marvell embodied their political views was, of course, the story of David in the Book of Samuel. This story may well have been the central political myth of seventeenth-century England. Perhaps it would not be too much to say that the essential struggle of this revolutionary century was reflected in the struggle for possession of the Davidic myth. Dryden's great coup was to capture the myth for the conservative side.

Although it was widely employed in the literature of controversy by both radicals and conservatives, until *Absalom and Achitophel* appeared, the myth of David was employed most effectively by Protestant reformers. They habitually identified leading figures with such characters in the story as David himself, Michal, Absalom and Achitophel, Saul, and so forth. Joseph Mazzeo has traced this interpretative tradition back to the early Middle Ages: "This tradition of Davidic kingship as model kingship which started with Pepin persisted through the Middle Ages into the Renaissance. Thomas Aquinas, for example, in *de regimine principium* gives David as an example of the ideal ruler, one who does what every ruler should and places his reward in God."[19] Mazzeo cites Kantorowicz (*The King's Two Bodies*) to witness that "Pepin's anointment as if he were a king of Israel was of great importance for the political evolution of Europe, for it is 'the keystone of this evolution and at the same time the cornerstone of medieval divine right and *Dei Gratia* kingship.' "[20] The use of the myth as a precedent establishing divine right may remind us of the range of interpretations and applications to which it was subjected.

Mazzeo goes on to trace another traditional interpretation of David as "humble psalmist," citing Dante's use of him as an example of *humilitas* in *Purgatorio* X, and as the dancer before the Ark, "who by his self-imposed humility before the Lord became less a king before such as Michal but more in the eyes of his Creator," thus providing "a perfect exemplum of the favourite Christian paradox of humilitas-sublimitas, supremely manifested in the life of Christ."[21]

Finally, Mazzeo traces a third tradition of Davidic interpretation which tends to play down David's humility and to emphasize his role as a great composer, applying to him "a well-developed conception of music as the art of cosmic harmony."[22] This music, he continues, was "an image of that unity in variety which is the essence of a well-ordered city."[23] It is this aspect of the Davidic myth that lies behind Marvell's presentation of Cromwell as Amphion in *The First Anniversary* (1655):

> The listning Structures he with Wonder ey'd
> And still new Stopps to various Time apply'd:
> Now through the Strings a Martial rage he throws,
> And joyning streight the *Theban* Tow'r arose;
> Then as he strokes them with a touch more sweet
> The flocking Marbles in a Palace meet;
> But, for he most the graver Notes did try,
> Therefore the Temples rear'd their Columns high:
> This, ere he ceas'd, his sacred Lute creates
> Th' harmonious City of the seven Gates.
>   Such was that wondrous Order and Consent,
> When Cromwell tun'd the ruling Instrument;
> While tedious Statesmen many years did hack,
> Framing a Liberty that still went back;
> Whose num'rous Gorge could swallow in an hour
> That Island, which the Sea cannot devour:
> Then our Amphion issues out and sings,
> And once he struck, and twice, the pow'rful Strings.   [57–74]

The Davidic myth was by no means primarily literary in its applications to seventeenth-century political and religious matters in England. Unlike the Virgilian elements in the conservative myth, which always retained a literary flavor and often some savor of intellectual snobbery, the Davidic myth sprang in part from popular acquaintance with the Bible. It was a way of interpreting contemporary issues in an oral tradition derived from pulpit, Parliament, and other arenas of discussion and debate. Some of the more bizarre instances of this widespread practice are examined by Louise Fargo Brown in *Baptists and Fifth Monarchy Men*. In the projected uprising of 1665, "The organization of the conspirators was as nearly as possible along biblical lines. The forces were to be divided into three bands, according to the precedent established by Abraham, Gideon, and David." A proclamation "outlined the government of the coming state. Christ was to be the supreme legislative power; the Scriptures, the body of the law, a Sanhedrin of Godly men was to be the chief magistracy, having control of the militia." On another occasion Venner, the radical mystagogue who led the uprising, and his associates were compared to Korah, Dathan, and Abiram, thus providing a precedent for Dryden's identification of the despicable Titus Oates as "Corah." Captain John Vernon under-

standably irritated Henry Cromwell, commander-in-chief of the forces in Ireland, when he preached a sermon comparing Henry to Absalom, remarking
"that Absalom grasped at unlawful power, and that such men might pretend
to be for the saints, but that it was as Pharaoh was for Joseph, and Herod for
John the Baptist." Henry cashiered another officer of his command for intimating that he was trying "Absalom-like, to steal the affections of his father's
people away from him." John Canne, the journalist, referred to the restoration
of the Rump in the spring of 1659 as "the work of an overturning Providence,
which had subverted the throne of iniquity and defeated the combinations of
Achitophels, thereby encouraging the saints to hope that the day of redemption was drawing nigh."[24] Thus Dryden, in his satirical attacks on "a thousand dreaming saints," exposed the abuses of apocalyptic scriptural interpretation of contemporary events, above all in the story of David. He had no need
to debase this use of the myth—the more far-out sectarians had obligingly
done that for him already. But in representing apocalyptic Christianity only
by members of the lunatic fringe (however numerous) and playing off against
them his cool, rational, established, secular Christianity, Dryden ignored a far
nobler apocalyptic version of the Davidic myth. Against Dryden's aging and
worldly David, who can only restore the status quo ante, we need to place the
apocalyptic David whom Marvell represented in *The First Anniversary*, a
unique hero who could become the final instrument of divine intervention in
history:

> . . . 'Tis he the force of scatter'd Time contracts,
> And in one Year the work of Ages acts;
> While heavie Monarchs make a wide Return,
> Longer and more Malignant than Saturn:
> And though they all Platonique years should raign,
> In the same Posture would be found again.
>
> . . . .
>
> Hence oft I think, if in some happy Hour
> High Grace should meet in one with highest Pow'r,
> And then a seasonable People still
> Should bend to his, as he to Heavens will,
> What we might hope, what wonderfull Effect
> From such a wish'd Conjuncture might reflect.
>
> Sure, the mysterious Work, where none withstand,
> Would forthwith finish under such a Hand:
> Fore-shortned Time its useless Course would stay,
> And some precipitate the latest Day.   [13–18; 131–40]

The death of Cromwell and his son's ignominious collapse demolished Marvell's millenarian hopes, however cautious, and tempered his belief in "the
power of providence to change the course, and thus the meaning of history."[25]
Yet Marvell still saw the hand of providence in the Restoration of Charles II,

and if he did not hail the event with Dryden's enthusiasm, he accepted it as a return to the traditional form of a mixed monarchy, with a balance of royal prerogative and parliamentary privilege. Marvell was quicker than Dryden to see a threat to this balance in the extension of power on one side at the expense of the other. For him the chief danger was the encroachment of royal power on the rights and privileges of Parliament and the increasingly arbitrary conduct of affairs by the king, who was (according to the usual fiction) the victim of bad ministers. This view was advanced as early as 1667 in the conclusion to *The Last Instructions to a Painter* with its double plea to the king to assume his responsibilities and to replace a corrupt and self-seeking ministry with loyal friends in the House of Commons:

> Bold and accurst are they all this while
> Have strove to isle our *Monarch* from his *Isle,*
> And to improve themselves, on false pretense,
> About the *Common-Prince* have rais'd a Fense. . . .
>
> .   .   .   .
>
> But they whom, born to Virtue and to Wealth,
> Nor Guilt to Flatt'ry binds, nor Want to Stealth;
> Whose gen'rous Conscience and whose Courage high
> Does with clear Counsells their large Soules Supply:
> That serve the *King* with their Estates and Care,
> And as in Love on *Parliaments* can stare,
> (Where few the Number, Choice is there lesse hard);
> Give us this *Court* and rule without a Guard.   [965–68; 981–88]

Such virtuous supporters of the king are remarkably like Barzillai, Dryden's ideal courtier:

> The Court he practis'd, not the Courtier's art:
> Large was his Wealth, but larger was his Heart:
> Which well the Noblest Objects knew to choose,
> The Fighting Warrior, and Recording Muse.   [825–28]

Dryden, however, persistently represented any attempt by the parliamentary opposition to check the extension of royal power as a usurpation, and he failed to see, or he ignored, the dangers emanating from Charles's entente with Louis XIV. Even before 1670 Marvell seems to have been alert to the autocratic tendencies of the regime. As John Wallace says, "politically, the farsightedness of *The Last Instructions* makes *Annus Mirabilis* look myopic."[26] Here one may raise the question as to whether the inveterate tendency of conservatives like Dryden to look to the past may blind them to the present and to probabilities in the future.

Yet if we would understand Dryden's moderation it is important for us to see how closely it resembles in principle the moderation of Marvell, a chief spokesman for the opposition. "God send us moderation and agreement," Marvell wrote in 1671, and this prayer "may stand as an epigraph to all his efforts during the last years of his life."[27] But the prayer could equally well 'represent Dryden's political position at the time of writing *Absalom and Achitophel:* "If I happen to please the more moderate sort, I shall be sure of an honest Party; and, in all probability, of the best Judges; for the least Concern'd are commonly the least Corrupt."[28] He shared with Marvell a deep aversion to the "particolor'd mind" and a habitually pragmatic approach to political questions. Both rejected republican government of any kind, with equal firmness, cleaving to the idea of monarchy, in the support of which Marvell was as unyielding (in the *Last Instructions*) as Dryden was in *Absalom* or *His Majesties Declaration Defended* (June 1681) or in his postscript to *Maimbourg's History of the League* (1684). Marvell's remark in a letter to Sir John Trott in 1667 states a central theme of *Absalom:* " 'Tis Pride that makes a Rebel. And nothing but the overweening of our selves and our own things that raises us against divine Providence."[29] Surely Dryden would have had no quarrel with Marvell's well-known reflections on the Civil Wars:

> I think the cause was too good to be fought for. Men ought to have trusted God; they ought and might have trusted the King with that whole matter. . . . The King himself, being of so accurate and piercing a judgment, would soon have felt where it stuck. For men may spare their pains where nature is at work, and the world will not go the faster for our driving. Even as his present Majestie's happy Restauration did it self, so all things else happen in their best and proper time, without any need of our officiousness.[30]

In his dedication to the Earl of Danby of *All for Love* (1678), Dryden celebrated "moderation" and "steadiness of temper" as the two requisites of a minister of state "that he may stand like an isthmus between the two lawless seas of arbitrary power and lawless anarchy." *To My Honour'd Kinsman, John Driden* (1699) emphasizes this moderating, mediating function:

> Well-Born and Wealthy; wanting no support,
> You steer Betwixt the Country and the Court.   [127–28]

How close Dryden's position was to Marvell's appears from Wallace's summary: "England had been blessed by its mixed or limited monarchy, and, humanly speaking, the equitable distribution of power among the estates of the realm afforded her a strength that probably could not be bettered, and which could only be endangered by the failure of the components to keep their proper place."[31]

Granted such a fundamental agreement on political principles, how can one explain the hostility that persisted between the two leading political poets of the age? Why, in 1672, did Marvell attack Dryden, by implication, as a champion of arbitrary power, using the laureate's nickname for the odious Samuel Parker? And why, in the same year, did he single out Dryden for obloquy as "the town Bayes" in his poem commending *Paradise Lost?* Why, ten years later, did Dryden attack the dead Marvell in his preface to *Religio Laici* as "a Presbyterian Scribler, who sanctify'd Libels to the use of the Good

Old Cause?" Marvell's antiprelatical bias is scarcely sufficient to motivate the antipathy of one whose feelings toward the clergy were as hostile as Dryden's. How, finally, could Dryden have justified his misrepresentation of Marvell as one of "a pack of sectaries and commonwealths-men?"

If there is any explanation for this persistent hostility, it must be sought in the specific interpretations Dryden and Marvell made of the main public issues and events of their time. The threat to the balance of constitutional forces which stemmed from covert extension of royal authority, beginning with the Secret Treaty of Dover in 1670, produced the dangers that Marvell revealed in *The Growth of Popery and Arbitrary Government* (1678): Louis XIV's sweeping triumphs in Flanders, the maintenance of a standing army to cow parliamentary opposition, the bribery of members of Parliament by French agents (among others), and Charles's short-circuiting of Parliament by repeated prorogations and by misappropriation of funds. Well before the sham Popish Plot broke out in 1678 there was a real plot, based on this secret pact with Louis, and the threat to English liberty was greatly exacerbated by the prospective heir to the throne, an inflexible bigot (in Scott's words) and hence all the more to be feared. By the time *Absalom and Achitophel* was written, this was common knowledge, but Dryden chose to ignore the threat of a Stuart tyranny and preferred to find the real danger exclusively in opposition activities. While Shaftesbury's ruthless and unprincipled exploitation of the sham plot greatly aggravated the danger of another civil war, the fact remains that the king, his brother, and his ministers had prepared the culture in which this poisonous plot was to flourish. From a modern perspective it is surprising, not that Marvell should have insisted on calling attention to these dangers, but that he should have done so in such a temperate way, and that Dryden, while proclaiming moderation, should constantly have supported the forces of arbitrary power. Though invoking the values of the traditional mixed monarchy, Dryden seems to have been willing to pay almost any price for the imagined stability of an inherently autocratic regime. As laureate and historiographer-royal he supported Charles II and the Stuart succession with a single-mindedness that astounds anyone who accepts his pleas for moderation in virtually everything he wrote in the 1670s and 1680s: in pamphlets such as *His Majesties Declaration Defended,* on the stage in *The Duke of Guise* and *Albion and Albanius,* in numerous prologues and epilogues, even in his translation of Maimbourg's *History of the League* and its highly partisan postscript, as well as in his explicitly political poems. In this unqualified support of the Stuarts and equally unqualified hostility to the opposition, in which loyalists and "rebels" were huddled together, Dryden's "moderation" turns out to be more manner than substance. Under the guise of a reasoned concern for a constitutional balance of power, the laureate belittled the all-too-real fears and grievances of the loyal opposition. Even after James's abdication and the accession of William and Mary, he maintained the Virgilian dynastic theme, which he translated into the myth of papal authority.

Dr. Johnson observed of Dryden's use of Davidic myth in *Absalom and Achito-phel* that "The original structure of the poem was defective: allegories drawn to great length will always break; Charles could not run continually parallel with David."[32] The observation is factually correct, for the final appearance of Charles, his speech and its affirmation by the Almighty, and the invocation of a "series of new time" following Charles's re-restoration have no counterpart in the Old Testament story of David.

This departure from the Davidic model is not, however, a defect. It was essential that Dryden modify the myth to allow for Charles/David's effective stroke against his enemies—by the dissolution of Parliament at Oxford—and to prophesy his final victory over them. The king's bloodless victory at the conclusion of the poem also suspends the implications of Absalom's Miltonic temptation and his movement in the direction of outright rebellion to suggest that this is not a *Paradise Lost* but a "Paradise Restored." The ultimate authority for this restoration, the Godlike David, is Charles II.

The absence of any violent denouement, which Charles and Dryden alike most wished to avoid, has led to the feeling that the ending is anticlimactic. Charles's enemies and friends alike vanish without a trace, as if, Dr. Johnson suggested, by magic:

The chiefs on either part are set forth to view; but when expectation is at the height the king makes a speech, and
> 'Henceforth a series of new times began.'
Who can forbear to think of an enchanted castle, with a wide moat and lofty battlements, walls of marble and gates of brass, which vanishes at once into air when the destined knight blows his horn before it?[33]

But the absence of a decisive contest at the end of the poem cannot be attributed solely to the fact that the necessary role of historical truth meant that "the action and catastrophe were not in the poet's power." Nor should we hasten to accept the explanation that the apparent anticlimax was due to discrepancies between the historical facts and the myth Dryden had employed.

As Godfrey Davies has shown, the concluding speech is modeled on Charles's declaration of June 1681 defending Parliament's dissolution and pre-senting the king as guardian of the constitutional government which the Whigs were trying to wreck.[34] Even more significant to the issue of the appropriateness of the ending is Dryden's decision to follow history in making the king reassert his authority by a speech. Since the issue at the heart of the poem is the question of legitimate monarchy and the succession, Dryden plays down the providential overtones predominant earlier in order to focus attention on the king. For one thing, it is Godlike David, not God, who announces the new dispensation, and the approving nod of Dryden's abstract Almighty is taken from Jupiter's most perfunctory—and, one is tempted to say, most trivial—intervention in the *Aeneid*. "Th' Almighty, nodding, gave Consent; / And Peals of Thunder shook the Firmament" translates literally the lines in which Jupiter agrees that Aeneas's ships (which are no longer of any use to him) shall be perserved at the request of Cybele: "adnuit et totum nutu tremefecit Olympum" (IX, 106). (The line occurs again at X, 115, when Jupiter agrees to a hands-off policy in the war.) In both cases we see the Olympian at his most detached. Furthermore, had he wished, Dryden could have emphasized the prophetic Christian overtones found in Virgil's fourth *Eclogue* (as he had done in *Astraea Redux*), but instead he contents himself with a nearly literal rendering of its Virgilian epigraph "magnus ab integro saeclorum nascitur ordo": "Henceforth a Series of new Times begun." The emphasis of the conclusion is thus doubly secular: it asserts a cyclical view of history that is essentially temporal rather than spiritual. The god in the machine is Charles Stuart confirming the succession of his brother, James. *Vox Regis vox Dei.*

This low-keyed secular theophany is also in tune with the historical circumstances of Charles's almost magically effective dissolution of the Whig-dominated Parliament at Oxford eight months before *Absalom and Achitophel* appeared. G. M. Trevelyan describes the scene in a terse but dramatic way:

Meanwhile, the leaders in the Commons hurried through the Exclusion Bill. . . . On the eighth day of the session the King appeared suddenly in the House of Lords. He had come in a sedan chair, closely followed by another, of which the drawn curtains prosumably concealed some attendant lord. The Commons, hastily summoned to the Upper House expecting to hear the King announce his surrender, came rushing tumultuously across the quadrangle, crowded up a steep and winding staircase, jostled through a narrow door, and passed down some steps into the body of the hall. Charles with a gay face watched his enemies defile. At length they stood there, as many as could fight their way in, below the throne, panting, a close-headed mob. The King was in the robes of State—the real contents of the second sedan. In those robes alone could he dissolve Parliament. He spoke the fatal words and left the room, while the Commons trooped back the way they had come with "dreadful faces" and "loud sighs". . . . A panic seized the undisciplined and braggart host that had ridden into Oxford.[35]

By the unexpected assertion of his royal prerogative in dissolving a Parliament bent on limiting that prerogative, the king scattered his enemies like chaff. What the Tories regarded as an attempt to destroy the king's authority by interfering in the succession was thwarted by the breath of royal authority. David's apparent passivity throughout the poem throws into relief the Godlike power of his word.

If one looks back over the poem from this perspective one can see how cunningly Dryden prepares us for the concluding theophany of Charles. "God-like David" appears at line 14 and often thereafter. At first it strikes us as a formal heroic epithet, and only at the end is the full force of the identification apparent. The poem starts out with the familiar typological identification of the king as God's vicegerent, but, little by little, he assumes godlike powers in his own person. This Royal grace is identified with divine grace, thus blurring the distinction between the two orders, in

> The Jews, a Headstrong, Moody, Murmuring race,
> As ever try'd th' extent and stretch of grace.   [45–46]

Also, by representing the Monmouth party as rebel angels, Dryden implicitly identifies the king with God:

> Some had in Courts been great, and thrown from thence,
> Like Fiends, were harden'd in Impenitence.
> Some by their Monarchs fatal mercy grown,
> From pardon'd Rebels, Kinsmen to the Throne.   [1016–19]

At the climax of the temptation scene the often-noted Miltonic rhetoric emphasizes the explicit identification of Achitophel with Satan and Absalom with Adam and the implicit identification of Charles/David with God the Father:

> Him Staggering so when Hells dire Agent found
> While fainting Vertue scarce maintain'd her Ground,
> He pours fresh forces in, and thus replies. . . .
>
> [373–75]

The cumulative effect of these largely subliminal and oblique identifications of Charles with God is unobtrusively to dismantle the conventional providential and supernatural framework of the Davidic and Miltonic myths and erect in its place an autonomous myth of divine right with Charles as its final cause. In the important passage which introduces the king's speech there is, to be sure, a perfunctory nod toward heaven, but the ultimate authority is really the speaker himself:

> With all these loads of injuries opprest,
> And long revolving, in his carefull Brest,
> Th' event of things; at last his patience tir'd,
> Thus from his Royal Throne by Heav'n inspir'd,
> The God-like David spoke: with awfull fear
> His Train their Maker in their Master hear.
>
> [933–38]

The whole tendency of Dryden's adaptation of traditional myth material in this poem is to remove—or at least obscure—the orthodox distinction between the divine maker and the secular master and to assert the godlike authority of King Charles.

In many ways I would agree with Leon Guilhamet, who sees "a revolutionary debasement of the traditional David story" in which "the king himself becomes the most significant figure, out-doing God, rather than relying on Him for support; and the Church is thrust into the background as a mere appurtenance of David-Charles' authority."[36] On the other hand "debasement" and "thrust into the background" overlook, I believe, the subtlety and quietness with which Dryden has effected the change of focus.

Guilhamet also sees Dryden as rejecting the David story in order to permit David-Charles "to emerge as Charles alone," thus reinterpreting the old myth "out of existence."[37] While it is hard to see how Dryden could have extended the Davidic parallel to cover the conclusion of the poem, in view of historical realities, it seems nevertheless inescapable that he has at the very least deemphasized the myth. In blending Virgilian references with his *Odyssey*-like finale, Guilhamet suggests, Dryden is giving us a secular, classical poetic style to match the new political age. *Absolom and Achitophel* thus marks the decline of the serious use of religious and classical myth in English poetry and, perhaps, the beginning of the myth of secular authority that has accompanied the development of the modern state.

CHAPTER SEVEN

Homeric Mockery in Milton and Pope

Among its many modes Homeric epic includes mock-epic. Not even the immortals are immune to absurdity. One thinks of the besotted Zeus beguiled by Hera in *Iliad* XIV, or the discomfiture of the braggart Ajax the Less in book XXII, or the Phaeacian song about the adultery of Aphrodite, or the periodic domestic squabbles that disturb the *dolce far niente* of Olympus. Homeric gods can be figures of fun because of their privileged status as *ámbrotoi,* the word that repeatedly defines them as *not*-mortals, for the privilege acts often as a limitation, since their immortality often deprives them of consequence. Hence comes their fascination, especially in the *Iliad,* with the doings and sufferings of the *brotoí,* those who die and who thus can achieve a more than godlike glory in sacrificing their lives in a noble cause. In pursuit of consequence the gods must turn from the inconsequential comic-strip repetitions of their activities to the conclusive experiences of those whose principal life choices may be death choices.

While the immortals are fascinated with the warring, dying mortals, mortals tend corresponding to seek surcease from their agonies in games that, for a time, free them from the normal limitations of time and place, from mortal wounds and pain, and join them in shared ritual illusions that emulate the carefree existence of divinities.

If games can bring man closer to the divine, war may serve a corresponding function for gods preoccupied with mortals, or for mortals who are quasi-divine. A prime example is the war between the sexes in *The Rape of the Lock,* which reaches a climax in an inconclusive battle between the partisans of Belinda, whose lock of hair has been cut, and the Baron, who has cut the lock and vows to keep it, despite the cries of Belinda's allies to "restore the lock." The contretemps is extensively modeled on the quarrel in *Iliad* I between Achilles and Agamemnon over the prize slave, Brisëis. In Pope the crisis is not resolved. Belinda's appeals go unheeded, despite the efforts of her emissary, Sir Plume, which adumbrate the famous embassy to Achilles in *Iliad* IX. In a display of immovable resolution that recalls Achilles' oath in book I the Baron declares:

> But by this Lock, this sacred lock I swear,
> (Which never more shall join its parted hair,
> Which never more its Honours shall renew,

> Clipt from the lovely Head where late it grew)
> That while my Nostrils draw the vital Air,
> This Hand, which won it, shall for ever wear.
> He spoke, and speaking, in proud Triumph spread
> The long-contended Honours of her Head.   [IV, 133–40]

Here Pope has ingeniously combined several Homeric motifs. The prized lock, which the intransigent Baron refuses to return despite the appeals of the assembled heroes, is also invoked as a sanction for his oath, in the manner of Achilles swearing on the scepter of Agamemnon. And just as Achilles stressed the irrevocable nature of his decision by reminding his audience that he was no more capable of going back on his oath than the scepter was of turning back into the tree from which it was cut, so the Baron stresses the irremediable nature of his act by reminding his audience that the lock can never again grow on Belinda's head. In the face of this irrefutable logic Belinda can only complain of what she regards as a violation of her honor, concluding her speech with the memorable couplet,

> Oh hadst thou, Cruel! been content to seize
> Hairs less in sight, or any Hairs but these!   [IV, 175–76]

Book IV ends in a deadlock similar to the one in the *Iliad* involving Agamemnon, who has sworn to keep the prize taken from Achilles, and Achilles, who has sworn to withdraw from battle until the Achaeans suffer terrible losses without him.

In book V Clarissa attempts to mediate the dispute in the manner of Nestor, but, unlike Nestor's even-handed speech, which finds faults on both sides, Clarissa's, however wise, is critical only of Belinda. Roused by the virago Thalestris, the beaux and belles form parties and proceed to do battle. At this point Pope compares the battle to certain theomachies in the *Iliad* during which the various Olympians intervene on behalf of their Achaean or Trojan favorites:

> No common weapons in their Hands are found,
> Like Gods they fight, nor dread a mortal Wound.   [V, 43–44]

In this drawing-room battle the warriors are not mere mortals and protégés of the gods, but enjoy a quasi-divine status. The distinction is all important because it is the foundation of Pope's mock-epic conception of this fashionable society, whose denizens live in a world of Olympian detachment from the pressures of time, decay, and the other unpleasant realities epitomized in "mortal wound." In the play world of Hampton Court, though the godlike beaux and belles are immune to mortal wounds, as are the Olympians, the overtones of the line go far beyond this obvious point, as Pope develops the sexual connotations of dying in the inconclusive battle that follows. After invoking the theomachies during which

'Gainst Pallas, Mars; Latona, Hermes arms;
And all Olympus rings with loud Alarms.   [V, 47–48]

Pope gives a curious twist to his parody. The godlike beaux actually court death!

While thro' the Press enrag'd Thalestris flies,
And scatters Deaths around from both her Eyes,
A Beau and Witling perish'd in the Throng,
One dy'd in Metaphor, and one in Song.
"O cruel Nymph! a living Death I bear,"
Cry'd Dapperwit, and sunk beside his Chair.
A mournful Glance Sir Fopling upward cast,
"Those Eyes are made so killing"—was his last.
Thus on Meander's flow'ry Margin lies
Th' expiring Swan, and as he sings he dies.   [V, 57–66]

While the death these immortals suffer may be limited to word-play and metaphor, the Baron seeks a more substantial consummation:

See fierce Belinda on the Baron flies,
with more than usual Lightning in her Eyes;
Nor fear'd the Chief th' unequal Fight to try,
Who sought no more than on his Foe to die.   [V, 75–78]

This paradoxical love-death sought by the Baron suggests the only conceivable resolution of the dispute. For Belinda it is the sole escape from an endless Olympian round of activities leading nowhere since, as Clarissa puts it, "She who scorns a Man must die a Maid." The weapon with which Belinda attacks the Baron ironically includes Clarissa's meaning and a great deal more:

"Now meet thy Fate," incens'd Belinda cry'd
And drew a deadly Bodkin from her side.
(The same, his ancient Personage to deck,
Her great-great Grandsire wore about his Neck
In three Seal-Rings; which after melted down,
Form'd a vast Buckle for his Widow's gown:
Her infant Grandame's Whistle next it grew,
The Bells she gingled, and the Whistle blew;
Then in a Bodkin grac'd her Mother's Hairs,
Which long she wore, and now Belinda wears.   [V, 87–96]

Belinda's bodkin and the history of its metamorphoses carry intimations of mortality, but intimations of marriage, birth, infancy, and old age as well. Everywhere in *The Rape of the Lock* the characters seem ageless, unchanging, eternally youthful. Their illusions of eternal youth allow them to play endlessly a mating game that never reaches a climax. Just as the Olympians, imprisoned in their immortality, are doomed to repetitive cycles of intrigues, quarrels, feasts, and inconclusive interventions in battle throughout most of the *Iliad,* Pope's belles and witlings are prevented by their unending cycles of treats, cards, balls, toilettes, and flirtation from escaping into life. The bodkin on which Belinda swears her oath is the comic counterpart of the scepter by which Achilles swears his irreconcilable hostility to Agamemnon, an oath fraught with catastrophic consequences. The scepter, with its bloody and monstrous entail upon generation after generation, is an appropriate symbol of irredeemable tragedy. The bodkin is no such thing, but rather a symbol of the natural cycles of human life from birth to death. Were she to understand it aright, Belinda would see the bodkin as an emblem of her human destiny. The Baron is equally uncomprehending in the oath he swears by Belinda's ravished lock.

There are faults, then, on both sides, and whether it is Belinda striving to recover the lock, or the Baron determined to retain it, both are fighting over something that is not the true object of contention between them. The lock is obviously a polite surrogate for Belinda's maidenhood and for the Baron's unsatisfied masculinity. For both to fulfill their destinies, Belinda's role would be to surrender to the Baron, after due rites of courtship and marriage, and the Baron's to cherish her, court her, and ease for her the transition from proud maiden to happy wife. The mating games with which they fill their days—the balls and treats and tea parties and rounds of cards— have lost their ritual functions and have turned into inconclusive frivolities. The lock, which can have only metaphoric value, is misconstrued by both Belinda and the Baron as an object of intrinsic worth. Pope's inspired use of the trite ambiguity of the word *die* gives the real clue to a happy issue out of this existential cul-de-sac. Acceptance of mortality is a precondition to living fully. The fashionable round, as Pope puts it in a more somber mood in his *Epistle to a Lady,* leads to a Dantesque circle in hell:

> See how the World its Veterans rewards!
> A Youth of frolicks, an old Age of Cards,
> Fair to no purpose, artful to no end,
> Young without Lovers, old without a Friend,
> A fop their Passion, but their Prize a Sot,
> Alive, ridiculous, and dead, forgot!   [243–48]

Belinda's insistence on winning and her intransigent hostility to the Baron are clearly the Augustan mock-epic counterparts of the narrow notion of heroic honor that nourished the quarrel between Agamemnon and Achilles. But since Belinda and the Baron remain irreconcilable on a point of false honor, the conflict remains a deadlock, climaxing in the Ovidian stellification of the lock.

The inconclusive mêlée of Pope's beaux and belles is an analogue to those equally inconclusive combats of the Olympians that occur at various points in the *Iliad.* What makes mortal combat significant, tragic, and conclusive—mortality—cannot raise Homer's theomachies to a level of equal importance. For the Olympians war is play, and it is for this reason that the gods in the *Iliad* become figures of fun, as C. M. Bowra remarked.[1] The battle of Pope's beaux and witlings is clearly founded on one of the most absurd of these theomachies, the battle-royal encouraged by Zeus in book XXI, a domestic farce in which Ares, trying to revenge himself on his sister, Athene, is laid low by a boulder from her ponderous hand, and Hera calls her daughter Artemis a "shameless hussy," boxes her ears, and scatters her arrows.

If the games for Patroclus mirror the serious concerns of the *Iliad* and provide a brief respite from them, in *The Rape of the Lock* the relation of games to serious concerns seems to be inverted. Where daily life is play, as in this hermetically sealed playground of Augustan society, what corresponds to the "reality" against which the confrontations of beaux and belles can be measured? There are a few pinholes in the otherwise impermeable membrane that encloses this timeless space, such as the intimations of mortality in Clarissa's speech, or the oft-quoted line "Then wretches hang that jurymen may dine," or the classic zeugmas juxtaposing the beau monde and the political world:

> Here Britain's Statesmen oft the Fall foredoom
> Of Foreign Tyrants and of Nymphs at home;
> Here Thou, Great ANNA! whom three Realms obey,
> Dost sometimes Counsel take—and sometimes Tea.   [III, 5–8]

Still, the fashionable life at this court is almost as free from the pressures of time and mortality as life on Olympus, with its round of drinking, squabbling, and intrigue. Having presented the ordinary life of beaux and belles *sub specie ludi,* Pope cast about, I believe, for an inner world that would reflect it, as the games in Homer reflect the ordinary world of war, and he found it in the game of Ombre.[2] One aspect of Pope's ingenious use of the game bears again on the important distinction between play and ordinary reality. Where the normal life of the court is inconsequential, the game of Ombre is decisive: Belinda wins, and her victory precipitates the main action of the poem. Moreover, the game seems more real and its playing-card combatants more vital and human than the etiolated youth who play the hands. The male court cards assume a virile substantiality that Sir Plume, the Baron, and the rest have not, while the queens are more truly feminine than the belles. In other words, sexual differentiation is strongly marked:

> Behold, four Kings in Majesty rever'd,
> With Hoary Whiskers and a forky Beard;
> And four fair Queens whose hands sustain a flow'r,
> Th' expressive Emblem of their softer Pow'r;
> Four Knaves in Garbs succinct, a trusty Band,
> Caps on their heads, and Halberds in their hand.   [III, 37–42]

Clearly a more rugged and simpler heroic world is evoked, in which the
passions and human attachments of the cardboard images are deeper and
stronger than those of the players, as seen in the final, winning, trick:

> And now, (as oft in some distemper'd State)
> On one nice Trick depends the gen'ral Fate.
> An Ace of Hearts steps forth: The King unseen
> Lurk'd in her Hand, and mourn'd his captive Queen.
> He springs to Vengeance with an eager pace,
> And falls like Thunder on the prostrate Ace!   [III, 93–98]

Thus, Pope's delicious and unobtrusive irony has endowed the royal cards, in
the interlude of Ombre, with a solidity of specification that outweighs their
epicene manipulators. It is a play within a play that shows nature its image
and erotic passion its features.

When gods fight each other or fight with mortals, they may suffer pain, but
immortality invariably renders the divine victim ludicrous. Immune to the
irreversible consequences that mortals must endure, the gods of classical pan-
theons can only make of war what Milton calls "a civil game." Dr. Johnson's
strictures on the war in Heaven in *Paradise Lost* VI as a "confusion of spirit
and matter"[3] have provided a useful departure for critical studies by Arnold
Stein, Merritt Hughes, Joseph Summers, Stella Revard, and others.[4] For
example, Stein's account of the war in Heaven as a "gigantic scherzo" takes
one a long way toward appreciating an episode formerly regarded as a failed
attempt at rendering a heroic conflict and a grotesque blot on the poem. Far
from being an unintentional and tasteless farce in which not only the devils
but the good angels are demeaned, the episode is defended as an expression of
Milton's characteristic aversion to attempts to settle moral issues by force,
while the discomfiture momentarily suffered by the loyal angels is both a
challenge to Abdiel's somewhat facile assumption that

> When Reason hath to do with force, yet so
> Most Reason is that Reason overcome   [VI, 125–26]

and a test of their loyalty under pressure, "by humiliation and strong suffer-
ance." Milton drew on theomachies in the *Iliad* to shape some of the key
incidents in the war in Heaven and, above all, to set the tone for its central
episodes.

   In addition to the touches of domestic farce that leaven Olympians'
combat in the *Iliad* —Athene flattening her brother, who happens to be the
god of war, with a rock, or Hera, when she grasps the wrists of her daughter
Artemis, the huntress queen, with one hand boxing her ears and scattering
her arrows—there are some ludicrous encounters that, in spirit and in detail,
lie behind certain key incidents in *Paradise Lost*. In *Iliad* V Diomedes, the
preux chevalier of the Achaeans during Achilles' absence, is incited by Athene
to make forays against two of the gods. The first is Aphrodite, who, unwisely

intervening on the Trojan side, has her hand pricked by the point of Diomedes' spear. With a shriek she flies up to Olympus and falls at the knees of
her father Zeus to complain of what those nasty mortals have done. Zeus's
response is a masterpiece of affectionate paternal irony: "Warfare is not for
you, child. Lend yourself / to sighs of longing and the marriage bed. / Let
Ares and Athena deal with war" (V, 428–30). Comforted by her father and
healed by her mother, Dione, Aphrodite decides to keep apart henceforth
from the struggle that is raging over her son, Aeneas. Apollo, however, now
urges Ares to intervene on the Trojan side and avenge his sister. But the god
of war is no more successful in the encounter than the goddess of love, as
Diomedes, assisted by the formidable force of Athene, drives his spear deep
into Ares' belly and pulls it out again.

> Then brazen Ares
> howled to heaven, terrible to hear
> as roaring from ten thousand men in battle
> when long battalions clash.   [V, 865–68]

Like his sister, the indignant Ares complains to his father, but this time
Zeus's response is anything but consoling:

> "Do not come whining here, you two-faced brute,
> most hateful to me of all the Olympians.
> Combat and brawling are your element.
> This beastly, incorrigible truculence
> comes from your mother, Hera, whom I keep
> but barely in my power, say what I will.
> Still, I will not have you suffer longer.
> I fathered you, after all;
> your mother bore you as a son to me.
> If you had been conceived by any other
> and born so insolent, then long ago
> your place would have been far below the gods."
>
> With this he told Paîeon to attend him,
> and sprinkling anodyne upon his wound
> Paîeon undertook to treat and heal him
> who was not born for death.   [V, 889–902]

Untaught by this painful experience, Ares reenters the battle in book xxi,
where, as shown above, he is laid low by Athene herself.

The two principal hand-to-hand engagements in the war in Heaven are
modeled on Ares' encounters with Diomedes and Athene. In the first of these
Michael wounds Satan grievously with his sword:

> it met
> The sword of *Satan* with steep force to smite
> Descending, and in half cut sheer, nor stay'd,
> But with swift wheel reverse, deep ent'ring shear'd

All his right side; then *Satan* first knew pain,
And writh'd him to and fro convolv'd; so sore
The griding sword with discontinuous wound
Pass'd through him, but th' Ethereal substance clos'd
Not long divisible, and from the gash
A stream of Nectarous humor issuing flow'd
Sanguine, such as Celestial Spirits may bleed,
And all his Armor stain'd erewhile so bright.
Forthwith on all sides to his aid was run
By Angels many and strong, who interpos'd
Defense, while others bore him on thir Shields
Back to his Chariot, where it stood retir'd
From off the files of war: there they him laid
Gnashing for anguish and despite and shame
To find himself not matchless, and his pride
Humbl'd by such rebuke, so far beneath
His confidence to equal God in power.
Yet soon he heal'd.   [VI, 323–44]

For the first time in the poem Satan's apparent imperturbability is shattered, and, though he does not bellow like Ares, he "writhes to and fro convolv'd" and "gnashes for anguish and despite and shame." The wound is a deep one, yet Milton surprisingly draws on the account of Aphrodite's scratch to describe the "stream of Nectarous humor issuing [that] flow'd / Sanguine." The corresponding detail in Homer is closely followed: "Now from the goddess that immortal fluid, / ichor flowed—the blood of blissful gods" (V, 339–40). Milton's allusion here to the wounding of Aphrodite, the goddess who instigated the Trojan War, not only introduces a satirical sidelight on Satan's conduct, but underscores his responsibility for starting the war in Heaven. The analogues to the wounding of Ares, "most hateful to me of the Olympians," are manifold, detailed, and too obvious to enumerate. An even richer example of Milton's adaptation of a mock-epic theomachy in Homer is the encounter between Abdiel and Satan. The first engagement, which begins the hostilities, is modeled on this purely mortal combat between Diomedes and Aeneas in the *Iliad:*

But Diomedes
bent for a stone and picked it up—a boulder
no two men now alive could lift, though he
could heft it easily. This mass he hurled
and struck Aineias on the hip, just where
the hipbone shifts in what they call the bone-cup,
crushing this joint with two adjacent tendons
under the skin ripped off by the rough stone.
Now the great Trojan, fallen on his knees,
put all his weight on one strong hand
and leaned against the earth: night veiled his eyes.
                                                        [V, 308–18]

The Miltonic encounter leaves Satan confounded and in the posture of the stunned Aeneas:

> So saying, a noble stroke he lifted high,
> Which hung not, but so swift with tempest fell
> On the proud Crest of *Satan,* that no sight,
> Nor motion of swift thought, less could his Shield
> Such ruin intercept: ten paces huge
> He back recoil'd; the tenth on bended knee
> His massy Spear upstay'd. [VI, 189–95]

Abdiel's mighty blow, however discomfiting to Satan and his cohorts (and all the more humiliating since it is struck by one whom Satan condemns as a "seditious angel"), is necessarily inconclusive, as is Michael's.

The third main hand-to-hand encounter is patterned on those of Ares. Between Gabriel and Moloch, it climaxes the first day's battle, and the palm goes to the good angels.

> Meanwhile in other parts like deeds deserv'd
> Memorial, where the might of *Gabriel* fought,
> And with fierce Ensigns pierc'd the deep array
> Of *Moloch* furious King, who him defi'd,
> And at his Chariot wheels to drag him bound
> Threat'n'd, nor from the Holy One of Heaven
> Refrain'd his tongue blasphémous; but anon
> Down clov'n to the waist, with shatter'd Arms
> And uncouth pain fled bellowing. [VI, 354–62]

As Addison was one of the first to observe, Milton here "had his eye on Mars in the *Iliad,*" adding that "the reader will easily observe how Milton has kept all the horror of this image without running into ridicule of it."[5] Yet the ridicule seems inescapable in view of Moloch's hyperbolic and blasphemous threats and all the more so in view of the close identification Milton has established between the most brutal of the rebel angels and Homer's most brutal god. Surely there is a comic discrepancy between Moloch here and Moloch as he conceives of himself in book II:

> His trust was with th' Eternal to be deem'd
> Equal in strength, and rather than be less
> Car'd not to be at all; with that care lost
> Went all his fear: of God, or Hell, or worse
> He reck'd not. [II, 46–50]

Clearly Moloch's pose as Stoic hero is as shattered as his arms, and one cannot doubt that at the council of the rebel chiefs that ends this first catastrophic day of battle, he would have to agree with Nisroch's observation:

> yet hard
> For Gods, and too unequal work we find
> Against unequal arms to fight in pain,

> Against unpain'd, impassive; from which evil
> Ruin must needs ensue; for what avails
> Valor or strength, though matchless, quell'd with pain
> Which all subdues, and makes remiss the hands
> Of Mightiest?   [VI, 452–59]

The rebel angels, like Homer's combative Olympians, suffer pain, but unlike .their Homeric counterparts, the devils learn from experience. To avenge their pain on their foes, and to defend themselves from any further hand-to-hand agonies, they resort to the secret weapon of cannon, invented, appropriately enough, by Satan. One should note that, according to the ancient Homeric code of heroic warfare, this is a gross violation of the rules of the game. None of the first-rate heroes in Homer employs a weapon that permits him to fight at a distance. Odysseus left his bow at home in Ithaca and never made use of the poisoned arrows that Mentes once brought him as a guest gift. True, bows are used in the Trojan war, but usually by heroes of dubious honor, like Pandarus and Paris. The unwritten protocol seems to be that a real hero only fights with a weapon that puts him in immediate range of his adversary. This point is underscored by the fact that a tentative truce between Trojans and Achaeans, to permit a settlement of the war by a combat between chosen champions, is breached by Pandarus's wounding Menelaus with an arrow. Not the least of the ironies surrounding Achilles' death, as anticipated in the *Iliad,* is that he dies from an arrow shot by Paris.

The concealed cannon employed by Satan's forces on the second day of the war in Heaven are simply a grosser violation of the rules of war. Against these unexpected weapons the loyal angels are helpless. The arch duplicity of Satan's puns is a marked departure from the forthright style in which contending heroes traditionally assert their claims to superior *areté*. (Not the least reprehensible product of the Satanic revolt is the labored and self-gratulatory ambiguity of their comments on their astonished victims.) A comparison of the vitality that Pope's wordplay on "die" accumulates at the core of *The Rape of the Lock* points up the sterility and frivolity of Satan's puns, born, as Conrad Hyers suggests, of deep despair.[6] If, then, the labored word-plays of Satan and his cohorts strike the reader as stupid, they ought to:

> O Friends, why come not on these Victors proud?
> Erewhile they fierce were coming, and when wee,
> To entertain them fair with open Front
> And Breast, (what could we more?) propounded terms
> Of composition, straight they chang'd thir minds,
> Flew off, and into strange vagaries fell,
> As they would dance, yet for a dance they seem'd
> Somewhat extravagant and wild, perhaps
> For joy of offer'd peace; but I suppose
> If our proposals once again were heard
> We should compel them to a quick result.   [VI, 609–19]

Not the least of the sufferings that the good angels must now endure are the scoffs of Satan's cowardly lieutenant, who dares in this moment of absolute military superiority to ape his master:

> To whom thus *Belial* in like gamesome mood.
> Leader, the terms we sent were terms of weight,
> Of hard contents, and full of force urg'd home,
> Such as we might perceive amus'd them all,
> And stumbl'd many; who receives them right,
> Had need from head to foot well understand;
> Not understood, this gift they have besides,
> They show us when our foes walk not upright.   [VI, 620–27]

The normal language of *Paradise Lost,* unexcelled in richness and imaginative grasp, provides an instructive comment on these devilish witticisms, which are characterized by imaginative poverty. True wit augments understanding with the powers of reason and fancy, but such false wit darkens understanding through a deliberate perversion of the metaphorical process. If wit enhances meaning, this systematic reductiveness is antiwit, ultimately reduced to an infantile practical joke that backfires. God's wit is true wit because it comprehends the universal context in which Satan's machinations inevitably rebound upon themselves.

The second day's fighting escalates the epic theomachy to its highest pitch. The loyal angels, whom the devil's artillery had bowled down like duckpins, cast aside weapons, shields, and armor and proceed to hurl enormous chunks of landscape at their foes. In this "jaculation dire," Milton carries the dialectic of immortal combat to its utmost conclusion, a deadlock that God sums up:

> sore hath been thir fight,
> As likeliest was, when two such Foes met arm'd;
> For to themselves I left them, and thou know'st,
> Equal in thir Creation they were form'd,
> Save what sin hath impair'd, which yet hath wrought
> Insensibly, for I suspend their doom;
> Whence in perpetual fight they needs must last
> Endless, and no solution will be found;
> War wearied hath perform'd what War can do,
> And to disorder'd rage let loose the reins,
> With Mountains as with Weapons arm'd, which makes
> Wild work in Heav'n, and dangerous to the main.
> Two days are therefore past, the third is thine;
> For thee I have ordain'd it, and thus far
> Have suffer'd, that the Glory may be thine
> Of ending this great War, since none but Thou
> Can end it.   [VI, 687–703]

Critics of Milton's God have charged him with disingenuousness in permitting his loyal angels to fight a war he knows they can't win. While it is true
that he seems to enjoy the spectacle somewhat like Zeus in *Iliad* XXI, who
"laugh'd in his heart for joy, seeing the gods / about to meet in strife" (389–
90), and while his behavior may be defended on the grounds that he permits
maximum freedom to men and angels alike, a more important reason for his
allowing this indecisive theomachy to disturb the peace of Heaven for two
days is that it provides a final and irrefutable demonstration of the futility of
heroic warfare. Here is the ultimate example of that "tedious and fabled
Havoc" Milton derides in the beginning of book IX, the ultimate criticism of
the heroic code as narrowly conceived by some of its Homeric and Virgilian
examplars. Interestingly enough, in *Paradise Lost* not a single decisive act is
achieved by force. Every deed of malevolent violence not only redounds upon
the doer, but is transmuted into good. Even in the hands of the virtuous,
violence is inneffectual. The angelic squadrons who patrol the circuits of Eden
with such vigilance, discipline, and panache are unable to prevent Satan's final
incursion, and none of God's champions—Abdiel, Michael, or Gabriel—
though armed with swords of ethereal temper, can win a decisive victory over
Satan or any of his cohorts. The farce of the war in Heaven, in which
irresistible forces collide with immovable bodies, produces a tremendous ex-
plosion in which the only serious casualty is the tradition of heroic warfare.[7]
Only the Son can break the futile dialectic of violence entailed on the angelic
armies by Satan, and the arms he uses are of the Spirit. "Exhausted, spiritless,
afflicted, fall'n" (VI, 852), the rebel forces, after much belligerent posturing,
nevertheless realize the hopelessness of force and, in their future undertakings,
resort to fraud—a decision that deeply undercuts their pretensions to heroic
virtue.

The war in Heaven, then, with its absurdity, farce, and bombastic
hyperbole, is indeed a confusion of spirit and matter. The devils, "since by
strength / They measure all, of other excellence / Not emulous" (VI, 820–
22), attempt in their folly to defeat immortal spirits with the ponderous
matter of their cannons (and the almost equally ponderous matter of their
jokes). The good angels, partly under the false assumption that right is
might, put their faith in arms that serve only to encumber and humiliate
them. The gigantic scherzo purges this epic at its very center from the
traditional epic fallacy of force. The poem is now free to move on to what
Milton considers to be the only real arena of combat, one in which victory is
won by "things deem'd weak / Subverting worldly strong, and worldly wise /
By simply meek" (XII, 567–69). The arena is transformed into the Paradise
within.

Pope's brilliant assimilation of Homer and Milton in *The Rape of the Lock,* with
its rich, implicit affirmation of a life of action and passion rather than acting,
resulted in a comic poem at once elegant, funny, and profound. After

Paradise Lost had exhausted the possibilities of an epic poem in the classical tradition, Pope salvaged a vital part of the Homeric and Miltonic tradition, and these great poets, with Virgil and Ovid, are the sources of his mock-epic imagination.

In the *Dunciad*, Pope creates, in a series of mock-epic episodes, a jocose-serious Virgilian style subsumed at the end by a tragic Miltonic apocalypse. The central event of the poem is patterned on Aeneas's descent into the underworld in the sixth book of the *Aeneid*, with the egregious Colley Cibber playing Aeneas to the Sibyl's Dulness. A central motif both in the *Aeneid* and the *Iliad* is the labyrinth, which owes its poetic origins to the famous Cretan labyrinth built by Daedalus. Pope exploits the analogies between the predominant Augustan subculture represented by Cibber and Virgil's heroic imperial vision to the hilt.

A critical aspect of the labyrinth motif is its function as a community ritual in the founding of a city, whose walls were consecrated by a threefold ploughing of the site where the foundations would be. In this respect the motif is apotropaic, defending the walls from intruders while giving access to initiates.

An opposite and more familiar aspect of the labyrinth is as a place of imprisonment or alienation, expressed in Ovid's and Virgil's phrases, *inextricabilis error* and *irremediabilis error*. Where Ariadne's labyrinthine dance, mentioned in Homer's description of Achilles' shield, celebrates Theseus' penetration of the Cretan maze, slaying of the Minotaur, and escape, and Daedalus' flight from his edifice marks his transcendence of the labyrinth's limits by a more potent art, it is primarily, for the unqualified, a place of confusion, danger, and confinement. As C. R. Deedes has written,

The Labyrinth was the center of the strongest emotions of the people—joy, fear, and grief were given the most intense forms of expression. These emotions were directed into certain channels, producing ritual and the earliest forms of art—not only music and dancing, but also sculpture and painting. The Labyrinth, as tomb and temple, fostered the development of all art and literature, activities which in those days possessed a religious and life-giving experience.[8]

The mock-epic emphasis of *Mac Flecknoe* and *The Dunciad* required a radical modification of the *Aeneid*'s pattern of descent and return. For the vertiginous descent there can be no corresponding ascent. Dryden's and Pope's dunces may aspire to "soar above th'*Aonian* Mount," but they are skilled only in the art of sinking. Father Flecknoe's final abrupt descent drops him "yet declaiming" through the trapdoor of what, in theatrical terms, was conventionally known as Hell. All that ascends is the bard's mantle, with which the new Prince of Dulness will be invested.

In Pope's more elaborately Virgilian and Miltonic mock epic, lateral motion is added to the pull of gravity, so that there is a pervasive downward-spiraling movement, especially in books III and IV, in addition to futile labyrinthine movements. In the somber climax it is not the patrons of Dulness who descend but her enemy, the Word.

The Dunciad seems to be disposed around books V and VI of the Aeneid. The games in book II are modeled on the games in Aeneid V and in Iliad XXIII, while Cibber's most adventurous experience is an Aeneas-like descent into an underworld of Dulness in Dunciad III, a descent characterized, however, by passivity and inertia, without a trace of heroic Virgilian labor. The facility of Cibber's passage and his inertness in the underworld define satirically the torpid and effortless character of the Dunces' literary productions. Pope has devised a suggestive image for these qualities by combining the bewildering features of the maze with the irresistible force of gravity. The result is a downward-spiraling vortex whose point may represent a number of themes, including the extinction of reason. Pope's downward gyre of bathos reflects the attractive power of egotism, unlike the upward spiral of Yeats, which leads to chaos because "the center cannot hold."

Pope's central conception of *dulness* as the offspring of pride, and of pride as a kind of rampant self-assertion that, paradoxically, leads to the obliteration of the self, finds its proper image in this vortex. Against the heroic and consecrated aspirations of Milton "to soar above th'*Aonian* Mount," he presents the Dunces as whirling downward to a non-place of darkness and disorientation.

We first encounter the labyrinth motif in book I, where Dulness pays a royal visit to Grub Street, a "Chaos dark and deep, / Where nameless Somethings in their causes sleep" (55–56). In this place of confusion—half Hell, half Garden of Adonis—she finds examples of a pullulating literary formlessness and nonsense:

> [Here] hints, like spawn, scarce quick in embryo lie
> [Here] new-born nonsense first is taught to cry,
> Maggots half-formed in rhyme exactly meet,
> And learn to crawl upon poetic feet.
> Here one poor word an hundred clenches makes,
> And ductile dulness new meanders takes;
> There motley images her fancy strike,
> Figures ill-pair'd and Similes unlike.
> She sees a Mob of Metaphors advance,
> Pleas'd with the madness of the mazy dance.   [I, 59–68]

At the center of Achilles' shield Homer had depicted the vital dance of Ariadne in a company of youths and maidens, a dance whose labyrinthine patterns ritualized the deliverance of Theseus from the Minotaur at the heart of the maze. Aesthetically and ritually the dance has profound cultural reverberations at the heart of Homer's epic. As the dance of the *géranos,* the crane, it has erotic and liberating power, and is probably the oldest vernacular dance in the West. (Joyce made it a thematic center of *The Portrait of the Artist as a*

Young Man, when Stephen encounters a birdlike girl wading in the sea off a beach called, significantly, the Bull.)

Pope's amorphous pageant, with its strangely precise but meaningless activities subsumed in "meanders" and "the mazy dance," finds its counterpart in Cibber's abortive struggle to write:

> Swearing and supperless the Hero sate,
> Blasphem'd his Gods, the Dice, and damn'd his Fate.
> Then gnaw'd his pen, then dash'd it to the ground,
> Sinking from thought to thought, a vast profound!
> Plung'd for his sense, but found no bottom there,
> Yet wrote and flounder'd on, in mere despair.
> Round him much Embryo, much Abortion lay,
> Much future Ode, and abdicated Play;
> Nonsense precipitate, like running Lead,
> That slipp'd through cracks and zigzags of the head;
> All that on Folly Frenzy could beget,
> Fruits of dull Heat, and Sooterkins of Wit. {I, 115–26]

The passage is obviously indebted to Satan's voyage through Chaos in *Paradise Lost* II, with its conflict of "embryon atoms." Cibber, "plunging for his sense," is a trivialized and antiheroic Satan bent upon a downward quest:

> At last his Sail-Broad Vans
> He spreads for flight, and in the surging smoke
> Uplifted spurns the ground, thence many a league
> As in a cloudy Chair ascending rides
> Audacious, but that seat soon failing, meets
> A vast vacuity: all unawares
> Flutt'ring his pennons vain plumb down he drops
> Ten thousand fadom deep. [II, 927–34]

Pope thus joins Satan's strenuous ascent to suggestions of the descent to the underworld, a motif he makes explicit in book III. He also carries over into his poem the Miltonic suggestion that for Satan the way up and the way down are the same:

> Which way I fly is Hell, myself am Hell;
> And in the lowest deep a lower deep
> Still threat'ning to devour me opens wide,
> To which the Hell I suffer seems a Heav'n. [IV, 76–79]

For the Prince of Dunces, Dulness—like Hell for the Prince of Devils—is a state of mind. The labyrinth in which Cibber is lost is in his head.

In his sacrifice to Dulness, Cibber's elaborate offerings of unreadable and unsellable books ("Redeem'd from tapers and defrauded pies") are topped off with a neat little Baroque motif of aspiration:

An hecatomb of pure, unsulli'd lays
That altar crowns: A folio common-place
Founds the whole pile, of all his works the base:
Quartos, octavos, shape the less'ning pyre;
A twisted Birth-day Ode completes the spire.   [I, 158–62]

The upward thrust is offset by the oblique and ponderous movements of a Dunce's mind:

O thou! of Bus'ness the directing soul!
To this our head like byass to the bowl,
Which, as more pond'rous, made its aim more true,
Obliquely wadling to the mark in view:
O! ever gracious to perplext mankind,
Still spread a healing mist before the mind;
And lest we err by Wit's wild dancing light,
Secure us kindly in our native night.
Or, if to Wit a coxcomb make pretence,
Guard the sure barrier between that and Sense;
Or quite unravel all the reas'ning thread,
And hang some curious cobweb in its stead.   [I, 169–80]

Into these thwart obliquities Pope has woven Shadwell's pseudo-Jonsonian humoresque (from *Mac Flecknoe*, "Obliquely wandering to the end in View"); crossed it with another telling echo from Dryden ("thy chase had a Beast in View"); and added an allusion to the protective mists that Venus from time to time throws about Aeneas, permitting him to see unseen (although here they prevent the hero from seeing). The brilliant cento culminates in images of the mazy dance: rather than "err by Wit's wild dancing light," Cibber implores his goddess-mother to "quite unravel all the reas'ning thread, / And hang some curious cobweb in its stead!" The goddess responds by extinguishing the barely combustible materials of Cibber's sacrifice with a sheet from Ambrose Philips's uncompleted poem, *Thule:*

Sudden she flies, and whelms it o'er the pyre;
Down sink the flames, and with a hiss expire.   [I, 259–60]

The motifs of sinking and falling are extended in book II to include a motley group of Dunces, most notably in the Fleet-ditch diving contests. Pope concludes the games with a reading from the "pond'rous books" of contemporary authors, which stupefies the audience:

Who sate the nearest, by the words o'ercome,
Slept first, the distant nodded to the hum.
Then down are roll'd the books; stretch'd o'er 'em lies
Each gentle clerk, and mutt'ring seals his eyes.
As what a Dutchman plumps into the lakes,
One circle first, and then a second makes;
What Dulness dropt among her sons imprest

> Like motion from one circle to the rest;
> So from the mid most the nutation spreads,
> Round and more round, o'er all the sea of heads. [II, 401–10]

While the lesser Dunces sleep, overcome by the contagious force of dull books, the goddess proceeds in book III to initiate her protégé into the *mysterium tremendum et fascinans* of her arts. In the opening scene, "in her Temple's last recess inclos'd," she combines (vis-à-vis her son Cibber) the role of the Sibyl in presiding over Aeneas's rites of passage with the protective, though obfuscating, maternal role of Venus. In this descent to the underworld there is, of course, no trace of Aeneas's strenuous ordeal: "And now, on Fancy's easy wing convey'd, / The King descending, views th'Elyzian shade" (13–14). Cibber is actually asleep.

Elkanah Settle, in the role of Anchises, reveals the metempsychotic wonders of this pseudo-Virgilian underworld to his unconscious heir:

> "Oh born to see what none can see awake!
> Behold the wonders of the oblivious Lake.
> Thou, yet unborn, hast touch'd the sacred shore;
> The hand of Bavius drench'd thee o'er and o'er.
> But blind to former as to future fate,
> What mortal knows his pre-existent date?
> Who knows how long thy transmigrating soul
> Might from Boeotian to Boeotian roll?
> How many Dutchmen she vouchsaf'd to thrid?
> How many stages thro' old Monks she rid?
> And all who since, in mild benighted days,
> Mix'd the Owl's ivy with the Poet's bays?
> As man's Maeanders to the vital spring
> Roll all their tides, then back their circles bring;
> Or whirligigs, twirl'd round by skilful swain,
> Suck the thread in, then yield it out again:
> All nonsense thus, of old or modern date,
> Shall in thee center, from thee circulate." [III, 43–60]

The mystery of reincarnation in Virgil, through which past and future are linked, is here collapsed into a futile cycle in which the soul of the archdunce obliviously threads and unthreads a labyrinthine chain of obtuse identities. Pope has subtly introduced Ariadne's guiding thread, which led Theseus out of the Cretan labyrinth, but here, since Cibber is the center of the maze, there is no way out for him. He has become the monster of the labyrinth, like Ovid's *monstrum biforme*.

The vision of Dulness's empire restored at the end of book III is exciting enough to rouse Cibber briefly. The book concludes with the only words he speaks in the entire episode: "Enough! Enough!" The "raptur'd Monarch" then ascends through the ivory gate of illusion, like Aeneas, and returns to the world.

Pope may be glancing at Adam's joy at the prospect of the Redemption in Cibber's rapture:

> O goodness infinite, goodness immense!
> That all this good of evil shall produce,
> And evil turn to good; more wonderful
> Than that which by creation first brought forth
> Light out of darkness! full of doubt I stand,
> Whether I should repent me now of sin
> By mee done and occasion'd, or rejoice
> Much more, that much more good thereof shall spring,
> To God more glory, more good will to Men
> From God, and over wrath grace shall abound.   [XII, 469–78]

In Cibber's ecstacy at the prospect of the restoration of the kingdom of Dulness Pope seems to imply an inversion of the felix culpa, the heart of Milton's providential scheme through which God converts evil to good. To Dulness and her devotees Pope's archpedant, Bentley, ascribes a corresponding power of the "uncreating word" to turn good into evil. He boasts himself to be

> Thy mighty Scholiast, whose unweary'd pains
> Made Horace dull, and humbled Milton's strains.
> Turn what they will to Verse, their toil is vain,
> Critics like me shall make it prose again.   [IV, 211–14]

For the creative power of the *Word*—Christ, as the *Logos* in the Gospel of St. John, as well as the poetic imagination—Bentley substitutes the stultifying power of *words:*

> Then thus: "Since Man from beast by Words is known,
> Words are Man's province, Words we teach alone.
> When Reason doubtful, like the Samian letter,
> Points him two ways, the narrower is the better.
> Plac'd at the door of Learning, youth to guide,
> We never suffer it to stand too wide.
> To ask, to guess, to know, as they commence,
> As Fancy opens the quick springs of Sense,
> We ply the Memory, we load the brain,
> Bind rebel Wit, and double chain on chain,
> Confine the thought to exercise the breath;
> And keep them in the pale of Words till death."   [IV, 149–60]

The metamorphoses worked by Dulness exhaust the symbolic and spiritual powers of language and reify it. In the course of the poem mind and meaning accumulate weight and density of a quasi-physical nature, which subjects them increasingly to the pull of gravity. Pope is continually suggesting that civilization depends on aspiration and inspiration, which the Dunces reduce to "breath." This reductive process makes the influence of Dulness and the responses of her sons a simple illustration of Newton's first law:

> And now had Fame's posterior trumpet blown,
> And all the Nations summon'd to the Throne.
> The young, the old, who feel her inward sway,
> One instinct seizes and transports away.
> None need a guide, by sure Attraction led,
> And strong impulsive gravity of Head:
> None want a place, for all their Centre found,
> Hung to the Goddess and coher'd around.
> Not closer, orb in orb, conglob'd are seen
> The buzzing Bees about their dusky Queen.
>   The gath'ring number, as it moves along,
> Involves a vast involuntary throng,
> Who gently drawn, and struggling less and less,
> Roll in her Vortex, and her pow'r confess.   [IV, 71–84]

The massive and compact involvement of the Dunces in the vortex of Dulness is evoked in the slow, labyrinthine movement of sound and sense in such a line as "Involves a vast involuntary throng." As the mass of Dulness is increased by the "conglobing" of the Dunces around her, an "attractive power" that draws more and more into its orbit at an accelerating pace resembles the black hole in outer space, which results from the tremendous gravitational force exercised by a huge and dense mass of dead matter that can reduce its volume almost to the point of annihilation. Black holes swallow light.

The gravitational vortex, fundamental and ubiquitous to the power of Dulness, is not limited by the law of the conservation of matter. It is imagined by Pope to have the power to annihilate, for Dulness is finally conceived of as something like Rochester's "Nothing." The final implication of this image, then, is that of a self-destroying artifact:

> Yet, yet, one moment, one dim Ray of Light
> Indulge, dread Chaos, and immortal Night!
> Of darkness visible so much be lent,
> As half to shew, half veil the deep Intent.
> Ye Pow'r whose Mysteries restor'd I sing,
> To whom Time bears me on his rapid wing,
> Suspend a while your force inertly strong.
> And take at once the Poet and the Song.   [IV, 1–8]

CHAPTER EIGHT

The Erosion of the Tradition

The Exclusion crisis and its aftermath represent yet another version of the profound constitutional struggle between royal prerogative and parliamentary privilege that had been a central issue of the Civil War. Charles's reimposition of his authority with the dissolution of the Oxford Parliament in 1681 could, however, only temporarily arrest the monarchy's decline in power. That decline inevitably undermined the myth that had sustained pro-Stuart poetry. James, who had none of Charles's tact and charm but all his stubbornness and deviousness, so embittered his subjects that it took him a mere four years to lose the kingdom that Charles had so shrewdly preserved and passed on to him. The birth of James's son in 1688 raised the specter of a Papist dynasty and led to an invitation that brought William and Mary to the throne. James had tried to govern by force and threats; he had violated the law of the land by introducing Catholic officers into the army and into positions of trust; he had employed the threat of Irish troops against his English subjects; and he had flaunted his adherence to the old religion and aroused the slumbering dread of a return to the period of the martyrs under Bloody Mary.

Dryden's final performance as laureate was to celebrate the birth of James Francis Edward Stuart on Trinity Sunday—June 10, 1688—as yet another manifestation of divine regard for the Stuart succession. The infant is first hailed, like Charles in *Astraea Redux,* as the fruit of the new season. Of Charles he had written:

> How shall I speak of that triumphant day
> When you renew'd the expiring pomp of May!.
> (A month that owns an int'rest in your name:
> You and the flow'rs are its peculiar claim.)
> That star, that at your birth shone out so bright
> It stain'd the duller sun's meridian light,
> Did once again its potent fires renew
> Guiding our eyes to find and worship you.   [284–91]

The topos of seasonal renewal occurs early in *Britannia Rediviva:*

> Departing spring could only stay to shed
> Her bloomy beauties on the genial bed,
> But left the manly summer in her stead

> With timely fruit the longing land to cheer
> And to fulfill the promise of the year.
> Betwixt two seasons comes th' auspicious heir,
> This age to blossom and the next to bear.   [12–18]

Dryden then amplifies the event as a joint creation of the Trinity and links unconvincingly the triune act to the preservation of England, Ireland, and Scotland:

> Three realms united, and on one bestow'd
> An emblem of their mystic union show'd
> The mighty Trine the triple empire shar'd,
> As every person would have one to guard.   [31–34]

But the optimism of *Astraea Redux* summed up in Dryden's Virgilian phrase, "And now time's whiter series is begun, / Which in soft centuries will smoothly run" (292–93), is absent, and the Stuart opposition is seen as the party of Satan. No longer can Dryden find in contemporary events the possibility of redemption that is so important in the forerunners of *Britannia Rediviva*. Like *Threnodia Augustalis,* as Stephen Zwicker observes, *Britannia Rediviva* "fails to achieve a convincing reading of contemporary events as an expression of sacred history."[1] Nor does Dryden place the event in a Virgilian context, even though *Eclogue IV* would supply appropriate analogies. So, as Zwicker concludes, "In *Britannia Rediviva* Dryden very consciously resigns the prophetic office in which he had so often performed: 'Poets are not Prophets to foreknow / What Plants will take the Blite, and which will grow' (71–72). And the ending of the poem, which is usually Dryden's occasion to recapitulate the meaning of English history in redemptive terms is noticeably secular in *Britannia Rediviva*."[2] In the performance of his last laureate duty we may assume that Dryden was fully aware of the popular reaction to the birth of an heir. Mary had suffered two miscarriages, and her five previous children had died in infancy, while it was widely believed that the king had contracted a "virulent distemper" that would have made the birth of James Edward improbable. The rumor spread that the baby had been introduced into the Queen's bed in a warming-pan. For those apprehensive of a Papist heir (his godfather was the Pope) what really mattered was that the baby was the heir to the throne. A host of satirical songs mocked the claim to legitimacy that the king tried to uphold by the testimony of forty-one witnesses. *Tom Tyler, or The Nurse* may be taken as representative of this subversion of the royal scenario. A tile-maker's wife named Cooper was brought to Richmond to nurse the ailing infant:

> His lady from the tiles and bricks
> Kidnapped to court in coach and six;
> Her arms a sucking prince embrace,
> Whate'er you think of royal race;
> A prince come in the nick of time

> (Blessed d'Adda!), 'tis a venial crime
> That shall repair our breach of state;
> While all the world congratulate,
> Shall, like his sire, suppress the just,
> Raise knaves and fools to place of trust.   [9–18]³

Three weeks after the birth Admiral Edward Russell, disguised as an ordinary seaman, had left for Holland with the invitation to William in his care.⁴ In a rustic dialogue, *The Plowman,* Ralph describes to Nick the reluctant soldiers charged with the defense of James's throne:

> For I shall tell thee such a story
> Will make thee laugh, and yet be sorry.
> Along the road the soldiers pass
> Like herds of cattle going to grass
> Or droves of sheep to Smithfield fair,
> In the same pickle, too, they are,
> And with like cheerfulness each goes.
> Poor men, their hearts are in their hose!
> Where one is silent, ten do curse;
> None goes by choice, but all perforce.   [40–49]⁵

For once the popular terror of a Popish plot has a real basis:

> They say the Jesuit priests have ordered
> That all the Protestants must be murdered;
> The faithless Irish with 'em join
> As partners in their black design,
> And though we now do reap and sow,
> They are come o'er to reap and mow.   [70–75]

Such was the backlash of James's unlawful maintenance of a standing army. The last lines convert the *Annus Mirabilis* theme in support of William, just as Dryden had appropriated it from the radical sects of the 1660s to support Charles:

> Then never 'gainst preservers pray,
> But let our bullocks bellow still,
> And Pro. prince act Heaven's high will.
> If this be still the year of wonder,
> Or they or we must truckle under;
> Therefore unyoke, let's home to dinner,
> There'll be two losses for one winner.   [103–09]

The plowman pronounces the end of the cycle Dryden had proclaimed almost thirty years earlier.

With the Revolution of 1688 England gained a monarch whose claim to the throne was relatively tenuous—at least as long as James or his son was alive—

and one whose powers, therefore, could be more strictly curbed by Parliament than those of Charles or James. If William of Orange and his wife Mary shared that Stuart passion for absolute power that had characterized their predecessors, they concealed it well, and it is indisputable that they brought to England an unprecedented and badly needed religious toleration. Their reign was marked by the establishment of a modus vivendi that nevertheless failed to reconcile extreme Tories and Jacobites to the Dutchman who was an inveterate and tenacious foe of Louis XIV.

Opposition to William and Mary at first found satirical expression in lampoons treating them as usurpers and virtual parricides, riding over the body of their uncle and father in the royal coach, like Tarquin and Tullia. Arthur Mainwaring, in a powerful satire by that title, applied the grisly episode from Roman history to display the king and queen as greedy murderers quite unmoved by claims of justice, loyalty to the de jure monarch, or filial duty:

> In times when princes cancelled nature's law
> And declarations (which themselves did draw),
> When children used their parents to dethrone
> And gnawed their way like vipers to a crown,
> Tarquin, a savage, proud, ambitious prince,
> Prompt to expel, yet thoughtless of defense,
> The envied scepter did from Tullius snatch,
> The Roman king, and father by the match. [1–8][6]

With a style that owes much to Dryden, Mainwaring proceeds to attack Bishop Gilbert Burnet, who had helped William come to the throne driven by the ambition, so his enemies said, of being made Archbishop of Canterbury:

> 'Mongst these, a pagan priest for refuge fled,
> A prophet deep in godly faction read,
> A sycophant that knew the modish way
> To cant and plot, to flatter, and betray,
> To whine and sin, to scribble, and recant,
> A shameful author and a lustful saint.
> To serve all times, he could distinctions coin,
> And with great ease flat contradictions join.
> A traitor now, once loyal in extreme,
> (And then obedience was his only theme)
> He sang in temples the most passive lays
> And wearied monarchs with repeated praise,
> But managed awkwardly that lawful part,
> For to vent lies and treason was his art,
> And pointed libels at crowned heads to dart. [16–30]

Tullia outdoes her savage mate in cruelty:

>   This king removed, the assembled states thought fit
> That Tarquin on the vacant throne should sit,
> Voted him regent in their senate house
> And with an empty name endowed his spouse.
> The elder Tullia, (some authors feign)
> Drove o'er her father's corpse a trembling wain,
> But she, more guilty, numerous wains did drive
> To crush her father, and her king, alive.   [97–104]

Mainwaring touches the note of Senecan horror one finds in the satires of
Ayloffe and Oldham but in a tempered style and without the hyperbolic
exclamations of the earlier satirists. The well-used topoi of earlier attacks on
Charles and James as tyrants are deployed once more against the new regime.
Perhaps what is most notable is the limited scope of the Roman story, a mere
episode, in contrast to the rich mythic allusiveness we encounter in Marvell
and Dryden.

There is little in the way of popular songs and ballads attacking William
and Mary, which suggests that they found strong and widespread support
from their subjects. *The Shash,* sung like so many pieces to the tune of "Old
Simon the King," celebrates a Shandean near-accident when a falling window
sash almost pilloried the monarch. When a statue with the king's head
thriftily set upon the body of the Protector was unveiled, the anonymous *On
the Late Metamorphosis* tried to expose William as another Cromwell (the sub-
stitution of Charles II's head for Cromwell's on another statue had provided
the occasion for one of Marvell's burlesques).

The duke of Marlborough, who outshone even William in the wars
against Louis XIV, became, by his defection from James II, his avariciousness,
and his alleged embezzlement of soldiers' pay, the prime target of satirists,
just as his redoubtable duchess would as the royal favorite in the next reign.
Thus the Jacobite ballad *The False Favorite's Downfall* (1690) ends with Marlborough's repentance of what the satirist sees as ruthless opportunism:

>   "At last to complete my life and my glory,
> And make me renowned for ever in story,
> I called foreign forces our religion to aid;
> And so by that cheat, king and country betrayed.
>   My master dethroned,
>   The true prince disowned,
> I fall by the man I unjustly have crowned.
> Then I the mark of ingratitude stand
> For betraying the church and enslaving the land."[7]   [52–60]

The duke's fall from grace was temporary, but he continued to be the main
butt of opposition satire through the reigns of William and Mary and of
Anne. The stability that came with the Revolution was largely due to a

widespread conviction that William's accession had marked the end of a sinister dynasty posing a major threat to political and religious freedom. We may take William's concluding speech from *A Dialogue between King William and King James* (probably by Charles Blount) as a representative expression of the relief with which most subjects greeted the Revolutionary settlement:

> When free-born men (by Providence designed
> Both to preserve and propagate their kind)
> Did first their brutish appetites pursue
> And force alone was all the law they knew,
> When sense was guardian, and when reason young,
> 'Twas then the weak submitted to the strong.
> Then, as the bull walks monarch of the ground,
> So Nimrod, Cyrus, and the rest were crowned.
> For he who could protect, and conquest bring,
> Was from a captain ripened to a king.
> Thus they the People's safety made their choice,
> And Heaven confirmed it by the People's voice.
> When you to France and priests the laws betrayed,
> The injured nation called me to their aid,
> And in their choice the noblest title brings,
> For subjects are the surest guard of kings.   [39 54][8]

Blount here traces the evolution of monarchy from Hobbesian absolutism—remember that Hobbes had been Charles's tutor—to a Lockean kind of social contract at the heart of which lies the sovereignty of the people. Such a "democratic" view of the sources of royal power indicates a fundamentally new concept of monarchy as derived from and limited by the people that comes close to the Venetian model of Harrington. It spells the end of divine right as the basis of monarchical authority and opens the way to a new concern with the lives of ordinary people, which we find expressed in the bourgeois realism of the novels of Defoe, Fielding, and Richardson as well as in the popular tradition of *Poems on Affairs of State*. It was that tradition that Benjamin Franklin honored when he printed *Last Instructions to a Painter,* of which a single copy is preserved in Philadelphia.

The king did not accept these limitations of his prerogative without a struggle, and when the "country party" in Parliament voted to curtail William's standing army and to dismiss the Dutch soldiers who had contributed so much to the defeat of Louis XIV's tyrannical ambitions, William, in 1698, was prepared to abdicate. The ideal of a mixed monarchy became the xenophobic and obstructive coalition of "Old Whigs" and Tory high churchmen, which had "no ideological basis but was simply a struggle for power."[9] In a mock *Encomium upon a Parliament* Defoe attacked the faction in a style more succinct and plain than we have found thus far in the *State Poems:*

Ye worthy patriots go on
　　To heal the nation's sores,
Find all men's faults out but your own.
Begin good laws, but finish none,
　　And then shut up your doors.
Fail not our freedom to secure,
　　And all our friends disband,
And send those fools to t'other shore
Who know no better than to come o'er
　　To help this grateful land.
And may the next that hear us pray,
　　And in distress relieve us,
Go home like those without their pay,
And with contempt be sent away
　　For having once believed us.   [1–15]

When John Tutchin published a pamphlet attacking William and his Dutch associates as foreigners, Defoe again took up the cudgels in *The True-Born Englishman,* where he exposed the racist fallacy that the English were a kind of pedigreed chosen people. Like the new limited monarchy Defoe's attack on the aristocratic tradition in "pointed truth . . . and down-right English" struck another blow at the dynastic tradition, with its conservative, neoclassical style favored by Dryden and his successor Tories. Lord Halifax, "the Trimmer," had to explain to the duchess of Marlborough that Defoe "has a great deal of wit, [and] would write very well if his necessities did not make him in too much haste to correct."[10] Nonetheless, Defoe's satire exposes the aristocratic fallacy effectively in a style that approximates Sprat's ideal of a "naked, plain and close way of speaking" in his *History of the Royal Society:*[11]

The civil wars, the common purgative,
Which always used to make the nation thrive,
Made way for all that strolling congregation,
Which thronged in pious Charles's Restoration.
The royal refugee our breed restores
With foreign courtiers and with foreign whores:
And carefully repeopled us again,
Throughout his lazy, long, lascivious reign,
With such a blessed and true-born English fry,
As much illustrates our nobility.
A gratitude which will so black appear,
As future ages must abhor to hear:
When they look back on all that crimson flood,
Which streamed in Lindsey's and Carnarvon's blood:
Bold Strafford, Cambridge, Capel, Lucas, Lisle,
Who crowned in death his father's fun'ral pile.
The loss of whom, in order to supply
With true-born English nobility,

Six bastard dukes survive his luscious reign,
The labors of Italian Castlemaine,
French Portsmouth, Tabby Scot, and Cambrian,
Besides the num'rous bright and virgin throng,
Whose female glories shade them from my song. [285–307]

Like much of his verse, Defoe's *True-Born Englishman* is somewhat invertebrate, a fault that may be ascribed in part to his rejection of conservative archetypes and narrative forms, but he does succeed in achieving an effectively ironic, vernacular, and naive realism, as in these lines spoken by Sir Charles Duncombe:

"With clouted shoon and skeepskin breeches,
More rags than manners, and more dirt than riches:
From driving cows and calves to Layton Market,
While of my greatness there appeared no mark yet,
Behold I come, to let you see the pride
With which exalted beggars always ride.
    "Born to the needful labors of the plow,
The cart-whip graced me as the chain does now.
Nature and fate in doubt what course to take,
Whether I should a lord or plough-boy make;
Kindly at last resolved they would promote me,
And first a knave, and then a knight they vote me." [1064–75]

Defoe's iconoclastic political and social views anticipated the increase of social mobility which accompanied the rise of democracy in the West, as his rejection of classical forms foreshadowed their abandonment in English poetry. But in the first year of Anne's reign there still appeared a prophetic imitation of Virgil's fourth eclogue, reinstating the classical presence Dryden had invoked more than forty years earlier. This work, *The Golden Age* (1702), employs some phrases from Dryden's translation of 1697. Once more we hear "Sicilian strains" celebrating the theme of renewal and restoration:

Sicilian Muse, thy voice and subject raise,
All are not pleased with shrubs and sylvan lays,
Or if we shrubs and sylvan lays prepare,
Let 'em be such as suit a consul's ear.
Now Merlin's propecies are made complete,
And Lilly's best events with credit meet;
Now banished Justice takes its rightful place,
And Saturn's days return with Stuart's race.
With its own luster now the church appears,
As one year makes amends for fourteen years,
And joys succeed our sighs, and hopes succeed our fears. [1–11]

As the headnote in the Yale *Poems on Affairs of State* observes, the poem

seeks a modern equivalent for each detail of the ancient prototype; it attempts to restate the classical antitypes in modern terms. The excitement derives from the poet's ingenuity in finding "modern instances": Partridge's almanac for the Sibylline books; Sir Samuel Dashwood, the new lord mayor of London, for C. Asinius Pollio, the new consul of Rome; Whig peculations for *priscae vestigia fraudis*.[12]

Whether one agrees with Trevelyan that it was "the Dutch schoolmaster" William who ushered in the peace of the Augustans, or with Plumb that its "adamantine strength and profound inertia" were established somewhat later with the accession of George I, there is no question that the period was marked by a great increase in party strife and a corresponding decrease in real violence.[13] Conspiracies, plots, and invasions, which had characterized English domestic politics throughout much of the seventeenth century, were now largely a thing of the past.

The peace of the Augustans was a vision—fleeting, as things turned out—hailed in Alexander Pope's early poem *Windsor-Forest* celebrating the imminent Treaty of Utrecht (1713), which was to put an end to decades of wars with Louis XIV:

> O fact accursed! What tears has *Albion* shed,
> Heavens! what new wounds, and how her old have bled?
> She saw her sons with purple deaths expire,
> Her sacred domes involved in rolling fire,
> A dreadful series of intestine wars,
> Inglorious triumphs, and dishonest scars.
> At length great *ANNA* said—Let Discord cease!
> She said, the world obeyed, and all was *Peace!*   [321–28]

Three-quarters of a century earlier, Marvell had similarly celebrated the phenomenal emergence of Cromwell and his impact upon the youthful poet in *An Horatian Ode on Cromwell's Return from Ireland:*

> The forward youth that would appear
> Must now forsake his Muses dear,
>   Nor in the shadows sing
>   His numbers languishing,
>
> 'Tis time to leave the books in dust,
> And oyl the unused armors rust:
>   Removing from the wall
>   The corslet of the hall.   [1–8]

Cromwell appears as an apocalyptic agent destroying the old order:

> Then burning through the air he went,
> And palaces and temples rent:
>   And Caesar's head at last
>   Did through his laurels blast.   [21–24]

In the conclusion of his poem, Pope—imitating Virgil, as Marvell had imitated Horace—brings the curtain down on decades of civil strife and returns to his shadows, his Muses, and his "numbers languishing":

> My humble Muse, in unambitious strains,
> Paints the green forests and the flowery plains,
> Where Peace descending bids her olives spring,
> And scatters blessings from her dovelike wing.
> Even I more sweetly pass my careless days,
> Pleased in the silent shade with empty praise;
> Enough for me, that to the listening swains
> First in the fields I sung the sylvan strains.   [427–34]

Between them, the Puritan poet who supported Cromwell and the Catholic poet who so indefatigably supported the Stuarts embrace the critical period covered by this volume. They also embrace a whole range of political attitudes, from apocalytic to paradise regained. But in hailing a new era Pope was unwittingly erecting a monument to an old one, for *Windsor-Forest* is one of the last attempts to invoke the traditional, classical, religiously oriented view of monarchy. Certainly Virgil's influence, in the *Georgics* especially, continued to be felt for some time in English poetry, but not with the profundity and passion exhibited here.

From the ruins of the Stuart dream after the death of Anne appears a malediction on the new Hanoverians. *Pasquin to the Queen's Statue,* a snarling invective in the manner of Ayloffe, terminates *Poems on Affairs of State:*

> Behold he comes to make thy people groan,
> And with their curses to ascend the throne;
> A clod-pate, base, inhuman, jealous fool,
> The jest of Europe and the faction's tool.
> Heaven ne'er heard of such a right divine,
> Nor earth e'er saw a successor like thine.   [1–6][14]

From such dunghill productions as this Pope revived for the last time, in the *Dunciad,* a tragic, mock-epic vision of the ruin of the "great work of Time."

In retrospect the real spokesman for the new age that was emerging after the Revolution of 1688 and that prevailed throughout the eighteenth century and after was not Pope but Defoe. A sociopolitical and economic revolution, which steadily increased the power of Whig money-men as against Tory landed gentry, undermined the traditional conservative concept of man and society embodied in "ancient right" and "the great chain of being." This myth, with its emphasis on subordination and fixed class structure, was challenged by new notions of social mobility fueled by the expanding wealth of Whig projectors, merchants, and businessmen. Conservative Augustan writers such as Bolingbroke, Pope, Swift, and Gay were appalled by the disintegration of the social ideal to which they had subscribed. At the center of their ethos was a fervent belief in "the hierarchical ordering of society and nature according to the divinely ordained chain of being" in contradistinction to the Lockean principle of "voluntary contract sponsored by the emerging middle class." Unlike the traditionalists, who tended to be Anglican, Tory, and, by their addiction to the classical writers, champions of the ancients against the moderns, the progressives, whose chief spokesman was Defoe, tended to be low church or Dissenting and Whiggish and to disparage the old order and humanist culture founded on Greek and Latin learning. Defoe embraced an individualistic concept of humanity freed from the restrictions of a social hierarchy:

In both his career and writings Defoe embodied the projecting spirit—the restless and optimistic desire to tinker with and change society and nature. Tradition, the inherited social order, and nature ceased to be sacred before the projector and the tinkerer. His wholly progressive spirit gloried in inventions and newness, in solving traditional problems, in conquering new worlds. His practical and utilitarian spirit enshrined the handy, the useful, the profitable; his was the spirit of self-interest, avarice, and individualism. Projecting man, free of any functional duty to any organic social structure, stood alone, creating and shaping his own world and his own destiny. His was the spirit of Locke's man, of Robinson Crusoe, a necessary ingredient of the capitalist creed.[15]

The growth of Augustan capitalism, hastened by the foundation of the Bank of England, debit financing, the issuance of paper money, and the proliferation of joint-stock companies, enabled a new class to rise to political and social power. Upward social mobility probably contributed to the expansion of a middle-class reading public, with distinctly unclassical tastes, that patronized the popular stage entertainments of Colley Cibber and Rich, supported the rage for opera and the new sentimental drama, and found a mirror of its own values and interest in the novels of Defoe. The time had come when any man who was clever, ambitious, and hardworking could aspire to wealth and power; the aristocratic bias of the old order had been reduced.

While many of the *State Poems* were written in defense of the old order, the total impact, regardless of the political viewpoints they represent, tended to erode that order. In the first place, it was subversive, by traditional standards, to invite public discussion of state secrets. In the second, these corrosive satires ate away traditional attitudes of awe and respect toward one's betters. In the third, the predominantly pessimistic and cynical tone of what must have appeared to be a never-ending flood of satires undermined confidence in institutions and public figures. In a rare attack on satire one anonymous poet put the case thus:

> Unhinge not governments except you could
> Supply us better ere you change the old.
> You would have all amended. So would I,
> Yet not deface each piece where faults I spy.
> 'Tis true I could find colors to expose

> Faulty grandees and over-paint a rose,
> But this checks me, that whatso'er is aimed,
> Few such are mended by being proclaimed.
> Public disgrace oft smaller sinners scares,
> But vice with greatness armed no colors fears.
> Besides, the rout grows insolent hereby,
> And slights the one disgraced authority,
> Whence, to paint all our betters' faults would be
> To hang up order in effigie.   [65–78][16]

The satirists of course failed to heed this advice but continued in their head-long pursuit of alleged or actual instances of folly, knavery, or tyranny among the great. The cumulative force of these thousands of poems was overwhelmingly antiheroic.

This spirit of freedom lies behind most of the better opposition satire. Among the many who did not hesitate to take risks, Defoe is probably the most famous because of his impudent transformation of what was intended to be a humiliating public punishment into a popular victory, an event commemorated in his *Hymn to the Pillory* "The indignity of the pillory," Defoe confided to the earl of Nottingham, "was worse to me than death," yet he struck out recklessly against "a merciless as well as unjust ministry," declaring that the punishment was "unjust, exorbitant, and consequently illegal."[17] Defoe anticipates Pope's snide inference in the *Dunciad* that the degrading punishment was appropriate to the victim by reminding his readers:

> But who can judge of crimes by punishment,
> Where parties rule, and law's subservient?
> Justice with change of interest learns to bow,
> And what was merit once is murther now:
> Actions receive their tincture from the times,
> And, as they change, are virtues made or crimes.   [25–30]

The despised mob, who were expected to aggravate Defoe's punishment, instead "expressed their affections by loud shouts and acclamations, when he was taken down."[18] These examples remind us that, despite the venality and cynicism of many party writers, some of them could see a crucial question of freedom behind the issues of church doctrine, foreign policy, and the contests of king and Parliament. I do not mean to suggest that infringements of freedom came only from conservatives and royalists: throughout the period that concerns us there was probably no greater threat to domestic order than the Popish Plot, so cynically nurtured by Shaftesbury and the exclusionists. Satires protesting tyranny, whether by a "radical" Defoe or a "conservative" Swift, helped keep freedom alive.

Mock-heroic, though it is responsible for most of the best satirical poetry in English, includes only a very small portion of *Poems on Affairs of State.* The paucity of mock-heroic in comparison with other styles such as burlesque and invective may be attributed in large part to the fact that so many of these satires are attacking institutions and traditions. Thus the opposition writers shunned, or were ignorant of, the classical learning that was the mainstay of the conservative writers. In rejecting the classical education of the nobility and gentry and promoting the practical training of the merchant, Defoe

mirrored values of the new age that so frightened men whose sights were set on the past.

He spoke for, and was read by a class totally alien to Bolingbroke, Swift, Pope, and Gay. These brothers of the Scriblerus Club thought Defoe's work socially and intellectually inferior, a fact indicated by its success with the new and bourgeois reading public. They regarded his work as another illustration of the progress of "dullness" that rejected their humanist political, social, and cultural ideals.[19]

Defoe's satirical poems have a utilitarian, journalistic, improvised air about them. They are not allusive or neoclassical, and the standards they bring to political experience are pragmatic and egalitarian. The air of improvisation is a characteristic of many of the best opposition satires. As opposed to the conservative preoccupation with correctness and form, the more radical writers were primarily concerned with getting a message across. Thus they resorted to ballad forms, doggerel, dialogues, mock litanies, and songs, shunning the more literary and elaborate forms of the animal fable, the mock pastoral, or the advice to the painter. It is significant that after Marvell wrote his last poem defending Charles II against his ministers, he turned from mock-heroic to antiheroic doggerel, to point up his loss of faith in the king. The Charles whom he had compared to the heroic King Minos in *The Last Instructions to a Painter* becomes an unruly and truant apprentice seven years later in *Upon His Majesty's Being Made Free of the City:*

> Beyond sea he began,
> Where such riot he ran,
> That all the world there did leave him;
> And now he's come o'er.
> Much worse than before,
> Oh what fools were you to receive him!
>
> . . . .
>
> He spends all his days
> In running to plays,
> When in his shop he should be poring;
> And wastes all his nights
> In his constant delights
> Of reveling, drinking, and whoring.   [19–24; 31–36][20]

The greatness of Dryden, Swift, and Pope has obscured or misrepresented much of what really happened in England between 1660 and 1714. "The Peace of the Augustans" was not due to the triumph of traditional social standards or Tory values but to political stability engendered by the Whig magnates. In *Windsor-Forest* Pope correctly predicted a period of peace and prosperity, starting with the Treaty of Utrecht (1713), but the architect of this unprecedented political stability was not to be his philosophical friend Bolingbroke bearing what Kramnick evocatively calls "the politics of nostalgia," but the creative and unprincipled Walpole and such political writers as Marvell and Defoe.

The classical presence of Homer, Virgil, and Horace as thematic and generic centers of English poetry dwindled after *Windsor-Forest* into a fashionable manner rather than a sustaining vision. The advent of the Hanoverians, where "Dunce the second reigned like Dunce the first," simply accelerated the decline of the English monarchy. Too weak to sustain a credible heroic image and too dull to warrant serious satire, the regime of the Georges posed a spectacle as unworthy of serious notice as the absurd dramatic productions of Cibber or Rich. It could be said that the metaphor of monarchy assimilated the Hanoverians to the lowest levels of popular taste, and writers of distinction turned away from these royal clowns to the more substantial fictional opportunities of the novel. Just as Milton exhausted the epic mode, Pope and Fielding took mock epic as far as it could go. "And universal Darkness buries all" was a prophetic conclusion to one classical tradition in English poetry until the Romantics attempted to revive it.

Notes

Introduction

1   Sprat, *The History of the Royal Society of London* (London, 1667), p. 113.
2   Quoted in *Anthology of Poems on Affairs of State,* ed. George deF. Lord (New Haven and London, 1975), p. 623.

Chapter One: Chapman's Renaissance Homer

1   W. B. Stanford, *The Ulysses Theme* (Oxford, 1954), p. 7.
2   Ibid., p. 211.
3   I have discussed this theme at length in "Homer and Home," a chapter in my *Trials of the Self: Heroic Ordeals in the Epic Tradition* (Hamden, Conn., 1984).
4   "Wished stay" has no corresponding phrase in the Greek, but Chapman (with me) clearly found the implication too strong to be ignored.
5   Janct Spens, "Chapman's Ethical Thought," *Essays and Studies by Members of the English Association* (1925), p. 150.
6   "Epistle Dedicatorie," *Homer's Odysses. Translated according to ye Greeke By Geo. Chapman* (London, 1615?), †1r.
7   Smalley, "The Ethical Bias of Chapman's *Homer,*" *SP* 36 (1939): 182.
8   Barlett, "The Heroes of Chapman's *Homer,*" *RES* 17 (1941): 270.
9   Idem, "Chapman's Revisions in his *Iliads,*" *ELH* 2 (1935): 107.
10 Schoell, *Etudes sur l'humanisme continentale en Angleterre* (Paris, 1926).
11 *Encheiridion. Item. Cebetis Thebani Tabula de vita prudente instituenda . . . Omnia H. Wolfie Interprete* (Cologne, 1595).
12 *Plutarchi Chaeronensis quae exstant omnia. Cum latina interpretatione Hermanii Cruserii: Gulielmi Xylandri, et doctorum virum notiis . . .* (Frankfurt, 1599); *Divini Platonis Opera omnia quae exstant. Marsilio Ficino interprete* (Frankfurt, 1602); *Marsilio Ficino's Commentary on Plato's Symposium: The Text and a Translation* (Columbia, Mo., 1944).
13 Schoell, p. 26, shows that although Comes's book was first published in 1551, not until 1581 did its widespread popularity in Europe begin, when two editions appeared, one in Venice and one in Frankfurt. I have used the edition of Arnold Sittart (Paris, 1583), who, Schoell says, "se contenta de 'pirater' l'édition très améliorée de Wechel (Paris, 1583) non sans vanter, toutefois, d'avoir amendé le texte et les citations." Sittart merely added his own *Mythologiae Musarum Libellus,* and the book is otherwise substantially the same as the first edition.
14 *Adagiorum Chiliades quatuor cum sesquicenturia . . . Henrici Stephani animadversiones* (Geneva, 1558). I have used this edition. First edition: Venice, 1508.
15 *Homeri quae exstant omnia, Ilias, Odyssea, Batrachomyomachia, Hymni, poemata aliquot cum Latina versione omnium quae circumferentur emendatissim{a} aliquot locis iam castigiatore. perpetuis item iustique in Iliada simul & Odysseam Io. Spondani . . . commentariis. Aureliae Allobrogum sumptibus Caldorianae Societatis,* MDCVI (hereafter cited as Spondanus, *Commentarius*).

16   Johannes Scapula, *Lexicon Graeco-Latinum novum in quo ex primitivorum & simplicium fontibus derivata atque composita ordine non minu naturali, quam alphabetico, breviter & dilucide deducuntur.* Basileae, MDCXV.

17   Quoted in McClure, *George Chapman: A Critical Study* (Toronto, 1960), p. 160.

18   Horne, "Remarks on Translation," *Classical Museum* (1844), p. 400.

19   Ellis, *Chapman with Illustrative Passages* (London, 1934), p. 42.

20   Arnold, *On Translating Homer* (London, 1861), pp. 42–50.

21   Hallett Smith, *Elizabethan Poetry* (Cambridge, Mass., 1952), pp. 303–12.

22   S. T. Coleridge, "Notes on Chapman's *Homer,*" *Notes and Lectures upon Shakespeare and Some of the Old Poets and Dramatists,* ed. Mrs. H. N. Coleridge (London, 1849), p. 231.

23   Regel, "Über George Chapman's Homerübersetzung," *Englische Studien* 5 (1882): 36.

24   Arnold, *On Translating Homer,* pp. 76–77.

25   Pound in *Hudson Review* 3 (1950): 60–61.

26   *The Poems of George Chapman,* ed. Phyllis Brooks Bartlett (New York, 1941), p. 392, 11. 37–40.

27   Ibid., p. 393, 11. 17–26.

28   Douglas M. Knight, *Pope and the Heroic Tradition: A Critical Study of his "Iliad"* (New Haven and London, 1951), p. 3.

29   Prose versions of the *Odyssey* are from A. T. Murray's translation (Cambridge, Mass., and London, 1925).

30   Smalley, "The Ethical Bias of Chapman's *Homer,*" p. 184.

31   Bartlett, "The Heroes of Chapman's *Homer,*" p. 71.

32   Chapman, following Scapula's faulty derivation, translates the Greek verb "swelled" as "labored in childbirth."

33   "Come, I pray thee, goddess, tell me truly whether there is any way I might escape from terrible Charybdis and ward off that other monster when she harms my comrades."
     So I spoke, and the beautiful goddess answered: "Rash fellow! Is thy heart still set on deeds of war and toil? Wilt thou not yield even to the immortal gods? She is not mortal, but an immortal bane, dread and terrible and fierce and not to be fought with. There is no defense: to flee from her is best. For, if thou tarriest to arm thyself beneath the cliff, I fear that she may leap out and attack thee with all her heads and seize as many men as before."

34   Spondanus, *Commentarius,* p. 78.

35   Scapula, col. 393. Scapula's derivation of *brotos* (col. 288) from *rheo* "flow" is wrong.

36   *Odysses* VI, 311*n.*

37   Spondanus, *Commentarius,* p. 84: "Non est hic vir humidus homo."

38   Schoell, p. 155.

39   Scapula, col. 154.

40   *Odysses* VI, 315*n.*

41   W. D. Geddes, *The Problem of the Homeric Poems* (London, 1878), p. 35*n.*

42   Margoliouth, *The Homer of Aristotle* (Oxford, 1923), p. 166.

43   Cf. *Odyssey* IX, 105–15: "Then we sailed on, grieved at heart, and we came to the land of the Cyclopes, lawless folk, who trust in the immortal gods, plant

nothing with their hands, nor plow; but all these things spring up for them without plowing or sowing—wheat and barley and vines which bear the clusters for wine, and the rain sent by Zeus makes them grow. They have neither assemblies to take counsel, nor appointed laws, but they dwell in hollow caves, and each one is lawgiver to his children and wives, and they care nothing for one another."

44   Cf. *Odyssey* IX, 125–28: "For the Cyclopes have at hand no ships with vermilion cheeks, nor are there shipwrights in their land to build them well-benched ships, which could carry them where they wished, passing to the cities of other men."

45   Cf. *Odyssey* IX, 173–76: "But I, with my own ship and comrades, will go and try these men to learn whether they are cruel and wild and unjust, or whether they love strangers and fear the gods."

46   Cf. *Odyssey* IX, 196–200: "With me I had a goatskin of the dark, sweet wine that Maro, son of Eveanthes, had given me. And he had given it to me because we had protected him and his children and wife out of reverence."

47   *Odyssey* IX, 252–55.

48   Cf. *Odyssey* IX, 259–68: "We, thou must know, are from Troy, Achaians, driven wandering over the great gulf of the sea by all manner of winds. Seeking our home, we have come by another way, as Zeus, I suppose, was pleased to devise. And we declare ourselves to be the men of Agamemnon, son of Atreus, whose fame is greatest under heaven, so great a city did he sack and so many people did he slay."

49   Cf. *Odyssey* IX, 269–71: " 'Nay, mightiest one, reverence the gods; we are thy suppliants, and Zeus is the avenger of of suppliants and strangers—Zeus, the stranger's god—who ever attends upon reverend suppliants.' "

50   Cf. *Odyssey* IX, 911–16: "He told me that all these things should come to pass in days to come and that by Odysseus' hand I should lose my sight. But I always looked for a tall and noble man to come here, but now a puny one, a thing of nought and a weakling blinded me when he had overpowered me with wine."

51   Comes, "De Circe," *Mythologiae,* Lib. VI, cap. vi, pp. 570–71.

52   Herakleitos, chap. 73, 11. 5–15.

53   *The Odyssey of Homer Translated from the Greek* (London, 1725–26), X, 361*n.*

54   Cf. *Odyssey* X, 373–74: "Then she bade me eat, but my heart was not thus inclined. Instead I sat with my thoughts, and my spirit boded ill."

55   Spondanus, *Commentarius,* p. 142.

56   Smalley, "The Ethical Bias of Chapman's *Homer,*" p. 190.

57   Spondanus, *Commentarius,* p. 327.

Chapter Two: Pretexts and Subtexts in Milton's Renaissance Homer

1   Spondanus and other Renaissance classical scholars Milton knew are referred to in the preceding chapter, nn. 14–16. Spondanus' *Homer,* first published in 1683, draws extensively on the commentary of Eustathius (fl. 1180), on the *Moralia* of Plutarch, on the *Mythologiae* of Natalis Comes, and, occasionally, on the sometimes far-fetched exegeses in the *Allegoricae Homericae* of an otherwise obscure Herakleitos. Selections from Eustathius' exhaustive compilation of Homeric criti-

cism were translated by Parnell and cited approvingly on almost every page of Pope's Homer. Pope also drew on versions by his French counterpart, Anne Dacier, whose commentary refers frequently to Spondanus. Stephanus' Greek-Latin dictionary in five folio volumes generally avoids fanciful etymologies like Scapula's, which badly misled Chapman.

2   Chapman, *Epistle Dedicatorie.*

3   Atkins, *Literary Criticism in Antiquity* (London, 1937), I: 14.

4   Comparetti, *Virgil im Mittelalter* (Leipzig, 1875), p. 99.

5   Harding, *Milton and the Renaissance Ovid* (Chicago, 1946).

6   Basil Willey, *The Seventeenth-Century Background* (New York, 1953) p. 251.

7   Spondanus, *Commentarius,* p. 333.

8   Kingsley Widmer, "The Iconography of Renunciation: The Miltonic Simile," *ELH* 35 (1958). Reprinted in *Critical Essays on Milton from ELH* (Baltimore, 1969), pp. 76ff.

9   N. J. Richardson, ed., *The Homeric Hymn to Demeter* (Oxford, 1974), p. 73. I posit Milton's knowledge of the archetype in full awareness of Richardson's observation that "As the manuscript of the Hymn was not apparently known to the world in general until the end of the eighteenth century, the Hymn exercised no influence over Renaissance literature. A paper was once written which endeavoured to identify Milton's debts to the Hymn." This, he concludes sternly, "should serve as a warning against the perils of any such attempt to trace literary influences."

10   My version is based on the text and translation in *Hesiod, the Homeric Hymns and Homerica,* ed. Hugh. G. Evelyn-White (Cambridge, Mass., 1914) and on the commentary of Richardson.

11   This conjecture about the felix culpa is developed by Mircea Eliade: "In the last analysis, the rape—that is, the symbolic death—of Proserpina had great consequences for humanity. As a result of it an Olympian goddess temporarily inhabited the kingdom of the dead. She annulled the unbridgeable distance between Hades and Olympus. Mediatrix between two divine worlds, she could thereafter intervene in the destiny of mortals. Using a favorite expression of Christian theology, we could say *felix culpa!* Just so, the failed immortalization of Demophöon brought on the shining epiphany of Demeter and the foundation of the mysteries" (*A History of Religious Ideas,* vol. I: *From the Stone Age to the Eleusinian Mysteries* [Chicago, 1978], p. 293). G. S. Kirk, though critical of what he regards as facile or repetitive in Eliade's work, finds a similar depth of significance in the hymn: "In the Greek canon the tale of Demeter and Persephone occupies a central place, and might be still more prominent in classical art and literature were it not restricted by its secret role in the Eleusinian mysteries (*Myth: Its Meaning and Function in Ancient and Other Cultures* [Cambridge, 1970], p. 197).

12   *Metamorphoses* V, 385–91. Text and translation are quoted from *Metamorphoses,* ed. F. J. Miller (Cambridge, Mass., 1916).

13   *Ovid's Metamorphoses Englished by G. S., Mythologiz'd, and Represented in Figures: An Essay to the Translation of Virgil's Aeneis* (Oxford, 1632), p. 254. The derivation has been questioned. See the *Oxford Classical Dictionary,* s.v. "Persephone."

14   In *Mystaguogus Poeticus* (London, 1648) Alexander Ross makes the identification

of Christ and Ceres explicit: "Christ is truly *Ceres;* which having lost mankinde, being carried away by the Devil, he came, and with the Torch of his Word, found him out; and being drawn by the flying serpents of Zeal and Prudence, dispersed his Seed through the World, went down to Hell, and rescued us from thence" (p. 69).

15 Comes, *Mythologiae* (1583), p. 175.

16 P. Ovidius Naso, *Metamorphosen,* commentary by Franz Bömer (Heidelberg, 1976) II: 238.

17 Karl Kerényi, *Eleusis: Archetypal Image of Mother and Daughter* (New York, 1967), p. 92.

18 Paul Schmitt, "The Ancient Mysteries in the Society of Their Times, Their Transformation and Most Recent Echoes" (1944). Reprinted in *The Mysteries: Papers from the Eranos Yearbooks,* ed. C. G. Jung (Princeton, 1955), p. 103.

19 The use of psychotropic drugs in the Eleusinian rituals is the subject of *The Road to Eleusis: Unveiling the Secret of the Mysteries,* by R. Gordon Wasson, Albert Hoffman, and Carl A. F. Ruck (New York, 1978).

20 Kerényi, *Eleusis,* p. 128.

21 Ibid., p. 12.

22 Ibid., p. 18.

23 Ibid., p. 12.

24 See especially Steadman, *Milton and the Renaissance Hero* (Oxford, 1967).

Chapter Three: Milton's Translation of Epic Conventions

1 Throughout this chapter I am indebted to Anne Davidson Ferry, *Milton's Epic Voice* (Cambridge, Mass., 1963); Joseph H. Summers, *The Muse's Method* (Cambridge, Mass., 1962); Louis L. Martz, *The Paradise Within* (New Haven, 1964); Rodney Delasanta, *The Epic Voice* (The Hague, 1967); William G. Riggs, *The Christian Poet in* Paradise Lost (Berkeley, 1972); and, most especially, to Walter Schindler, *Voice and Crisis: Invocation in Milton's Poetry* (Hamden, Conn., 1984).

2 Homer, *Iliad,* trans. A. T. Murray (Cambridge, Mass., and London, 1924).

3 This and all subsequent quotations are from the edition of *Paradise Lost* by M. Y. Hughes (New York, 1962).

4 This point is developed by Martz in "The Voice of the Bard," *The Paradise Within,* pp. 105–10.

5 *The Odyssey of Homer,* trans. Robert Fitzgerald (New York, 1963).

6 Riggs, *The Christian Poet in* Paradise Lost, p. 45.

7 Hanford, *John Milton, Englishman* (New York, 1949), p. 179.

8 Ibid., p. 146.

9 Ibid., p. 9.

10 Quoted in ibid., p. 147.

11 Ibid.

12 Ibid., p. 149.

13 Brisman, "Serpent Error: *Paradise Lost* X, 216–18," *Milton Studies* 2 (1970): 27–35.

14 Barbara Lewalski's article on *Paradise Regained* provides a comprehensive historical and critical account of the poem and a judicious survey of the best secondary sources. See *A Milton Encyclopedia,* ed. by William B. Hunter, Jr., John T. Shawcross, and John M. Steadman, 8 vols. (Lewisburg, Me. and London, 1978–80), VI: 80–105.

15 Campbell, *The Hero with a Thousand Faces* (Princeton, 1968), p. 30.

16 Ibid., pp. 37–38.

17 The text of *Paradise Regained* used throughout is from *Paradise Regained, the Minor Poems, and Samson Agonistes,* ed. M. Y. Hughes (New York, 1957).

18 Campbell, *The Hero with a Thousand Faces,* p. 79.

19 Ibid., pp. 77–78.

Chapter Four: Andrew Marvell and the Virgilian Triad

1 The text used through is from my edition of *Andrew Marvell: Complete Poetry* (London, 1984).

2 Joseph Summers takes a more sanguine view: "The body wins and ironically resolves the argument with its final additional four lines. Without the soul the body would be truly a part of nature and could not sin. Yet architecture, whether external or internal, is the product and desire of a higher part of man, even though many 'Green Trees' may be destroyed for it." From "Marvell's 'Nature,' " reprinted in *Andrew Marvell: A Collection of Critical Essays,* ed. George deF. Lord (Englewood Cliffs, N.J., 1968), p. 49.

3 Klause, *The Unfortunate Fall: Theodicy and the Moral Imagination of Andrew Marvell* (Hamden, Conn., 1983), p. 75.

4 Leishman, *The Monarch of Wit* (London, 1951).

5 *The Odes of Horace,* trans. James Michie ([New York]: Orion, n.d.).

6 Steele Commager, *The Odes of Horace: A Critical Study* (New Haven, 1962), p. 91.

7 Coolidge, "Marvell and Horace," reprinted in *Andrew Marvell: A Collection of Critical Essays,* p. 86.

8 *Eclogue 1,* from Virgil, *Eclogues, Georgics, Aeneid,* ed. and trans. H. R. Fairclough (Cambridge, Mass., and London, 1928).

9 Michael O'Loughlin draws a different conclusion: "What is most striking of course is the fact that as a result of its *human* configuration the house attains a more perfect *architectural* form, the central cupola where, transcending geometry, a circle has been immured in a quadrature." From *Andrew Marvell: A Collection of Critical Essays,* p. 126.

10 Maren-Sofie Røstvig, *The Happy Man: Studies in the Metamorphoses of a Classical Ideal,* 2d ed. (Oslo, 1962), 1:173.

11 Cf. Harold Skulsky, "*Upon Appleton House:* Marvell's Comedy of Discourse," *ELH* (1985): 602: "What the guide does best is to serve as a kind of *magister ludi* adept at suggesting games of imaginative projection."

12 John Klause, *The Unfortunate Fall: Theodicy and the Moral Imagination of Andrew Marvell* (Hamden, Conn., 1983), p. 100.

13 Patterson, *Marvell and the Civic Crown* (Princeton, 1978), pp. 81–86.

14 Ibid., p. 93.

Chapter Five: Satire and Sedition

1 C. V. Wedgwood, *Poetry and Politics under the Stuarts* (Cambridge, 1960), pp. 1–2.

2 *The Rebell Scot,* ll. 27–28.

3 John Freke, *The History of Insipids,* ll. 7–10. In Lord, *Anthology of Poems on Affairs of State,* pp. 136–42.

4 Full text in Lord, *Anthology of Poems on Affairs of State,* pp. 121–29.

5 *Calendar of State Papers Domestic* (hereafter *CSPD*), *1666–67,* p. 430. Cited by H. M. Margoliouth, ed., *Poems and Letters of Andrew Marvell* (Oxford, 1927; 2d ed., Oxford, 1952) (hereafter Margoliouth).

6 *CSPD, 1667,* p. 330. Cited by Margoliouth.

7 *Historical Manuscripts Commission Reports* (hereafter *HMCR*) 7: 517.

8 Narcissus Luttrell, *A Brief Historical Relation* (Oxford, 1857), I: 311.

9 *CSPD, 1683–84,* p. 43.

10 *Portledge Papers,* ed. R. J. Kerr and Ida C. Duncan (London, 1928), p. 24.

11 *A New Song for the Times, 1683* (Case 189 [2], p. 12).

12 *A Familiar Epistle to Mr. Julian, Secretary of the Muses,* ll. 1–4. In the Yale edition of *Poems on Affairs of State* (New Haven and London, 1963–75; hereafter referred to as Yale *POAS*), I: 388–91.

13 Luttrell, *A Brief Historical Relation,* I: 319–20. Cited by Brice Harris, "Captain Robert Julian, Secretary to the Muses," *ELH* 10 (1943): 301.

14 North, *Examen* (1740), p. 139.

15 H. Thynne to T. Thynne, 19 Sept. 1677, in B.M. Add. MS. 32095, f. 38. Cited by David Ogg, *England in the Reign of Charles II* (Oxford, 1956), p. 102.

16 James I, *Political Works,* ed. C. H. McIlwain (London, 1918), p. 62. Cited by J. R. Tanner, *English Constitutional Conflicts in the Seventeenth Century, 1603–1689* (Cambridge, 1928), p. 20.

17 See *The Earl of Rochester's Verses for Which He Was Banished* in Lord, *Anthology of Poems of Affairs of State,* p. 248.

18 Pepys, *Diary,* 14 Dec. 1666.

19 Ibid., 20 Jan. 1667.

20 Ibid., 1 July 1667.

21 Ibid., 16 Sept. 1667.

22 Muddiman Newsletter, 13 Feb. 1668.

23 *HMCR* 7: 486, letter dated 13 Feb. 1668.

24 Muddiman Newsletter, 15 Feb. 1668.

25 Anchitell Grey, *Debates of the House of Commons from the Year 1667 to the Year 1694,* 10 vols. (London, 1769), 14 Feb. 1668.

26 Lord, *Anthology of Poems on Affairs of State,* pp. 49–50.

27 Ibid., p. 180.

28 George Savile, marquis of Halifax, *A Character of King Charles II* (London, 1723).

29 Percy, *Reliques of Ancient Poetry* (London, 1910), II: 157.

30 Thomas Babington Macaulay, *The History of England from the Accession of James II,* ed. C. H. Firth, 6 vols. (London, 1913–15), III: 1072.

31 Hume, *History of England* (London, 1762), V: 455.

32 From Lord, *Anthology of Poems on Affairs of State,* pp. 486–87.

33 Alvin Kernan, *The Cankered Muse: Satire of the English Renaissance* (New Haven, 1959), p. 2.

34   Strachey, *Pope. The Leslie Stephen Lecture for 1925* (New York, 1926).

35   Frye, *Anatomy of Criticism* (Princeton, 1957).

36   Randolph, "The Structural Design of Formal Verse Satire," *PQ* 21 (1942): 368–84; Mack, "The Muse of Satire," *Yale Review* 41 (1951–52): 80–92.

37   Kernan, *The Cankered Muse,* p. 4; Robert C. Elliott, *The Power of Satire: Magic, Ritual, Art* (Princeton, 1960).

38   Jean Hagstrum, *The Sister Arts,* pp. 179, 180.

39   Ibid., p. 180.

40   Commonplace book of George Villiers, second duke of Buckingham, in the library of the earl of Jersey. I am indebted to the earl for permission to quote and to J. Harold Wilson for lending a microfilm of the book.

41   From Lord, *Anthology of Poems on Affairs of State,* p. 106.

42   Ibid., p. 32.

43   Ibid., p. 23.

44   *Bulletin of the Institute for Historical Research* (London, 1923–25).

45   Macaulay, *History,* II: 520.

46   *The Life of Edward, Earl of Clarendon . . .* [and] *a Continuation of His History of the Grand Rebellion* (Oxford, 1827), bk. II, para. 44.

47   *Correspondence of the Family of Hatton,* ed. E. M. Thompson (London, 1878), I: 118.

48   Haley, *William of Orange and the English Opposition, 1671–74* (Oxford, 1953), pp. 58–59, 63.

49   The poem is assigned to the year 1674 by Godfrey Davies in "The Date of *Britannia and Raleigh,*" *HLQ* 9 (1946): 311–18.

50   Charles James Fox, *A History of the Early Part of the Reign of James II* (London, 1808), p. 226.

51   [John Tutchin], *A New Martyrology: or, The Bloody Assizes* (London, 1689), p. 181.

52   With the exception of the manuscript poems on Armstrong and *Oceana and Britannia,* the texts are from Yale *POAS,* I. The text for *Oceana and Britannia* is from vol. II of this collection, ed. Elias F. Mengel, Jr.

53   Z. S. Fink, *The Classical Republicans,* 2d ed. (Evanston, Ill., 1962), p. 127.

54   In Lord, *Anthology of Poems on Affairs of State,* pp. 145–46.

55   *Bulletin of the Institute for Historical Research* XXII: 65.

Chapter Six: Dryden, the New Virgil

1   *The Rehearsal Transprosed,* Part II, in *Complete Works of Andrew Marvell,* ed. A. B. Grosart (1872–75), III: 211.

2   Preface to *Religio Laici.*

3   Bradbrook and Lloyd Thomas, *Andrew Marvell* (Cambridge, 1961), p. 102.

4   *Complete Works,* ed. Grosart, III: 382.

5   Ibid., p. 370.

6   Bradbrook and Thomas, *Andrew Marvell,* p. 109.

7   Jürgen Moltmann, *Religion, Revolution, and the Future* (New York, 1969), p. 24.

8   Sutherland, *English Literature of the Late Seventeenth Century* (New York and Oxford, 1969), pp. 303–04.
9   Eliade, *Cosmos and History* (New York, 1959), p. 34.
10 Davies, "The Conclusion of Dryden's *Absalom and Achitophel*," *HLQ* 90 (1946): 69–82.
11 Schilling, *Dryden and the Conservative Myth: A Reading of "Absalom and Achitophel"* (New Haven, 1961), p. 50.
12 *The Authours Apologie for Heroic Poetry and Heroic License,* in Watson, I: 207.
13 Quoted in George Williamson, "The Restoration Revolt against Enthusiasm," *Seventeenth-Century Contexts* (Chicago, 1960), p. 212.
14 Ernest H. Kantorowicz, *The King's Two Bodies: A Study in Medieval Political Theology* (Princeton, 1957).
15 Dryden, *Works,* I: 307.
16 Ibid., p. 258.
17 Schilling, *Dryden and the Conservative Myth,* p. 2.
18 Ibid., p. 4.
19 Mazzeo, *Renaissance and Seventeenth-Century Studies* (New York and London, 1964), p. 188.
20 Ibid.
21 Ibid., p. 191.
22 Ibid., p. 192.
23 Ibid.
24 L. F. Brown, *The Political Activities of the Baptists and Fifth Monarchy Men in England during the Interregnum* (Washington, 1912), pp. 112, 113, 155, 167, 184.
25 John M. Wallace, *Destiny His Choice: The Loyalism of Andrew Marvell* (Cambridge, 1968), p. 102.
26 Ibid., p. 173.
27 Ibid., p. 184.
28 *Absalom and Achitophel* "To the Reader."
29 Quoted in Wallace, *Destiny His Choice,* p. 182.
30 *The Rehearsal Transprosed* in *Complete Works,* ed. Grosart, III: 436–37.
31 Wallace, *Destiny His Choice,* p. 204.
32 Johnson, *Lives of the Poets,* ed. G. B. Hill (Oxford, 1905), III: 436–37.
33 Ibid.
34 Davies, "The Conclusion of Dryden's *Absalom and Achitophel*," pp. 69–82.
35 George Macaulay Trevelyan, *England under the Stuarts* (London, 1949), p. 346.
36 Guilhamet, "Dryden's Debasement of Scripture in *Absalom and Achitophel*," *SEL* 9 (1969): 407.
37 Ibid., p. 412

Chapter Seven: Homeric Mockery in Milton and Pope

1   Bowra, *Tradition and Design in the "Iliad"* (Oxford, 1930), p. 239.
2   See William K. Wimsatt, Jr., *"Belinda Ludens:* Strife and Play in *The Rape of the Lock,"* *New Literary History* 4 (1972–73): 357–74.
3   Johnson, *Lives of the Poets,* I: 185.

4   Arnold Stein, "The War in Heaven," in *Answerable Style: Essays on "Paradise Lost"* (Minneapolis, 1953), pp. 17–37; Merritt Y. Hughes, "Milton's Celestial Battle and the *Theogonies*," in *Studies in Honor of T. W. Baldwin*, ed. D. C. Allen (Urbana, Ill., 1958); Summers, *The Muse's Method*; Stella Revard, "Milton's Critique of Warfare in *Paradise Lost* V and VI," *SEL* 7 (1967): 119–39.

5   Joseph Addison, *The Spectator*, ed. Donald F. Bond (Oxford, 1969), III: 232.

6   M. Conrad Hyers, "The Comic Profanation of the Sacred," in *Holy Laughter: Essays on Religion in the Comic Perspective*, ed. Hyers (New York, 1969), pp. 9–27.

7   "Milton has followed some of the heroic assumptions to their ultimate conclusions: what if two heroic forces, equal in number and in strength, did meet? If one were 'impaired,' the other would have some advantage, but neither could finally 'win'; neither could achieve the unconditional surrender of the other. The alternate possibilities are, for human warriors, mutual destruction and death; for angelic ones, 'in perpetual fight they needs must last / Endless and no solution will be found.' The analogy holds too, I believe, for the spiritual warfare without divine intervention. Human and angelic wars are absurd if one expects them really to resolve uncertain issues" (Summers, *The Muse's Method*, p. 152).

8   Deedes, "The Labyrinth," in *The Labyrinth: Further Studies in the Relations between Myth and Ritual in the Ancient World*, ed. S. H. Hooke (London, 1935), p. 42.

Chapter Eight: The Erosion of the Tradition

1   Zwicker, *Dryden's Political Poetry* (Providence, 1972), p. 114.

2   Ibid., p. 117.

3   From Lord, *Anthology of Poems on Affairs of State*, p. 467.

4   Ibid., p. 463.

5   Ibid., p. 482.

6   Ibid., p. 489.

7   Ibid., p. 534.

8   Ibid., pp. 526–27.

9   Ibid., p. 587; headnote to *An Encomium upon a Parliament*.

10 Ibid., p. 623; headnote to *The True-Born Englishman*.

11 Sprat, *History of the Royal Society of London*.

12 From Lord, *Anthology of Poems on Affairs of State*, p. 662.

13 Trevelyan, *England under the Stuarts*, p. 372; J. H. Plumb, *The Origins of Political Stability: England, 1675–1724* (Boston, 1967), p. xviii.

14 From Lord, *Anthology of Poems on Affairs of State*, p. 751.

15 This quotation and the two preceding ones are from Isaac Kramnick, *Bolingbroke and His Circle: The Politics of Nostalgia in the Age of Walpole* (Cambridge, Mass., 1967), pp. 214, 193.

16 *The Answer of Mr. Waller's Painter to His Many New Advisers* (1667), from Lord, *Anthology of Poems on Affairs of State*, pp. 60–73.

17 Introduction to Lord, *Anthology of Poems on Affairs of State*, p. xxvii.

18 Ibid., p. xxviii.

19 Kramnick, *Bolingbroke and His Circle*, p. 196.

20 From Lord, *Anthology of Poems on Affairs of State*, p. 131.

Index

217